Praise for O

"Insightful, witty, and accessible prose. [Gay] has an ability to blend the personal and political in a way that feels simultaneously gentle and brutal. . . . For 1,400 or so words you look at a cultural moment through Gay's eyes and, by the end, you see the world differently."

—*The Guardian*

"A true star in the literary world known for her uncompromising opinions, timely takes on modern American culture, and in-depth profiles."

—Shondaland

"Gay made a name for herself with her pieces, which often turned conventional opinion writing on its head—decisive, funny takes that sat squarely in the space between logic and empathy, and eschewed conventional pundit wisdom. These pieces have been gathered in *Opinions*, and they showcase her work as a thinker, grappling with the questions of our time."

—*Harper's Bazaar*

"This sharp, thought-provoking anthology will delight Roxane Gay's devotees and draw new readers to this inimitable talent."

—*USA Today*

"Gay's essays are brilliant and incisive. . . . Each piece on its own is worthy of attention. Taken collectively, this title is not to be missed."

—*Library Journal* (starred review)

"This is a must-read for not only fans of Gay's work, but for everyone interested in reading intellectual, accessible, and important takes on timely topics."

—*Booklist* (starred review)

"Essays, op-eds, and pop-culture pieces from the acclaimed novelist and memoirist. . . . [Gay] has a gift for clean, well-ordered prose, and strong feelings on matters of race, gender, and sexuality. Most important, she possesses a fearlessness essential to doing the job right; though she can observe an issue from various angles, she never wrings her hands or delivers milquetoast commentaries. . . . Fierce and informed riffs on current events and enduring challenges."

—*Kirkus Reviews*

Praise for *Not That Bad*

"A diverse and unvarnished collection of personal essays reckoning with the experiences and systemic dysfunction that produced Me Too."

—*O, The Oprah Magazine*

"From the author of *Bad Feminist* and *Hunger* (drop everything if you haven't read this) comes a collection of first-person essays about rape, assault, and sexual harassment. It couldn't be more timely. Gay's introduction moved me to tears, as did many of the pieces contributed by household names—Gabrielle Union, Ally Sheedy—but accounts from 'regular' women moved me even more. Perhaps that's the lesson we're meant to take away from *Not That Bad*: we're all "regular." Shocking as they are, many of these stories will be familiar to us all—and we all deserve better."

—*Glamour*

"A profoundly personal anthology."

—*Harper's Bazaar*

"Critical reading."

—*Paste* magazine

"This is a devastating book, heartbreaking in how familiar and relatable each story is—yet there's power and solidarity in it, too."

—Shondaland

"*Not That Bad* is essential reading."

—*Refinery29*

"Timely. . . . It is a critical work that makes this much clear: The violations Me Too rages against can and do damage people for a lifetime."

—*Globe and Mail*

"It's hard to imagine a more fitting editor for a collection like this . . . everyone *should* read it."

—*The Brooklyn Rail*

Praise for *Hunger*

"A gripping book, with vivid details that linger long after its pages stop. . . . *Hunger* is arresting and candid. At its best, it affords women, in particular, something so many other accounts deny them—the right to take up space they are entitled to, and to define what that means."

—*The Atlantic*

"A work of staggering honesty. . . . Poignantly told."

—*The New Republic*

"On nearly every page, Gay's raw, powerful prose plants a flag, facing down decades of shame and self-loathing by reclaiming the body she never should have had to lose."

—*Entertainment Weekly*

"Bracingly vivid. . . . Remarkable. . . . Undestroyed, unruly, unfettered, Ms. Gay, live your life. We are all better for having you do so in the same ferociously honest fashion that you have written this book."

—*Los Angeles Times*

"Searing, smart, readable. . . . *Hunger*, like Ta-Nehisi Coates's *Between the World and Me*, interrogates the fortunes of black bodies in public spaces. . . . Nothing seems gratuitous; a lot seems brave."

—*Newsday*

"Luminous. . . . Intellectually rigorous and deeply moving."
—*New York Times Book Review*

"An amazing achievement in more ways than I can count."
—Ann Patchett

"Her spare prose, written with a raw grace, heightens the emotional resonance of her story, making each observation sharper, each revelation more riveting. . . . It is a thing of raw beauty."
—*USA Today*

"Powerful. . . . Gay has a vivid, telegraphic writing style, which serves her well. Repetitive and recursive, it propels the reader forward with unstoppable force."
—Associated Press

"Anyone who has a body should read this book."
—Isaac Fitzgerald on *Today*

"Unforgettable. . . . Breathtaking. . . . We all need to hear what Gay has to say in these pages. . . . Gay says hers is not a success story because it's not the weight-loss story our culture demands, but her breaking of her own silence, her movement from shame and self-loathing toward honoring and forgiving and caring for herself, is in itself a profound victory."
—*San Francisco Chronicle*

"*Hunger* is Gay at her most lacerating and probing. . . . Anyone familiar with Gay's books or tweets knows she wields a dagger-sharp wit."
—*Boston Globe*

"Wrenching, deeply moving. . . . A memoir that's so brave, so raw, it feels as if [Gay's] entrusting you with her soul."
—*Seattle Times*

"It is a deeply honest witness, often heartbreaking, and always breathtaking. . . . Gay is one of our most vital essayists and critics."
—*Minneapolis Star Tribune*

"Searing."

—*Miami Herald*

"This raw and graceful memoir digs deeply into what it means to be comfortable in one's body. Gay denies that hers is a story of 'triumph,' but readers will be hard-pressed to find a better word."

—*Publishers Weekly* (starred review)

"A heart-rending debut memoir from the outspoken feminist and essayist. . . . An intense, unsparingly honest portrait of childhood crisis and its enduring aftermath."

—*Kirkus Reviews* (starred review)

"Displays bravery, resilience, and naked honesty from the first to last page. . . . Stunning. . . . Essential reading."

—*Library Journal* (starred review)

"It's hard to imagine this electrifying book being more personal, candid, or confessional. . . . a generous and empathic consideration of what it's like to be someone else: in itself something of a miracle."

—*Booklist* (starred review)

"A work of exceptional courage by a writer of exceptional talent."

—*Shelf Awareness* (starred review)

Praise for *Bad Feminist*

"A strikingly fresh cultural critic."

—Ron Charles, *Washington Post*

"Perfectly imperfect, Gay is an unforgettable voice, coming at just the right time."

—NPR

"Arresting and sensitive. . . . An author who filters every observation through her deep sense of the world as fractured, beautiful, and complex."

—*Slate*

"Roxane Gay is the brilliant girl-next-door: your best friend and your sharpest critic. . . . She is by turns provocative, chilling, hilarious; she is also required reading."

—*Time*

"Roxane Gay may call herself a bad feminist but she is a badass writer."

—Associated Press

"Fascinating. . . . An important and pioneering contemporary writer. . . . An important contribution to the complicated terrain of gender politics."

—*Boston Globe*

"Gay playfully crosses the borders between pop culture consumer and critic, between serious academic and lighthearted sister-girl, between despair and optimism, between good and bad."

—Melissa Harris-Perry

"Roxane Gay is so great at weaving the intimate and personal with what is most bewildering and upsetting at this moment in culture. She is always looking, always thinking, always passionate, always careful, always right there."

—Sheila Heti

"Trailblazing."

—*Salon*

"Gay is nothing short of a critical genius."

—*Bustle*

"A prolific and exceptionally insightful writer."

—*Globe and Mail* (Toronto)

"As a culture critic, Gay has X-ray eyes. Her writing is smart and trenchant, but she has something else as well, a hard-to-define quality that makes her readers root for her. She's disarming and one of us, only smarter. She has a tumblr and she writes about Internet dating. We love her, you know?"

—*Philadelphia Inquirer*

"One of the most astute critics writing today."

—*Boston Review*

ALSO BY ROXANE GAY

Nonfiction

Hunger

Bad Feminist

Not That Bad (editor)

Fiction

Difficult Women

An Untamed State

Ayiti

Opinions

[
A Decade of
Arguments, Criticisms, and
Minding Other People's Business
]

Roxane Gay

HARPER ● PERENNIAL

NEW YORK ● LONDON ● TORONTO ● SYDNEY ● NEW DELHI ● AUCKLAND

HARPER ● PERENNIAL

A hardcover edition of this book was published in 2023 by Harper, an imprint of HarperCollins Publishers.

HarperCollins books may be purchased for educational, business, or sales promotional use. For information, please email the Special Markets Department at SPsales@harpercollins.com.

FIRST HARPER PERENNIAL EDITION PUBLISHED 2024.

Designed by Leah Carlson-Stanisic

Library of Congress Cataloging-in-Publication Data has been applied for.

ISBN 978-0-06-334147-0 (pbk.)

24 25 26 27 28 LBC 5 4 3 2 1

For my mother, who first taught me that my opinions matter

He licked his lips. "Well, if you want my opinion—"
"I don't," she said. "I have my own."

—Toni Morrison, *Beloved*

Opinion has caused more trouble on this little earth
than plagues or earthquakes.

—Voltaire

Contents

CIVIC RESPONSIBILITIES

FOR THE CULTURE

MAN PROBLEMS

MINDING OTHER FOLKS' BUSINESS

SOLICITED ADVICE

Introduction

I have a lot of opinions and I come by them honestly. From an early age, I watched my mother confidently expressing her opinions with wit and intellect. She always stood her ground and was unapologetic about her beliefs. As someone who is relatively shy and quiet, I was impressed and I admired her greatly for her forthrightness. While I had opinions, I didn't necessarily have the confidence to share them, so I wrote them down, usually for myself, and that was good enough. My mom didn't necessarily know it at the time, but she consistently modeled what it means to have convictions and the confidence to express them. She still does. In my own work, I have aspired to do so, too.

Throughout my career, I've had the privilege of being able to share some of my opinions with a large audience. I built an ever-growing body of work one word at a time, writing on everything from contemporary fiction to police brutality to the *Fast & Furious* franchise. This book pulls together selections from a decade of opinion writing. It has been a decade of massive social upheaval. We continue to deal with a pandemic that reshaped our lives in many ways. This decade saw the rise of Donald Trump and his peculiar brand of ego-driven politics. We are drowning in misinformation. The battle for reproductive freedom has lost too much ground. The trans community is more imperiled than they were five years ago, as several states pass legislation that, essentially, outlaws everything from drag queen events to gender-affirming health care. This does not bode well for the rest of the LGBTQ community. Many states are experiencing a resurgence of book banning, and state legislatures are trying to dictate what is taught in schools and colleges and universities, trying to change history by ignoring it.

The climate into which I write my opinions is incredibly fraught but I write, nonetheless. I write to express outrage or bear witness or express admiration. I write knowing many people will disagree with me for one reason or another, sometimes reflexively. When I publish a new essay that's provocative in some way, my father will reach out, in a concerned but also teasing manner, about how I'm making too many enemies. He worries that by virtue of expressing opinions, I am burning bridges. He's probably right, though that is never my intention. And, frankly, any bridge my work might burn is not a bridge I have any interest in traversing.

The internet has long been an open-air bazaar for sharing opinions. And the ubiquity of those opinions is chaotic and intriguing and sometimes tiresome and overwhelming. There is a whole lot of noise and we probably know far too much about one another and what we think in this modern age. We can review almost any product from the point of purchase. On Amazon, some shoppers take their reviewing so seriously, you'd think they worked for *Consumer Reports*. What I'm saying is that our voluntary labor is rigorous. We can share our thoughts about a hotel, motel, or resort property. I am obsessed with TripAdvisor in particular, and consult it religiously when deciding where I want to lay my head in a given city. On that site, people discuss everything from the hotel restaurant to the quality of room service or housekeeping or the linens, to how polite or impolite the bellhops were during their stay. When reviewing higher-end hotels, people love to start by explaining that they regularly stay in luxury hotels, so we know they are very fancy. Yelp is a world unto itself; if someone has an exceptional meal or a bad meal and also has some disposable time, they can recount just how good or bad the meal was in exquisite or excruciating detail.

Entire Reddit forums are given over to people opining on anything and everything from relationship woes to old-school mommy bloggers. In one such Reddit community called "Am I the Asshole?," users share a relationship conflagration and how they behaved and open themselves up to the judgment of the public. Nine times out of ten, the answer is, "Yes, YTA (you're the asshole)," immediately followed by Redditors urging the original poster's partner or relative to abandon said relationship forthwith. And, there is social media, where all of this happens in real time—an unending stream of everyone's thoughts and feelings and desires and frustrations, great and small.

Then, of course, there are the more formal expressions of opinions, where writers synthesize and prognosticate on the most pressing issues of the day in a rapidly dwindling number of publications. The work that tackles the present and its concerns garners the most attention, which can be both a blessing and a curse. Readers turn to opinion writing because they want help in parsing complex issues. In times of strife or tragedy, they may be seeking solace and community. They want to learn and be exposed to diverse modes of thought. They want help finding clarity on issues they find confusing or feel ambivalent about. And they want to read thoughtful, provocative, beautiful writing.

As I have developed something of an audience, readers have reached out to me publicly or privately, asking what I—specifically—think about a given issue. It can be flattering. It can be stressful, too, because while I am opinionated, I don't necessarily have an opinion on everything. Or I may have an opinion on a given topic but not be well-informed enough because I am not an expert on everything. Understanding when to speak on an issue and when to listen and learn is an invaluable skill I continue to hone. At times, people treat me like an opinion vending machine, asking me what I think about their favorite television show or a politician running for office or a recent calamity, as if opinion writing is merely emotional utterance rather than a practice that requires care and consideration. Alas.

When I first started writing essays, I was often writing to the news cycle. Something would happen, and I'd know I had something to say, and I'd know I had to say something. I sat with my laptop and wrote furiously until I reached the end. I tried to revise these into something I felt reasonably confident sharing with an editor and waited to see what happened next. In the late aughts and 2010s, I published such pieces in *HTMLGIANT* or *The Rumpus* or *Salon*, the first publications that took a chance on my nonfiction. Some of that work ended up in my first essay collection, *Bad Feminist*. I never really anticipated people reading or engaging with my work, but they did.

As I built more of a career, editors started to seek me out, which was pretty thrilling after so many years writing in obscurity. These solicitations were flattering and kind of terrifying and an interesting challenge. Something tragic and/or culturally significant would happen like a mass shooting in a Black church or the death of a towering public figure or an unexpected election outcome and an editor would email me, often immediately, asking if I could write something within a few hours, a day at the most. Somehow, I was able to do so, though in retrospect, I'm not sure how I managed for as long as I did. After I agreed to an assignment, I thought through what I had to say about the matter at hand, did as much research as time allowed, and tried my best to compose a lucid, compelling argument. Sometimes, I already knew what I wanted to say, and sometimes I wrote my way into what I needed to say. For all of this writing, I was rewarded with the handsome sum of $50 or $150, maybe $250 if I was really lucky.

Early on, I tried to engage in the discourse my work instigated. I read comments, a grave mistake, and sometimes responded, also a grave mistake. Rarely do good things happen in comment sections, particularly when they are unmoderated. These toxic engagements had little to do with what I actually wrote and they made me brittle and overly defensive. It has taken a long time to undo that calcification, to recognize that my work is to write as well as I can, and that I don't have to debate random internet strangers simply because they want to have a conversation.

What was once flattering eventually started to feel like something of a burden. Editors, wanting to stay ahead of the news cycle, prioritized getting the first reactions published without really caring if those reactions were also the best or most thoughtful. One of the greatest gifts of my career has been to finally reach a place where I can take time to write, where I can prioritize quality over speed.

I have enjoyed the opportunity to share my perspective or to argue against something I find intolerable or abhorrent or for something I passionately believe in. I don't take it for granted. I have access to a world I previously could only imagine—one where I have a voice and dare to use it and know my voice is being heard. On the page, I get to be the boldest, most audacious version of myself.

After more than a decade of opinion writing, I understand, most of the time, that the only thing I can control is what I put on the page. I know not everyone will engage in good faith. A lot of the time, an alarming amount of the time, people will only read a headline I had no hand in crafting. They will respond to that headline in ways that reinforce their own opinions, biases, and pet positions. People will criticize me for what I don't say instead of what I do, expecting me to account for the whole of human experience in any given piece.

Sometimes, when I express an opinion, readers assume I have far more power than I do. If I don't find a comedian funny, they make a bizarre, (il)logical leap, suggesting that I am somehow silencing that comedian or materially affecting their career. They presume that, as a writer who does well enough for herself but is still just a writer, I have the kind of power held by the most famous and wealthiest people in the world. They misunderstand fairly straightforward concepts like privacy or free speech or democracy or autonomy in self-serving ways. Ultimately, such responses to my work are more reflective of their discomfort with who is expressing certain opinions rather than the opinions themselves.

I am often accused of being angry because I write about infuriating problems. I bristle at this accusation, because it is one. There is always the implication that anger is wrong, unbecoming, inappropriate. Being called angry is not a compliment; it is a warning that I'm overstepping, that I don't know my place—even though I absolutely know that my place is wherever I choose to be. Sometimes I try to defend myself, because anger is not the primary engine of my work. And other times I get angry, because anger is an entirely appropriate response to bigotry, systemic bias, and injustice.

Opinionated people of a certain ilk often lament the "good old days" of discourse when everyone, regardless of affiliations and persuasions, listened to and respected one another. I'm not really sure those days ever existed for women or people of color or queer people or anyone else living in the margins. Those seeking a platonic ideal of discourse want people to be able to freely express their thoughts in a vacuum, without context or consequence. They want the airing of opinions to be nothing more than a harmless intellectual exercise. And I suppose, for those whose lives are not materially affected by the issues on which they opine, that might be possible. If the right people agree with your opinions, or if they believe you have the right to express your opinions, they will respect them. They will engage with what you actually wrote rather than some shallow, facile reconstruction that better suits their own beliefs and agendas.

But if they don't think you have a right to an opinion—if they resent who you are and what you represent—your opinions are a problem. The reach and power of those opinions expands exponentially. Suddenly, you are a threat. Suddenly, free speech, for example, no longer applies. Suddenly, *ad feminam* attacks are the dominant response.

When you have opinions, particularly opinions that challenge the status quo, people are going to react. Unfortunately, most of that reaction is offered in deeply bad faith. There are the trolls who look for your most tender weaknesses, the places where you are too vulnerable, and then they dig and dig at you. If you're a woman or a person of color or queer or fat or disabled or any kind of different, that's what they will home in on. The cruelty can be relentless and heartbreaking. Sometimes I dread publishing a given essay. Sometimes I write something and choose not to publish it simply because I don't want to deal with the bullshit. I hate when that happens, when I hold back my intellectual work because I am unwilling to pay the price I know will be exacted.

I don't know what an ideal discursive culture should look like, and if such a thing is even remotely possible on the internet, which is raucous and often ungovernable. Then again, as a writer, I, too, am raucous and often ungovernable. And so I write toward spaces where being raucous and ungovernable is seen as an asset rather than a liability. I write with care and consideration. I write knowing I am fallible. Sometimes I get things wrong, but my intentions are good, and my curiosity about the world is genuine.

In these pages, you will find writing about the issues that have shaped my professional and personal lives for the past ten years. There is connective tissue across many of these essays. I am often interested in identity politics. That phrase is often weaponized to dismiss the concerns and lived experiences of marginalized people. It is used to derail conversations about how identity shapes the way we move through the world and the way the world moves through us. It is an accusation that implies that we can somehow separate ourselves from the very things that contribute to who we are. It implies that we can't both acknowledge and embrace our identities and be part of a broader community. To decry identity politics, to suggest you are not political, that you are simply human before anything else is, in fact, an identity politic. And that in itself interests me, as one of the ways that people can so utterly lack self-awareness while denying the lived experiences of everyone different from them.

Race is another common theme, though I wish it weren't, given the breadth of my intellectual interests. When another Black person has been murdered by police or has otherwise suffered the ills of racism, I often think, *I don't have another thing to say about the insidiousness of racism.* I and many other writers have written eloquently and furiously and thoughtfully about how Black lives matter, how unchecked police brutality must end, about how we have had enough. We write and write and write and very little changes because the people who truly need to hear these words are not listening, are incapable of listening. They do not believe Black lives matter and so regardless of how many times they hear those words, they cannot be reached. Writing about race can feel repetitive, but then, racism is repetitive. Generation after generation, our culture perpetuates toxic bigotries. Those in power try to hold dominion over those they feel are lesser. It is a vicious cycle, and while writing feels like a profoundly inadequate response, it's what I know best. To say nothing in the face of rank injustice, as I've written many times over, would be unacceptable.

The political climate in the United States is fractured, and I don't know that those fractures are reparable. We are not merely divided across party lines. We are divided between those who recognize and honor our differences and those who despise and seek to condemn them. During each election cycle, we are reminded of how much is at stake, how women's bodies and trans lives and queer lives and Black and Latino and Asian and Indigenous and South Asian and Muslim lives hang in the balance. We don't really get to root for the best candidates. We are forced to agitate, instead, for the candidates who can beat the most odious, vacuous, and myopic opponents. The "electables" are always rather old white men with patrician good looks and moderate politics and a passion for civility and "reaching across" the proverbial aisle. They lack the backbone to serve the best interests of the majority of Americans. Meanwhile, the compelling candidates, the grassroots organizers and inventive mayors and upstart lawyers who rise up through the political ranks, are dismissed as unviable, when in fact they offer solutions for the problems we're facing and hope for a better future.

When I write about politics, I am expressing my frustration about the terrible political choices we're forced to make, how we cannot succumb to despair however tempting it is, how there are exciting political candidates we should be paying attention to who aren't receiving the support they deserve from the establishment, and how desperately we need change.

Some of my favorite writing is cultural criticism, whether it's a book review or the exploration of a cultural trend or an appreciation of a beloved movie franchise. I am writing in a time where brilliant cultural artifacts are being made in professional circumstances where the systemic issues that affect creators' personal lives are equally present. I write about that, too, about the burden of representation, the pressures it can place on marginalized creators, and what it takes to thrive in a system where we are not meant to thrive. Once in a while, I profile a celebrity. It's not my favorite genre of writing, mostly because it's hard to know what to say about people who are written about exhaustively, but it is admittedly fun to wait for Madonna in her living room or sit across from Charlie Hunnam in a cramped booth in a Jewish deli in Hollywood or watch Janelle Monáe twirling around her swimming pool while her Ivy Park coat billows in the gentle breeze.

Gender politics informs a lot of my work, because as much progress as we have achieved with regard to gender equity, there is still so much work to do. It's a tricky thing, trying to find the right balance between addressing the circumstances women contend with while acknowledging the progress we've made. Feminist activists are actively engaged in defending women's bodily autonomy and protecting our choices. They strive to ensure a future where our lives are not constrained by systemic bias. It's important to acknowledge that, too.

The book closes with a few examples of solicited advice from my Ask Roxane and Work Friend columns in the *New York Times*, simply because I love giving advice. It's so satisfying, even if that advice is not taken. I consider the questions I am asked seriously, because when people reach out for counsel they want to be seen and heard and cared for in some small way.

In each of the sections besides the last, the work appears chronologically, from earliest to most recent. With few exceptions, the pieces included in *Opinions* appear as they did in their original publications. Any changes have been made only for the sake of clarity.

Because I've been writing for quite some time, I am often asked if I have changed my mind about any of my opinions. Generally, people want to hear that yes, I have, as if an opinion is a temporary thing to be overcome. And though I hate to disappoint anyone, I cannot say I have. I still believe we need stricter gun laws and that people with uteruses should have bodily autonomy and that extrajudicial murder is wrong and that democracy is vastly better than fascism. That said, I would like to believe my opinions have evolved, that my thinking grows more nuanced. And so I say that while my opinions haven't changed, I did the best I could with the knowledge and skill I had at the time. And I continue to write that way. Regardless of how I'm expressing my opinions, I am always, always trying my best.

[IDENTITY/POLITICS]

Tragedy Plays on an Infinite Loop

The expansive anarchy of the internet continues to lull us into believing that, because we can see something, that something should be seen. Because we can say something, there is something that must be said. When there's nothing to be seen, we are more than willing to create a spectacle so that we might have something to say.

On August 9, 2014, unarmed, 18-year-old Mike Brown was killed by Darren Wilson. In the days since, Ferguson, Missouri—where the shooting occurred—became the site of an occupation by militarized police, a series of protests and exploitation by opportunists of all stripes. Before long, the media will leave, and Ferguson will remain a troubled town with a police force that disproportionately targets its black citizens: a town where the majority of the residents are black and the majority of the elected officials and police officers who should be protecting and serving are white.

Before too long, another city will become another spectacle because another unarmed black man will be gunned down by another overzealous police officer.

In the wake of the events in Ferguson, we want information. We want to understand why Michael Brown was killed. We want to understand the events leading up to it. We are all forensic analysts. We are all detectives. We are all journalists. We are anything we want to be in any given moment because we have so much access to the spectacle—live feeds from citizen journalists, tweets from reporters and people who are in the thick of it all, images splashed across the internet, information from news feeds and, once in a while, on the major news networks.

And then we have the commentary. There is the spectacle, and then we must deliberate on the spectacle. We must demand that our favorite thinkers offer their deliberations, whether they are qualified or not, as if we cannot truly make sense of a spectacle until we are told how to do so.

Much of what we now know as spectacle is mediated through technology. We have cellphones and smartphones and iDevices and laptops and the ability to be perpetually connected. We never have to miss anything significant or insignificant.

In some ways, this unprecedented access means injustice is no longer customarily ignored or brushed aside. We do not remain silent as we mourn and rage against, for example, the deaths of Troy Davis, Renisha McBride, Trayvon Martin and Eric Garner. In other ways, it means we see too much, and are forced into spaces where it is hard to feel an appropriate amount of horror or make sense of anything.

We bear witness to the worst of human brutality, retweet what we have witnessed, and then we move on to the next atrocity. There is always more atrocity.

Journalist James Foley was kidnapped in 2012 while on assignment in Syria. On Tuesday, terrorists from the Islamic State posted a video of what appears to be Foley being beheaded. The video was posted on YouTube and Al-Furqan media (though YouTube quickly took the video down). It didn't matter. Once this sort of thing slithers into the world, the spectacle swells. The images are shared and re-shared and discussed—mostly in horror. But is it horror, really? To click on the video, knowing what you are about to see is to make yourself, in some small way, part of the story. It is to invite the horror upon yourself. We cannot absolve ourselves.

Of course, the terrorists understand this perfectly. They knew what they were doing when they uploaded the video. They understand the economics of spectacle. They supplied an insatiable demand.

In St. Louis, Kajieme Powell was also killed by a police officer, in broad daylight. The police said that he had a knife raised over his head but, in a video released on Wednesday, we see that, though Powell was agitated and demanding, "Shoot me," he was several feet away from the police officers. And then, in the video, on YouTube, there is the staccato of 12 gunshots.

The entire tragedy became spectacle because a passerby was filming the incident before, during and after. He was armed with his cellphone. He was primed for a spectacle because this is the culture we have wrought, one in which we are perpetually ready to bear witness even if we do not know, in advance, what we will bear witness to. "I got everything on tape," says the man with his cellphone, over and over and over again.

In the last minutes of the video of the killing of Kajieme Powell, several other witnesses are seen holding their cellphones up so that they, too—so that we, too—might have a piece of the testimony. No matter where we are, no matter who we are, we can be part of the spectacle. Far too few of us question whether or not we should be.

Originally published in *The Guardian*, August 22, 2014

Am I a Bad Person If *Je Ne Suis Pas Charlie*?

In the wake of terrorist attacks in Paris last week, many people in France and elsewhere have declared, *Je suis Charlie* ("I am Charlie") after heavily armed gunmen broke into the headquarters of *Charlie Hebdo*, a satirical French magazine, and killed eight staff members, two police officers, a building maintenance worker and wounded several others.

On Sunday, hundreds of thousands of people including a number of world leaders such as Angela Merkel, Benjamin Netanyahu and David Cameron gathered in Paris for a unity rally, to stand in mourning, in defiance. There were cries of *Je suis Charlie, Je suis Ahmed* (I am Ahmed, the Muslim police officer who lost his life in the attack), *Je suis juif* (I am a Jew).

These declarations were a display of solidarity with those who lost their lives and those who survived. They allowed people to try and place themselves in the lives of others by using the power of language. We have seen this kind of remembrance before in the face of tragedy: I am Troy Davis; I am Mike Brown; I am Eric Garner; I am Renisha McBride.

But we are none of these people. We can and do empathize with the plights of the dead, the survivors and their loved ones. We can and do empathize with how fragile we all are, and with how we cannot be ruled by terror, but why the rhetorical urge to take the place of the fallen? What does it bring them? I, too, have ached since hearing the news of what happened in Paris but *je ne suis pas Charlie et je ne suis pas Ahmed et je ne suis pas juif.*

There are times when silence equals consent, but is the loss of someone else's life really such an instance? Is it reasonable to assume that if *je ne suis pas Charlie*, I tacitly endorse terrorism?

I believe in the freedom of expression, unequivocally—though, as I have written before, I wish more people would understand that freedom of expression is not freedom from consequence. I find some of the work of *Charlie Hebdo* distasteful, because there is a preponderance of bigotry of all kinds in many of their cartoons' sentiments. Still, my distaste should not dictate the work the magazine produces or anything else. The cartoonists at *Charlie Hebdo*—and writers and artists everywhere—should be able to express themselves and challenge authority without being murdered. Murder is not an acceptable consequence for anything.

Yet it is also an exercise of freedom of expression to express offense at the way satire like *Charlie Hebdo*'s characterizes something you hold dear—like your faith, your personhood, your gender, your sexuality, your race or ethnicity.

Demands for solidarity can quickly turn into demands for groupthink, making it difficult to express nuance. It puts the terms of our understanding of the situation in black-and-white—you are either with us or against us—instead of allowing people to mourn and be angry while also being sympathetic to complexities that are being overlooked.

It has been disheartening to see calls for the Muslim community to denounce terrorism. It has been disheartening to see journalists highlighting the stories of "good" Muslims, as if goodness is the exception to the rule of an entire people.

We will continue to see discussions of satire, the freedom of expression and its limits. We will see speculations as to how such a tragedy can be avoided because it is easier to speculate than it is to accept that we cannot prevent terrorism. We cannot sway extremists with rational thought or with our ideas of right and wrong.

Life moves quickly but, sometimes, consideration does not. And yet, we insist that people provide an immediate response, or immediate agreement, a universal, immediate me-too—as though we don't want people to pause at all, to consider what they are weighing in on. We don't want to complicate our sorrow or outrage when it is easier to experience these emotions in their simplest, purest states.

The older (and hopefully wiser) I get, the more I want to pause. I want to take the time to think through how I feel and why I feel. I don't want to feign expertise on matters I know nothing about for the purpose of offering someone else my immediate reaction for their consumption.

The demand for response from all of us through the means available to us, most often our social networks, rises in part because we can feel so impotent in our day-to-day lives. We are people with jobs and families and our quotidian concerns. It is easy to feel impotent in the face of terrorism in Paris or hundreds of girls being kidnapped in Nigeria or a bombing at an NAACP building in Colorado or an unarmed black man being killed by a police officer.

Within our social networks, we can feel less alone. We can feel less impotent. We can make these gestures of solidarity. *Je suis Charlie.* We can change our avatars. We can share our anger, our fear or devastation without having to face that we may not be able to do much more.

But we still feel impotent and we still feel inadequate. When we see people not participating in our expressions of solidarity—not showing their awareness of their own impotence—we see something we can possibly change. That is why we demand allegiance.

Originally published in *The Guardian*, January 12, 2015

The Seduction of Safety, on Campus and Beyond

I have been searching for safety for most of my life. I experienced a brutal assault when I was young, and in that terrible moment I learned I was vulnerable in unimaginable ways. I have come to crave safety, the idea that I can live free from physical or emotional harm. As an adult, I understand that there is no such thing as safety, that safety is promised to no one, but oh the idea of it remains so lovely, so elusive.

When it comes to human resilience, our culture has grand ideas about the nobility of hardship and suffering. "The world breaks every one and afterward many are strong at the broken places," Ernest Hemingway wrote. And certainly, I became the woman I am today, for better and worse, because of the hardships I have endured. If I had to choose, though, I would prefer to have not lost my sense of safety in the way I did.

I am now always searching for safety, and I appreciate safe spaces—the ones I create for my students in a classroom, the ones I create with my writing and the ones others create, too—because there is so much unsafe space in this world.

This past week, the news media has energetically discussed student unrest at Yale and at the University of Missouri, where students are protesting administrative insensitivity or inaction in the face of troubled racial climates. At Mizzou, in particular, student activists have demanded safe space. A student journalist, Tim Tai, was denied access to the protesters' tent city in a public area of the campus. The protesters didn't want to be photographed or interviewed, possibly not trusting journalists to tell their story accurately.

The next day, they rightly changed their stance, opened their space to the media, and a debate on free speech and safe spaces found new life.

Quickly, the student protesters were accused of not tolerating free speech in regard not only to Mr. Tai but also to those who use racial epithets and otherwise engage in hate speech. They were accused of being weak, of being whiny for having the audacity to expect to attend college without being harassed for their blackness.

As a writer, I believe the First Amendment is sacred. The freedom of speech, however, does not guarantee freedom from consequence. You can speak your mind, but you can also be shunned. You can be criticized. You can be ignored or ridiculed. You can lose your job. The freedom of speech does not exist in a vacuum.

Many of the people who advocate for freedom of speech with the most bluster are willing to waste this powerful right on hate speech. But the beauty of the freedom of speech is that it protects us from subjectivity. We protect someone's right to shout hateful slurs the same way we protect someone's right to, say, criticize the government or discuss her religious beliefs.

And so the students at Mizzou wanted a safe space to commune as they protested. They wanted sanctuary but had the nerve to demand this sanctuary in plain sight, in a public space. Rather than examine why the activists needed a safe space, most people wrapped themselves in the Constitution, the path of less resistance. The students are framed as coddled infants, as if perhaps we should educate college students in a more spartan manner—placing classrooms in lions' dens.

Feminism is largely responsible for introducing safe space into our cultural vernacular as a means of fostering open, productive dialogue. In the late 1980s, queer groups began safe space programs that have since flourished on college campuses. When a faculty member puts the safe space symbol on her door, L.G.B.T. students know they have a place on campus where they will not be judged or persecuted for their sexuality or gender identity, where they are safe.

Safe spaces allow people to feel welcome without being unsafe because of the identities they inhabit. A safe space is a haven from the harsh realities people face in their everyday lives.

All good ideas can be exploited. There are some extreme, ill-advised and simply absurd manifestations of the idea of safe space. And there are and should be limits to the boundaries of safe space. Safe space is not a place where dissent is discouraged, where dissent is seen as harmful. And yet. I understand where safe space extremism comes from. When you are marginalized and always unsafe, your skin thins, leaving your blood and bone exposed. You live at the breaking point. In such circumstances, of course you might be inclined to fiercely protect yourself, at any cost. Of course you might become intolerant. Of course you might perceive dissent as danger.

There is also this. Those who mock the idea of safe space are most likely the same people who are able to take safety for granted. That's what makes discussions of safety and safe spaces so difficult. We are also talking about privilege. As with everything else in life, there is no equality when it comes to safety.

While no one is guaranteed absolute safety, and everyone knows suffering, there are dangers members of certain populations will never know. There is a degree of safety members of certain populations will never know. White people will never know the dangers of being black in America, systemic, unequal opportunity, racial profiling, the constant threat of police violence. Men will never know the dangers of being a woman in America, harassment, sexual violence, legislated bodies. Heterosexuals will never know what it means to experience homophobia.

Those who take safety for granted disparage safety because it is, like so many other rights, one that has always been inalienable to them. They wrongly assume we all enjoy such luxury and are blindly seeking something even more extravagant. They assume that we should simply accept hate without wanting something better. They cannot see that what we seek is sanctuary. We want to breathe.

On college campuses, we are having continuing debates about safe spaces. As a teacher, I think carefully about the intellectual space I want to foster in my classroom—a space where debate, dissent and even protest are encouraged. I want to challenge students and be challenged. I don't want to shape their opinions. I want to shape how they articulate and support those opinions. I do not believe in using trigger warnings because that feels like the unnecessary segregation of students from reality, which is complex and sometimes difficult.

Rather than use trigger warnings, I try to provide students with the context they will need to engage productively in complicated discussions.

I consider my classroom a safe space in that students can come as they are, regardless of their identities or sociopolitical affiliations. They can trust that they might become uncomfortable but they won't be persecuted or judged. They can trust that they will be challenged but they won't be tormented.

When students leave my classroom, any classroom, they have to and should face the real world, the best and worst of it. I can only hope they are adequately prepared to navigate the world as it is rather than how we wish it could be. But I also hope they are both realistic and idealistic. I hope that, like me, they search for safety, or work to create a world where some measure of safety, not to be confused with anything as infantile as coddling, is an inalienable right.

Originally published in the *New York Times*, November 13, 2015

White Crime

On June 10, 2016, singer Christina Grimmie was shot and killed by a white man who then killed himself. There was no security at Plaza Live, the venue where Grimmie was performing. Orlando police chief John Mina said, in a *Buzzfeed News* interview, "This isn't a crowd that you would suspect would be carrying guns into an event like this." What goes unsaid is that there is a crowd "you" would suspect would be carrying guns into a different kind of concert. At a rap concert, for example, security is always visibly present. There are often metal detectors. This kind of security is simply a reflection of this country's overall attitude toward race and crime.

When black men commit crimes or are alleged to have committed crimes, we immediately learn of their every misdeed from the womb forward. We see their mug shots. We are treated to a recitation of statistics on race, criminality, and incarceration rates. Rarely are these men seen as human, treated as human. They are not sons, fathers, brothers, or friends. They are not men. Instead, they are criminals, and worse, there is no hope for their redemption, there is no possibility that they are anything more than their misdeeds, their mistakes.

Black men receive sentences that are 20 percent longer than white men's sentences for the same crimes. There are disparities along racial lines for all issues related to sentencing, including who gets life without parole for both violent and nonviolent crimes and who is sentenced to death.

Even when black men are victims of crimes, they are scrutinized and treated as criminals in waiting. Black boys in particular are never allowed to be boys. Manhood is ascribed to black boys because we are part of a culture where innocence and blackness are seen as antithetical. Look at

Trayvon Martin. Look at Tamir Rice. Look, even, at the preschooler who climbed into the Gorilla World exhibit at the Cincinnati Zoo. A gorilla from the exhibit, Harambe, was killed in order to save the boy, and immediately afterward speculation began about why he entered the enclosure, as if there could be a reason beyond a child's curiosity and naïveté.

White men who commit crimes don't have to suffer such indignities. Instead, they get the Brock Turner treatment. Turner—someone convicted of sexual assault—who was sentenced to a paltry six months in county jail for the crime of rape. He will likely serve only half that sentence. In justifying the inadequate jail time, judge Aaron Persky said, shamelessly, "A prison sentence would have a severe impact on him. I think he will not be a danger to others."

Manhood is ascribed to black boys because we are part of a culture where innocence and blackness are seen as antithetical.

This is how whiteness works. Turner is seen as human, as a victim in the crime he committed. He is a "good young man." He is allowed to have both a past and a future and this past and future are worthy of consideration. His crime is a mistake, not a scarlet letter, not a reflection of his character.

Brock Turner assaulted a woman behind a Dumpster in an alley. His victim was unconscious. He lifted her dress. He removed her underwear. He penetrated her without her consent. Turner took at least one picture of her breasts with his cellphone. Brock Turner was only stopped because two passersby noticed him and intervened. Before Turner committed this sexual assault, he had tried to kiss the victim's sister, who rejected him. Twice. That's when he found the victim, who was drunk and alone, and before long, unconscious. Brock Turner's crime is revolting. His crime is deliberate.

The victim wrote an eloquent and impassioned statement about her experience, about how she has suffered, about the repercussions of Brock Turner's crime. Her words were not enough to overcome the power of Brock Turner's whiteness.

In the aftermath, Brock Turner is remorseless for everyone but himself. He doesn't seem to understand that he has committed a crime. In his statement to the court, he was preoccupied with how his life has been changed. He states, with flagrant arrogance and immaturity, "I wish I never was good at swimming or had the opportunity to attend Stanford, so maybe the newspapers wouldn't want to write stories about me." He says this as if he was simply in the wrong place at the wrong time, as if he is a victim of his blessings and good fortune, as if the true travesty here is the damage to his reputation. That sort of deluded attitude is what whiteness allows—a haven from reality and consequence.

Letters of support from Turner's family and friends illuminate his willful ignorance. His supporters mourn for how he is suffering, for how his life has changed, how unfair this all is. Turner's grandparents wrote, "Brock is the only person being held accountable for the actions of other irresponsible adults." His father lamented how Brock is a changed person, how the man's life has been ruined for "20 minutes of action." His mother is so upset she cannot bear to redecorate her new home and she is bereft that her son's "dreams have been shattered." His sister made it clear that Turner's actions were "alcohol-fueled." A friend, Leslie Rasmussen, doesn't think Turner's life should be ruined because of "the decision of a girl who doesn't remember anything but the amount she drank."

This is how whiteness works. It provides instant redemption and unearned respect.

This is how whiteness works. It provides shelter. In most of these letters of support, everyone and everything must shoulder the blame but Brock Turner, the convicted sex offender.

This is how whiteness works. It provides protection. It took months for the Santa Clara County Sheriff's Office to release Brock Turner's mug shot. Instead, the most prominent image of Turner was a school photo in a suit jacket and tie, his hair cut neatly, his smile wide. He wasn't referred to as a violent criminal but as a Stanford student, a talented swimmer with ambitions of reaching the Olympics.

This is how whiteness works. It provides instant redemption and unearned respect. Too many articles refer to Turner as the ex–Stanford swimmer instead of labeling him as the rapist he is. Too many articles enthusiastically offer his résumé of accomplishments even though he is only 20 years old. He hasn't been alive to accomplish that much.

I grew up in quiet, "idyllic" communities like Oakwood, Ohio, where Turner is from. I know all about these upper-middle-class environments where white children are raised believing they can do no wrong, where those same children are denied nothing, and where they grow up entitled and never learn that they should be otherwise. These are communities where good, wholesome kids drink and do drugs and make trouble. Everyone looks away because they are good kids who are "just having fun." High grades and athleticism and sharp haircuts and "good" families excuse all manner of bad behavior.

I was a victim once. The boys who raped me were boys like Brock Turner. They were athletes, popular, clean cut. They came from *good families* and so did I. There is some benefit in reminding people that criminality lurks in all kinds of places and that goodness provides cover for all kinds of badness.

As sad as it is to say, there is nothing surprising about Brock Turner, his family, and their reluctance to place the responsibility for Turner's crime squarely on their son's shoulders. That's not how they were raised. His whiteness allows his family, his friends, and far too many people who are following news about his crime to see Brock Turner as the boy next door. The white boy next door cannot possibly be a criminal, and so he isn't.

Were it that black men received such indulgence. Everyone lives next door to someone.

Originally published in *Lenny Letter*, December 6, 2017

The Case Against Hope

———

"Now what?" is a question I ask myself often. It's a question many recent graduates are asking themselves this spring, after collecting their hard-earned diplomas. And it is a good question for them to contemplate as they try to figure out how to move forward.

Because I write about difficult subjects—gender, sexual violence, sexuality, race—people wondering "Now what?" often ask me about hope. They want me to offer assurances that though we are facing many challenges, everything will be O.K., the world will keep on turning. It is very seductive, this hope people yearn for.

I don't traffic in hope. Realism is more my ministry than is unbridled optimism. Hope is too ineffable and far too elusive. Hope allows us to leave what is possible in the hands of others. And now, more than ever, as we consider the state of the world, as we consider the many candidates running for president in 2020, we don't need to leave possibility to others. So much of what is possible is, in fact, in our hands. We can choose which parts of the political process—in our local communities, in our states and in our country—we directly participate in.

The current political climate is overwhelming. With each passing day, the administration advances its agenda, unimpeded. The Senate has confirmed more than 100 of President Trump's judicial nominees. The tariffs the president has imposed are, essentially, a significant tax hike that will, if they persist, contribute to the demise of many American businesses, which will contribute to the demise of many Americans. As with most problems in this country, the working class, people of color and women will be disproportionately affected.

The Mueller report has been released, but we will most likely never see the fully unredacted report unless a whistleblower leaks it. Mr. Mueller stood in front of cameras on May 29 and reminded us that "there were multiple, systematic efforts to interfere in our election." That allegation, he said, "deserves the attention of every American."

Meanwhile, Mr. Trump has continued to focus on insisting that the report absolves him personally, tweeting, "Nothing changes from the Mueller Report. There was insufficient evidence and therefore, in our Country, a person is innocent. The case is closed! Thank you." This is despite Mr. Mueller saying, "If we had had confidence that the president clearly did not commit a crime, we would have said so."

Too many Democrats in Congress refuse to take a stand of any kind. Other politicians are polling to see how the American people feel about impeachment instead of taking definitive action. They want to make a political decision about impeachment instead of holding the president accountable for his actions. It is politics as usual. Politicians offer meaningless words about what an outrage this all is, but refuse to do anything that would compromise their own agendas.

The news cycle doesn't allow for memory anymore, so you may have forgotten that the governor of Virginia apologized for appearing in a yearbook photo of a man in blackface and a man in a Ku Klux Klan outfit before changing his tune and insisting that he was not in the picture (after which an investigation into the image proved inconclusive). You may have forgotten that the Virginia attorney general preemptively admitted that he had donned blackface at some point in his life. You may have forgotten that the state's lieutenant governor was accused of sexual misconduct (he's denied the allegations). These men are still in office. It's amazing what political expedience will tolerate.

Last month, there was a school shooting in Highlands Ranch, Colorado. Within 48 hours, the news cycle had moved on. You could have easily missed the fact that an 18-year-old boy, Kendrick Ray Castillo, died trying to stop one of the shooters. Just last week, a public works employee in Virginia Beach killed 12 people. We now live in a world in which most mass shootings capture our attention for only a matter of hours or days. Do politicians prioritize enacting effective gun control legislation? Of course not.

Footage from Sandra Bland's ill-fated arrest in 2015 was recently released, and in it, we can see a Texas state trooper yelling at Ms. Bland with increasing ferocity. He says to her, "I will light you up." A routine traffic stop was anything but routine. Three days after this video was taken, she was found dead in her jail cell. Police brutality remains a major threat to black and brown life. Police brutality continues to happen in plain sight. It is documented time and again, but rarely are there consequences.

In Georgia, Alabama, Ohio, Missouri and several other states, elected officials have fixated on using draconian abortion legislation to control women and our bodies. When the television series *The Handmaid's Tale*, based on Margaret Atwood's disturbingly prescient novel, debuted in 2017, many of us who fight for reproductive freedom, myself included, abstained from watching it because there was nothing entertaining about a show set in a world where women have no rights, where women are chattel, only as valuable as what their wombs issue. Back then I said we weren't that far from such a reality. I and others were told we were exaggerating, hysterical, that we were nowhere near such a possibility. And yet, here we are.

A United Nations report indicates that a million plant and animal species are in danger of extinction, as global warming continues to reshape the planet and how we live. It used to be that when we discussed global warming, we were talking about how the peril was a few generations away. Instead, the danger is now. It seems apocalyptic, but waters are rising. Weather is becoming wildly unpredictable. On the West Coast, forest fires are raging. Temperatures are rising. Glaciers are melting. Too many politicians do nothing. Too many of us do nothing. And we can no longer afford all this nothing.

I put these thoughts together recently for a commencement address, one that started with asking the question "What now?" and contemplating how hope could possibly relate to that question. I was not trying to depress anyone. I was not trying to make those graduates feel like the world is on fire but . . . the world is on fire both literally and figuratively. This is the world into which these new graduates are entering and the world in which they'll begin their careers. They are going to have to grapple with all of it. And so are we.

Thinking about graduation this year, I read the news about the billionaire Robert F. Smith's gift to the graduates of Morehouse, paying the student loans of the graduating class of 2019. His generous gift was framed as hopeful. I know that for years to come, college students will hope a billionaire is their commencement speaker and will give them the gift of the freedom from student loan debt. They will hope because really, that's all they can do. The cost of tuition, room and board, and books is something beyond their control. Hope isn't.

But instead of thinking about hope, I want to continue thinking about possibility. When we hope, we have no control over what may come to pass. We put all our trust and energy into the whims of fate. We abdicate responsibility. We allow ourselves to be complacent. We are all just people living our lives as best we can, aren't we? It is easy to feel helpless. It is much harder to make ourselves uncomfortable by imagining the impossible to be possible. But we can do that. We can act, even in the smallest of ways.

Democracy is faltering. The actions of the executive branch are being insufficiently checked and balanced. Many of us have surrendered to numbness or apathy in this political moment because our politicians seem to be refusing to act in our best interests. If we are being honest, we also aren't acting in the best interests of the people we should be serving, which is one another. No matter who we are, where we come from, what we believe, who we vote for, how we worship, we live in this world together. And so maybe we should do everything in our power to make sure things don't get worse.

This question of "Now what?" is an important one to ask, wherever we are in our lives. One thing I didn't say to those new graduates I addressed was "Good luck." Luck is like hope—too far beyond our control, too ephemeral. What we really must wish for one another is the power of all that might be possible if we do anything more than hope.

Originally published in the *New York Times*, June 6, 2019

Cops Don't Belong at Pride

My wife, Debbie, came out as a lesbian when she was 50 years old. Her first Pride parade in New York City was also the first time, she told me early in our courtship, that she was able to understand what it feels like to be proud. There is a picture of her on Christopher Street, beaming. She is wearing a T-shirt that says, "Yep, I'm Gay." Around her are hundreds of people from the L.G.B.T.Q. community, and allies, celebrating our right to be.

I came out as a lesbian when I was 19 and would, in later years, identify as bisexual. It was a relatively unremarkable experience. But after a misadventure in Arizona, I found myself in Lincoln, Nebraska, my home state. I didn't know many people, and I certainly didn't know other queer people. I had no role models. I didn't know how to ask a girl out on a date or where to get the right haircut. My first Pride parade, in Omaha, was a modest one—but there were rainbow flags everywhere and beautiful queer people of every stripe. There was music and dancing. There were pamphlets about marriage equality and activists giving fiery speeches. I knew, deep in my bones, that I was among my people.

Our experiences mirror those of millions of other queer people who have needed, at some point in their lives, to find their people. Pride parades are and have been a way for the L.G.B.T.Q. community to march proudly through the streets of our cities, to claim our identity in a world that criminalized our sexuality, demanded our shame, expected us to hide in the dark.

Modern Pride celebrations began with a rebellion against the police. In June 1969, at the Stonewall Inn, a gay bar in Greenwich Village, there was yet another police raid—but this time it was met with a raucous protest. The bar patrons fought back and continued to protest for the next several days. A movement, largely ignited by Black trans women and young gay hustlers, was born. The first gay pride parade was held the following year in New York City.

Now, after Pride organizers asked police officers to refrain from marching in uniform as a group in the New York parade (as Pride organizations have done in other cities), there has been an outcry and complaints that L.G.B.T.Q. officers are now the ones being marginalized. But many of us want no part of a display of police pride. Our history is young, and we have not forgotten it. For decades, the police have tormented our communities. They enforced laws about how we dressed, where we congregated and whom we had sex with. They beat us, blackmailed us and put us in jail.

Police harassment didn't begin or end in 1969—nor did queer resistance. Ten years before the Stonewall uprising, there was a similar incident in Los Angeles. The police began harassing patrons at Cooper Donuts, a cafe that welcomed not only gays and lesbians but also transgender patrons. When the police tried to arrest several people, they were pelted with debris until they fled the area.

And even now, the police across the United States can be incredibly hostile to the L.G.B.T.Q. community, whether it is mishandling intimate partner violence in our relationships, physically and verbally assaulting us, refusing to investigate the crimes we suffer or abusing their power when they police our events.

Violence against Black trans women remains disproportionately high, with many reporting that they don't feel safe going to the police for fear of encountering more violence or facing disbelief and indifference. According to the Human Rights Campaign, at least 27 trans or gender-nonconforming people, most of them Black or Latinx, have been murdered so far in 2021, and many of their killings have gone unsolved. And then, of course, a year after the murder of George Floyd, it's hard to ignore the ever-growing list of Black and brown people killed by police officers.

Over the past 50 years, Pride has evolved. At times, it feels unrecognizable because it has gone so mainstream. It has taken on the feel of a holiday, but with corporate sponsorship. What began in New York City is now celebrated in cities all across the world. Pride is a month of marches, parties and events. The celebrations are dynamic and broadly inclusive. Straight allies bring their children. Queer people bring our children. I love seeing how Pride has grown, but it sometimes feels as if we have forgotten who Pride is for. And it is frustrating that some corporations have commodified it, drenching their marketing materials with rainbow colors but doing little to celebrate and support the L.G.B.T.Q. community during the rest of the year. Nonetheless, at its best, Pride celebrations continue to offer space for us to know we belong to a community in which we are embraced for who we are.

We are a sprawling, unruly community. As we continue to think about who belongs at Pride, questions and, inevitably, controversies arise. Some people, for example, want to exclude the kink community or at least expect kinky queers to tone down their public expressions of sexuality to make Pride more family-friendly. This kind of respectability politics is nothing new. There have always been calls for the L.G.B.T.Q. community to neuter the sex from our sexuality, to temper our flamboyance, to bend to heterosexual norms. Let's be clear: We should not have to contort ourselves to make straight people more comfortable with our lives. Assimilation cannot be the price we must pay for freedom.

The idea that we should now forgive the past and make peace with oppressive police forces is ludicrous. It is infuriating. In an essay for the *Washington Post*, the columnist Jonathan Capehart wrote a vigorous entreaty for L.G.B.T.Q. officers to be welcomed at Pride celebrations. The *New York Times* editorial board took a similar stance. Mr. Capehart empathizes with people who don't want police officers at Pride, but he argues that they are wrong, calling it "beyond troubling that a community made up of so many who've been rejected by their families because of who they are is now turning on its members because of what they do for a living."

This false equivalence defies credulity. We are not turning on anyone. Law enforcement is not an innate identity. The police are not marginalized. They aren't disowned by their families for carrying a gun and badge. They haven't been brutalized or arrested because of how they make a living.

And they aren't actually being rejected; they are being asked to respect boundaries. L.G.B.T.Q. officers are more than welcome to join

Pride celebrations—unarmed and in civilian clothing. They are being asked to confront their complicity with an institution that does more harm than good to vulnerable communities. It is telling that some of these officers refuse to do so. We don't need the police marching alongside us. We don't need them at Pride providing security.

What we need, what we've always wanted and deserved, is what Debbie and I found when we first marched at Pride: a welcoming space where we can be safe and free.

Originally published in the *New York Times*, May 29, 2021

Why People Are So Awful Online

When I joined Twitter 14 years ago, I was living in Michigan's Upper Peninsula, attending graduate school. I lived in a town of around 4,000 people, with few Black people or other people of color, not many queer people and not many writers. Online is where I found a community beyond my graduate school peers. I followed and met other emerging writers, many of whom remain my truest friends. I got to share opinions, join in on memes, celebrate people's personal joys, process the news with others and partake in the collective effervescence of watching awards shows with thousands of strangers.

Something fundamental has changed since then. I don't enjoy most social media anymore. I've felt this way for a while, but I'm loath to admit it.

Increasingly, I've felt that online engagement is fueled by the hopelessness many people feel when we consider the state of the world and the challenges we deal with in our day-to-day lives. Online spaces offer the hopeful fiction of a tangible cause and effect—an injustice answered by an immediate consequence. On Twitter, we can wield a small measure of power, avenge wrongs, punish villains, exalt the pure of heart.

In our quest for this simulacrum of justice, however, we have lost all sense of proportion and scale. We hold in equal contempt a war criminal and a fiction writer who too transparently borrows details from someone else's life. It's hard to calibrate how we engage or argue.

In real life, we are fearful Davids staring down seemingly omnipotent Goliaths: a Supreme Court poised to undermine abortion and civil rights; a patch of sea on fire from a gas leak; an incoherent but surprisingly effective attack on teaching children America's real history; the dismantling of the Voting Rights Act; a man whom dozens of women have accused of sexual assault walking free on a technicality. At least online, we can tell ourselves that the power imbalances between us flatten. Suddenly, we are all Goliaths in the Valley of Elah.

It makes me uncomfortable to admit that I have some influence and power online, because it feels so foreign or, maybe, unlikely. My online following came slowly, and then all at once. For years, I had a couple hundred followers. Those numbers slowly inched up to a couple thousand. Then I wrote a couple of books, blinked, and suddenly hundreds of thousands of people were seeing my tweets. Most of them appreciate my work, though they may disagree with my opinions. Some just hate me, as is their right, and they follow me to scavenge for evidence to support or intensify their enmity. Then there are those who harass me for all kinds of reasons—some aspect of my identity or my work or my presence in the world troubles their emotional waters.

After a while, the lines blur, and it's not at all clear what friend or foe look like, or how we as humans should interact in this place. After being on the receiving end of enough aggression, everything starts to feel like an attack. Your skin thins until you have no defenses left. It becomes harder and harder to distinguish good-faith criticism from pettiness or cruelty. It becomes harder to disinvest from pointless arguments that have nothing at all to do with you. An experience that was once charming and fun becomes stressful and largely unpleasant. I don't think I'm alone in feeling this way. We have all become hammers in search of nails.

One person makes a statement. Others take issue with some aspect of that statement. Or they make note of every circumstance the original statement did not account for. Or they misrepresent the original statement and extrapolate it to a broader issue in which they are deeply invested. Or they take a singular instance of something and conflate it with a massive cultural trend. Or they bring up something ridiculous that someone said more than a decade ago as confirmation of . . . who knows?

Or someone popular gets too close to the sun and suddenly can do nothing right. "Likes" are analyzed obsessively, as if clicking a button on social media is representative of an entire ideology. If a mistake is made, it becomes immediate proof of being beyond redemption. Or if the person is held mildly accountable for a mistake, a chorus rends her or his garments in distress, decrying the inhumanity of "cancel culture."

Every harm is treated as trauma. Vulnerability and difference are weaponized. People assume the worst intentions. Bad-faith arguments abound, presented with righteous bluster.

And these are the more reasonable online arguments. There is another category entirely of racists, homophobes, transphobes, xenophobes and other bigots who target the subjects of their ire relentlessly and are largely unchecked by the platforms enabling them. And then, of course, there are the straight-up trolls, gleefully wreaking havoc.

As someone who has been online for a long time, I have seen all kinds of ridiculous arguments and conversations. I have participated in all kinds of ridiculous arguments and conversations. Lately, I've been thinking that what drives so much of the anger and antagonism online is our helplessness offline. Online we want to be good, to do good, but despite these lofty moral aspirations, there is little generosity or patience, let alone human kindness. There is a desperate yearning for emotional safety. There is a desperate hope that if we all become perfect enough and demand the same perfection from others, there will be no more harm or suffering.

It is infuriating. It is also entirely understandable. Some days, as I am reading the news, I feel as if I am drowning. I think most of us do. At least online, we can use our voices and know they can be heard by someone.

It's no wonder that we seek control and justice online. It's no wonder that the tenor of online engagement has devolved so precipitously. It's no wonder that some of us have grown weary of it.

I don't regret the time I've spent on social media. I've met interesting people. I've had real-life adventures instigated by virtual relationships. I've been emboldened to challenge myself and grow as a person and, yes, clap back if you clap first.

But I have more of a life than I once did. I have a wife, a busy career, aging parents and a large family. I have more physical mobility and, in turn, more interest in being active and out in the world. I now spend most of my time with people who are not Very Online. When I talk to them about some weird or frustrating internet conflagration, they tend to look at me as if I am speaking a foreign language from a distant land. And, I suppose, I am.

Originally published in the *New York Times*, July 17, 2021

Why I've Decided to Take
My Podcast Off Spotify

———

Sometimes, I watch a reality TV show called *Building Off the Grid*, about people who decide to make homes for themselves in remote places where they can live sustainable lives. Over the course of an hour, I'll watch someone build a yurt or a mud hut with cob walls or a house on a mountain outside of Denver, powered by solar panels. It's clear that what these modern-day hermits want is to exist in a vacuum, where they are not affected by nor do they affect anything beyond the boundaries of their home. That is, certainly, an illusion, but I can see the appeal.

I'm a writer. I often write about my opinions, and I know I can't do that in a vacuum, as tempting as that sometimes seems. I believe we should be exposed to a multitude of interesting ideas and perspectives, including those that challenge our most fiercely held beliefs.

But engaging with the world with intellectual honesty and integrity is rarely simple. Several years ago, I pulled out of a book deal with Simon & Schuster because the publishing company had bought a book by a white supremacist provocateur. (Eventually, it dropped Milo Yiannopoulos's book.) He had every right to air his political beliefs, but he didn't have a right to a lucrative book contract. Nor did I, for that matter. The right I did have was to decide who I wanted to do business with.

I made a stand because I could. I had the means to do so. But it was symbolic, as most such stands are: Most of my books have been published at HarperCollins, which is owned by News Corp, the company started by Rupert Murdoch, whose manipulation of the media has done great harm to public discourse over the last several decades. HarperCollins has published all kinds of people I find odious, dangerous and amoral. Would I walk away from my body of work because I find those people loathsome?

No. I don't live in a vacuum. And the most toxic voices should not be the only ones that are heard.

Every day, I try to make the best decisions possible about what I create, what I consume, and who I collaborate with—but living in the world, participating in capitalism, requires moral compromise. I am not looking for purity; it doesn't exist. Instead, I'm trying to do the best I can, and take a stand when I think I can have an impact.

Joe Rogan has been handsomely rewarded for these efforts, to the tune of a reported $100 million deal when he moved his podcast to Spotify. The company clearly believes that's a worthy investment. He has a large, enthusiastic audience of an estimated 11 million willing listeners, none of whom are forced to listen to the podcast. Clearly, something about his feigned curiosity and ignorance and his embrace of conspiracy theorists and quacks resonates with a lot of people. That, too, is disturbing.

In the face of the outcry and boycotts begun by the musicians Neil Young and Joni Mitchell, both the company and Mr. Rogan have made conciliatory gestures. On an earnings call this week, Spotify's chief executive and co-founder, Daniel Ek, defended the company's efforts to combat misinformation, which include working to create content warnings for shows that discuss Covid-19—but not removing Mr. Rogan's podcast from the platform. He added, "I think the important part here is that we don't change our policies based on one creator nor do we change it based on any media cycle, or calls from anyone else."

Spotify does not exist in a vacuum, and the decisions it makes about what content it hosts have consequences. To say that maybe Mr. Rogan should not be given unfettered access to Spotify's more than 400 million users is not censorship, as some have suggested. It is curation.

Misinformation has contributed to tens of millions of people believing the 2020 election was stolen from Donald Trump. It contributed to the January 6 insurrection. And misinformation has helped prolong the Covid-19 pandemic and encouraged people to do dangerous things such as injecting bleach or taking Ivermectin, a horse dewormer paste.

The platforms allowing this misinformation to flourish and intensify consistently abdicate their responsibility to curate effectively. Instead, they offer tepid, ambiguous and ineffective policies. They frame doing nothing as a principled stand to protect free speech, but really, they're protecting their bottom line.

I have a podcast where I talk to interesting people. Until Tuesday, it was available on Spotify, but I have decided to make another stand. A small one. Joining Mr. Young, Ms. Mitchell and a growing group of creators, I took *The Roxane Gay Agenda* and its archives off Spotify, though it will be available on other platforms. It was a difficult decision—there are a lot of listeners on the platform, and I may never recoup that audience elsewhere.

I am not trying to impede anyone's freedom to speak. Joe Rogan and others like him can continue to proudly encourage misinformation and bigotry to vast audiences. They will be well rewarded for their efforts. The platforms sharing these rewards can continue to look the other way.

But today at least, I won't.

Originally published in the *New York Times*, February 3, 2022

It's Time to Rage

My wife's stepfather began raping her when she was 11 years old. The abuse went on for years, and as Debbie got older, she was constantly terrified that she was pregnant. She had no one to talk to and nowhere to turn.

Her stepfather often threatened to kill her younger brother and her mother if Debbie told anyone, so when the fear of pregnancy became too consuming, she told her mother she was assaulted at school. Her mother took Debbie to a doctor, who said that because of her scar tissue, she was sexually active and must have a boyfriend. It was the early 1970s.

A pregnancy would have, in Debbie's words, ruined her life. Today, she is 60 years old. She is still dealing with the repercussions of that trauma. It is unfathomable to consider how a forced pregnancy would have further altered the trajectory of her life.

I was sexually assaulted by several young men when I was 12. I have told the story and am tired of telling it, and the story is not the point. I had not yet had my first period. And still, in the weeks and months after, of course I worried I was pregnant. I worried I would not know who the father was.

If I had been pregnant, I don't know what I would have done. I was Catholic. Abortion was a sin. But a 12-year-old is not equipped for childbirth or parenthood. The trauma I endured would have only been compounded by a forced pregnancy. And the trajectory of my life, too, would have been further altered.

It is stunning that a draft of a Supreme Court ruling that would overturn *Roe v. Wade* was leaked before the justices planned to announce their decision, likely next month. It is also telling. Whoever leaked it wanted people to understand the fate awaiting us.

At least, that is what I am telling myself. And thank God somebody did, so we know. So we can prepare. So we can rage.

We should not live in a world where sexual violence exists, but we do. Given that unfortunate reality, we should not live in a world where someone who is raped is forced to carry a pregnancy to term because a minority of Americans believe the unborn are more important than the people who give birth to them.

And we should defend abortion access not only in cases of sexual violence. All those who want an abortion should be able to avail themselves of that medical procedure. Their reasons are no one's business. People should not have to demonstrate their virtue to justify a personal decision about how to handle a life-altering circumstance.

We should not live in a country where bodily autonomy can be granted or taken away by nine political appointees, most of whom are men and cannot become pregnant. Any civil right contingent upon political whims is not actually a civil right.

Without the right to abortion, women are forced to make terrible choices. These burdens disproportionately fall upon poor and working-class women without the means to travel across state lines to receive the care they need. Despite promises from the anti-abortion movement to support pregnant women and children, the "pro-life" lobby appears to be invested only in the unborn. The same mostly male politicians who oppose abortion so often do everything in their power to oppose rights to paid parental leave, subsidized child care, single-payer health care or any kind of social safety net that could improve family life.

The leaked document is a draft. Abortion is still legal, though it is largely inaccessible in parts of the country. The Supreme Court has issued a statement emphasizing that the draft, while authentic, may still change. Still, it is a harbinger of terrible things to come. As many as 25 states are poised to ban abortion the moment *Roe v. Wade* is overturned.

And there are other disturbing considerations in the draft decision, written by Justice Samuel Alito. Some have expressed the concern that by extending Justice Alito's reasoning, other hard-won rights—such as the rights to contraception and marriage equality—could be struck down too. That is to say, this decision is opening the door for social progress and civil rights to be systematically dismantled on the most absurd of pretexts.

And this is not a theoretical threat. We are already seeing how several states are trying to legislate trans people out of existence with laws banning gender-affirming health care for children, and in Missouri, a proposed law could extend that denial to adults.

I do not know where this retraction of civil rights will end, but I do know it will go down as a milestone in a decades-long conservative campaign to force a country of 330 million people to abide by a bigoted set of ideologies. This movement seeks to rule by hollow theocracy, despite our constitutional separation of church and state. The people behind this campaign do not represent the majority of this country, and they know it, so they consistently try to undermine the democratic process. They attack voting rights, gerrymander voting districts and shove unpopular legislation through so that they can live in a world of their choosing and hoard as much power and wealth as possible.

Where do we go from here? To protect women's bodily autonomy, the right to abortion must be codified in federal law. But the possibility of that seems very distant. In their joint statement, issued after the Supreme Court leak, the Senate majority leader, Chuck Schumer, and the House speaker, Nancy Pelosi, did not use the word "abortion" even once. President Biden has barely uttered it during his presidency. It's hard to believe they are as committed as they need to be to protecting a right whose name they dare not speak. Until the Democrats stop lounging in the middle of the political aisle—where no one is coming to meet them—nothing will change.

The possibility of so many civil rights being rolled back is terrifying. Millions of Americans now wonder which of our rights could be stripped away from us, our friends and family, our communities. The sky is falling, and a great many of us are desperately trying to hold it up.

As Debbie and I discuss the strong likelihood of *Roe v. Wade* being overturned, we have started worrying about potential legal consequences for our very happy marriage. In June, we will celebrate our second wedding anniversary.

When we exchanged our vows, everything changed. We were already committed, but our commitment deepened. There was a new and satisfying gravity to our relationship. In an instant, I understood that marriage is far more than a piece of paper—but that having that paper mattered.

We have each worked very hard to overcome the traumas we endured as children, to allow ourselves to love and be loved wholly. This life we share would not be possible had we ended up pregnant far too young and against our will, with no recourse. This life we have made together isn't political. It is deeply personal. And yet our lives and our bodies remain subject to political debate. In one way or another, they always have.

How are we free, under these circumstances? How can any of us be free?

Originally published in the *New York Times*, May 3, 2022

Don't Talk to Me About Civility. On Tuesday Morning, Those Children Were Alive.

———

There is a cultural obsession nowadays with civility, with the idea that if everyone is mannered enough, any impasse or difference of opinion can be bridged. But these are desperately uncivil times. And there is nothing more uncivilized than the political establishment's inurement to the constancy of mass shootings in the United States: 60 deaths in Las Vegas, 49 deaths in Orlando, 26 deaths at Sandy Hook, 13 deaths in Columbine, 10 deaths in Buffalo. Adults, schoolchildren, concertgoers, nightclub revelers, grocery shoppers, teachers.

The scale of death in Uvalde, Texas, is unfathomable. At least 19 children and two teachers are dead. These staggering numbers will not change one single thing.

Time and again we are told, both implicitly and explicitly, that all we can do is endure this constancy of violence. All we can do is hope these bullets don't hit our children or us. Or our families. Or our friends and neighbors. And if we dare to protest, if we dare to express our rage, if we dare to say enough, we are lectured about the importance of civility. We are told to stay calm and vote as an outlet for our anger.

Incivility runs through the history of this country, founded on stolen land, built with the labor of stolen lives. The document that governs our lives effectively denied more than half of the population the right to vote. It counted only three-fifths of the enslaved population when determining representation. If you want to talk about incivility, let us be clear about how deep those roots reach.

The United States has become ungovernable not because of political

differences or protest or a lack of civility but because this is a country unwilling to protect and care for its citizens—its women, its racial minorities
and especially its children.

When politicians talk about civility and public discourse, what they're
really saying is that they would prefer for people to remain silent in the
face of injustice. They want marginalized people to accept that the conditions of oppression are unalterable facts of life. They want to luxuriate in
the power they hold, where they never have to compromise, never have to
confront their consciences or lack thereof, never have to face the consequences of their inaction.

Gun violence is one of the problems with which they need not concern
themselves because they believe these calamities will never affect them or
their families. Instead, these politicians talk about protecting our Second
Amendment rights—and they have reimagined the Second Amendment
as something that will accommodate whatever the gun lobby wants, rather
than what the Constitution actually says. With a conservative majority on
the Supreme Court, the continued reinvention of the Second Amendment
will likely flourish, unchecked.

When asked for solutions, Republicans talk about arming teachers and
training them to defend their classrooms. We hear about how good guys
with guns will valiantly stop mass shootings, even though there have been
good guys with guns at several mass shootings and they have not pre-
vented these tragedies.

These politicians offer platitudes and prayers and Bible verses. But
they do not care to do what must be done to stop the next gun massacre
or the average of 321 people shot a day in the United States—including
42 murders and 65 suicides. It is critical that we state this truth clearly
and repeatedly and loudly. That we don't let them hide behind empty
rhetoric. That they know we see through their lies. They must know that
we know who they truly are.

They called for civility again and again, as they did during protests
after Black people were shot or killed by the police in Ferguson and
Kenosha and Minneapolis and Louisville. They called for civility when
a draft of a Supreme Court decision that would overturn *Roe v. Wade*
leaked this month. The draft decision tells people of childbearing age
that they have no bodily autonomy. It is barbaric.

In the wake of the leak, there were lawful, peaceful protests outside some of the justices' homes. Journalists and politicians proceeded to fall all over themselves to condemn these protests as incivility—as if the protests were the problem. The *Washington Post* editorial board wrote that justices have a right to private lives, that public protests should never breach certain boundaries.

They call for civility, but the definition of civility is malleable and ever-changing. Civility is whatever enables them to wield power without question or challenge.

In March of last year, Senator Christopher Murphy of Connecticut reintroduced the Background Check Expansion Act. The bill is common-sense legislation mandating federal background checks for all firearm purchases, including private sales and transfers. Nothing has happened with this bill. The vast majority of voters support background checks, but Republicans in Congress are preventing the bare minimum of gun legislation.

Their obstruction is vile malfeasance. These are not people who value life, no matter what they say. They value power and control. This too we must state clearly and loudly and repeatedly.

There have been at least 213 mass shootings in the first 145 days of 2022. The politicians on both sides of the aisle who have enabled this convey no real sense of understanding or caring about the incivility of children practicing active-shooter drills and wearing bulletproof backpacks to school. They care nothing, it seems, about children being instructed to throw things at a gunman who might enter their classroom. They care about nothing but their own political interests.

On Tuesday morning, at least 19 children's parents woke them up and helped them brush their teeth, fed them breakfast, made sure they had their little backpacks packed. They held their children's small hands as they walked or drove them to school. Those children were alive when their parents waved to them and handed them their lunches and kissed their cheeks. Their lives were precious, and they mattered.

The greatest of American disgraces is knowing that no amount of rage or protest or devastation or loss will change anything about this country's relationship to guns or life. Nothing will change about a craven political system where policy is sold to the highest bidder. Language is inadequate for expressing this lack of civility.

Originally published in the *New York Times*, May 25, 2022

THE MATTER OF
BLACK LIVES

Why I Can't Forgive Dylann Roof

I *do not* forgive Dylann Roof, a racist terrorist whose name I hate saying or knowing. I have no immediate connection to what happened in Charleston, South Carolina, last week beyond my humanity and my blackness, but I do not foresee ever forgiving his crimes, and I am wholly at ease with that choice.

My unwillingness to forgive this man does not give him any kind of power. I am not filled with hate for this man because he is beneath my contempt. I do not believe in the death penalty, so I don't wish to see him dead. My lack of forgiveness serves as a reminder that there are some acts that are so terrible that we should recognize them as such. We should recognize them as beyond forgiving.

I struggle with faith but I was raised Catholic. I believe God is a God of love but cannot understand how that love is not powerful enough to save us from ourselves. As a child, I learned that forgiveness requires reconciliation by way of confession and penance. We must admit our sins. We must atone for our sins. When I went to confession each week, I told the priest my childish sins—fighting with my brothers, saying a curse word, the rather minor infractions of a sheltered Nebraska girl. When I didn't have a sin to confess, I made something up, which was also a sin. After confession, I knelt at a pew and did my penance, and thought about the wrong I had done and then I tried to be better. I'm not sure I succeeded all that often.

Ever the daydreamer, I spent most of my time in Sunday Mass lost in my imagination. The one prayer that stayed with me was "Our Father" and the line "and forgive us our trespasses as we forgive those who trespass against us." I always got stuck on that part. It's a nice idea that we could forgive those who might commit the same sins we are apt to commit, but surely there must be a line. Surely there are some trespasses most of us would not commit. What then?

Forgiveness does not come easily to me. I am fine with this failing. I am particularly unwilling to forgive those who show no remorse, who don't demonstrate any interest in reconciliation. I do not believe there has been enough time since this terrorist attack for anyone to forgive. The bodies of the dead are still being buried. We are still memorizing their names: Cynthia Hurd, Susie Jackson, Ethel Lance, DePayne Middleton Doctor, Clementa C. Pinckney, Tywanza Sanders, Daniel L. Simmons Sr., Sharonda Coleman-Singleton and Myra Thompson.

We are still memorizing these names but the families who loved the people who carried these names have forgiven Dylann Roof. They offered up testimony in court, less than 48 hours after the trauma of losing their loved ones in so brutal a manner. Alana Simmons, who lost her grandfather, said, "Although my grandfather and the other victims died at the hands of hate, everyone's plea for your soul is proof that they lived in love, and their legacies will live in love." Nadine Collier, who lost her mother, said, "You took something very precious away from me. I will never talk to her ever again. I will never be able to hold her again. But I forgive you and have mercy on your soul."

I deeply respect the families of the nine slain who are able to forgive this terrorist and his murderous racism. I cannot fathom how they are capable of such eloquent mercy, such grace under such duress.

Nine people are dead. Nine black people are dead. They were murdered in a terrorist attack.

Over the weekend, newspapers across the country shared headlines of forgiveness from the families of the nine slain. The dominant media narrative vigorously embraced that notion of forgiveness, seeming to believe that if we forgive we have somehow found a way to make sense of the incomprehensible.

We are reminded of the power of whiteness. Predictably, alongside the forgiveness story, the media has tried to humanize this terrorist. They have tried to understand Dylann Roof's hatred because surely, there must be an explanation for so heinous an act. At the gunman's bond hearing, the judge, who was once reprimanded for using the N-word from the bench, talked about how not only were the nine slain and their families victims, but so were the relatives of the terrorist. There are no limits to the power of whiteness when it comes to calls for mercy.

The call for forgiveness is a painfully familiar refrain when black people suffer. White people embrace narratives about forgiveness so they can pretend the world is a fairer place than it actually is, and that racism is merely a vestige of a painful past instead of this indelible part of our present.

Black people forgive because we need to survive. We have to forgive time and time again while racism or white silence in the face of racism continues to thrive. We have had to forgive slavery, segregation, Jim Crow laws, lynching, inequity in every realm, mass incarceration, voter disenfranchisement, inadequate representation in popular culture, microaggressions and more. We forgive and forgive and forgive and those who trespass against us continue to trespass against us.

Mr. Roof's racism was blunt and raggedly formed. It was bred by a culture in which we constantly have to shout "Black lives matter!" because there is so much evidence to the contrary. This terrorist was raised in this culture. He made racist jokes with his friends. He shared his plans with his roommate. It's much easier to introduce forgiveness into the conversation than to sit with that reality and consider all who are complicit.

What white people are really asking for when they demand forgiveness from a traumatized community is absolution. They want absolution from the racism that infects us all even though forgiveness cannot reconcile America's racist sins. They want absolution from their silence in the face of all manner of racism, great and small. They want to believe it is possible to heal from such profound and malingering trauma because to face the openness of the wounds racism has created in our society is too much. I, for one, am done forgiving.

Originally published in the *New York Times*, June 23, 2015

On the Death of Sandra Bland and Our Vulnerable Bodies

I am tired of writing about slain black people, particularly when those responsible are police officers, the very people obligated to serve and protect them. I am exhausted. I experience this specific exhaustion with alarming frequency. I am all too aware that I have the luxury of such exhaustion.

One of the greatest lies perpetrated on our culture today is the notion that dash cameras on police cruisers and body cameras on police officers are tools of justice. Video evidence, no matter the source, can document injustice, but rarely does this incontrovertible evidence keep black people safe or prevent future injustices.

Sandra Bland, 28 years old, was pulled over earlier this month in Waller County, Texas, by a state trooper, Brian T. Encinia. She was pulled over for a routine traffic stop. She shouldn't have been pulled over but she was driving while black, and the reality is that black women and men are pulled over every day for this infraction brought about by the color of their skin.

We know a lot about Ms. Bland now. She was in the prime of her life, about to start a new job at Prairie View A&M University. She had posted on Facebook earlier this year that she was experiencing depression. She was passionate about civil rights and advocacy. According to an autopsy report, she committed suicide in her jail cell after three days. What I find particularly painful is that her bail was $5,000. Certainly, that is a lot of money, but if the public had known, we could have helped her family raise the funds to get her out.

As a black woman, I feel this tragedy through the marrow of my bones. We all should, regardless of the identities we inhabit.

Recently, my brother and I were talking on the phone as he drove to work. He is the chief executive of a publicly traded company. He was dressed for work, driving a BMW. He was using a hands-free system. These particulars shouldn't matter but they do in a world where we have to constantly mourn the loss of black lives and memorialize them with hashtags. In this same world, we remind politicians and those who believe otherwise that black lives matter while suffocated by evidence to the contrary.

During the course of our conversation, he was pulled over by an officer who said he looked like an escapee from Pelican Bay State Prison in California. It was a strange story for any number of reasons. My brother told me he would call me right back. In the minutes I waited, my chest tightened. I worried. I stared at my phone. When he called back, no more than seven or eight minutes had passed. He joked: "I thought it was my time. I thought 'this is it.'" He went on with his day because this is a quotidian experience for black people who dare to drive.

Each time I get in my car, I make sure I have my license, registration and insurance cards. I make sure my seat belt is fastened. I place my cellphone in the handless dock. I check and double-check and triple-check these details because when (not if) I get pulled over, I want there to be no doubt I am following the letter of the law. I do this knowing it doesn't really matter if I am following the letter of the law or not. Law enforcement officers see only the color of my skin, and in the color of my skin they see criminality, deviance, a lack of humanity. There is nothing I can do to protect myself, but I am comforted by the illusion of safety.

As a larger, very tall woman, I am sometimes mistaken for a man. I don't want to be "accidentally" killed for being a black man. I hate that such a thought even crosses my mind. This is the reality of living in this black body. This is my reality of black womanhood, living in a world where I am stripped of my femininity and humanity because of my unruly black body.

There is a code of conduct in emergency situations—women and children first. The most vulnerable among us should be rescued before all others. In reality, this code of conduct is white women and children first. Black women, black children, they are not afforded the luxury of vulnerability. We have been shown this time and again. We remember

McKinney, Texas, and a police officer, David Casebolt, holding a young black girl to the ground. We say the names of the fallen. Tamir Rice. Renisha McBride. Natasha McKenna. Tanisha Anderson. Rekia Boyd. We say their names until our throats run dry and there are still more names to add to the list.

During the ill-fated traffic stop, most of which was caught on camera, Mr. Encinia asked Ms. Bland why she was irritated and she told him. She answered the question she was asked. Her voice was steady, confident. Mr. Encinia didn't like her tone, as if she should be joyful about a traffic stop. He told Ms. Bland to put her cigarette out and she refused. The situation escalated. Mr. Encinia threatened to light her up with his Taser. Ms. Bland was forced to leave her car. She continued to protest. She was placed in handcuffs. She was treated horribly. She was treated as less than human. She protested her treatment. She knew and stated her rights but it did not matter. Her black life and her black body did not matter.

Because Sandra Bland was driving while black, because she was not subservient in the manner this trooper preferred, a routine traffic stop became a death sentence. Even if Ms. Bland did commit suicide, there is an entire system of injustice whose fingerprints left bruises on her throat.

In his impassioned new memoir, *Between the World and Me*, Ta-Nehisi Coates writes, "In America, it is traditional to destroy the black body—it is heritage." I would take this bold claim a step further. It is also traditional to try and destroy the black spirit. I don't want to believe our spirits can be broken. Nonetheless, increasingly, as a black woman in America, I do not feel alive. I feel like I am not yet dead.

Originally published in the *New York Times*, July 24, 2015

Of Lions and Men: Mourning
Samuel DuBose and Cecil the Lion

Like many others, I was stunned by the story of the Minnesota dentist who hunted and killed a 13-year-old lion, Cecil, in Zimbabwe. It was a brutal, senseless thing.

The story has gone viral because it offers a strange alchemy of arrogant privilege, an animal's being lured out of safety and slaughtered, and something onto which we can project outrage without having to contend with the messiness of humanity. Animals are not stained by original sin.

On Twitter, I joked, "I'm personally going to start wearing a lion costume when I leave my house so if I get shot, people will care."

The columnist Erma Bombeck once said, "There is a thin line that separates laughter and pain, comedy and tragedy, humor and hurt."

When people die in police custody or are killed by the police, there are always those who wonder what the fallen did to deserve what befell them.

He shouldn't have been walking down that street.

She should have been more polite to that police officer.

He shouldn't have been playing with a toy gun in a park.

We don't consider asking such questions of a lion. We don't speculate as to why Cecil was roaming the savanna.

In Cincinnati, there was a news conference on Wednesday to announce grand jury findings in the case of Samuel DuBose. He was an unarmed man, shot in the head on July 19 by a University of Cincinnati police officer, Ray Tensing. Before the news conference, the school shut down for the day, anticipating riots, anticipating human messiness.

The prosecutor, Joseph T. Deters, was visibly angry during the news conference. "It was a senseless, asinine shooting," he said.

And then there was the video. Less than two minutes into speaking to him at a routine traffic stop, Officer Tensing pulls his gun on Mr. DuBose and shoots him in the head. Mr. DuBose is fatally wounded, and the car begins rolling because the man behind the steering wheel is no longer able to control it. Officer Tensing falls, gets up and absurdly gives chase, shouting unintelligibly.

It's a bewildering scene. When Officer Tensing catches up to the car, which has crashed, another officer has arrived. Officer Tensing says he shot after Mr. DuBose began rolling away despite the incontrovertible video evidence. This other officer writes in a report that he, too, saw this thing that did not occur.

Greetings from an alternate reality.

I did not want to watch this video but I did. I felt a compulsion. I needed to see what led to such a senseless killing. I hoped this was all a misunderstanding, an accident. I have no idea where such foolish hope comes from.

Often, when I write about race or gender, people offer apologies.

They say, I apologize for my fellow white people.

They say, I apologize for my fellow men.

I understand this desire to say, "We are not all like that," or, "I wish the world were a better place."

Sometimes, saying sorry is, at least, saying something. It is acknowledging wrongs that need to be addressed.

These apologies, however, also place an emotional burden on the recipient. You ask the marginalized to participate in the caretaking of your emotions. You ask them to do the emotional labor of helping you face the world as it truly is.

When we talk about injustice, the conversation always comes back to: What do we do? How do we move forward? How do we create change?

I don't have answers to these questions. I don't think anyone does, but there are actions that would accomplish more than offering an apology to those who cannot provide you with the absolution you seek.

When you hear "black lives matter," don't instinctively respond that all lives matter, as if one statement negates the other. Instead, try to understand why people of color might be compelled to remind the world that their lives have value.

When others share their reality, don't immediately dismiss them because their reality is dissimilar to yours, or because their reality makes you uncomfortable and forces you to see things you prefer to ignore.

Avoid creating a hierarchy of human suffering as if compassion were a finite resource. Don't assume that if one person says, "These are the ways I am marginalized," they are suggesting you know nothing of pain and want.

Understand that the seemingly endless list of black people who have died at the hands of law enforcement or racist zealots or other bringers of violence is not just a news peg or a matter of "identity politics." This is the world we live in. The traumatic blur of videos, this stark imagery of how little black life matters, takes its toll. It creates a weariness I worry will never go away.

It feels impossible to talk about race or other kinds of difference. But if we don't have difficult conversations, we will be able to reconcile neither this country's racist past nor its racist present.

I am thinking about how and when people choose to show empathy publicly. Cecil the lion was a majestic creature and a great many people mourn his death, the brutality of it, the senselessness of it. Some people also mourn the deaths, most recently, of Sandra Bland and Samuel DuBose, but this mourning doesn't seem to carry the same emotional tenor. A late-night television host did not cry on camera this week for human lives that have been lost. He certainly doesn't have to. He did, however, cry for a lion and that's worth thinking about. Human beings are majestic creatures, too. May we learn to see this majesty in all of us.

Originally published in the *New York Times*, July 31, 2015

Where Are Black Children Safe?

Black children are not allowed to be children. They are not allowed to be safe, not at home, not at pool parties, not driving or sitting in cars listening to music, not walking down the street, not in school. For black children, for black people, to exist is to be endangered. Our bodies receive no sanctity or safe harbor.

We can never forget this truth. We are never allowed to forget this truth.

On Monday, in Columbia, South Carolina, Ben Fields, a sheriff's deputy assigned to Spring Valley High School, was called to a classroom to exert control over an allegedly disobedient student—a black girl. She wouldn't give up her cellphone to her teacher, an infraction wholly disproportionate to what came to pass. There are at least three videos of the incident. When Mr. Fields approaches the girl, she is sitting quietly. He quickly muscles her out of her seat and throws her across the room.

The video of this brutality is unbearable in its violence, in what it reminds us, once again, about the value of black life in America, and about the challenges black children, in particular, face.

Schools are not merely sites of education; they are sites of control. In fact, they are sites of control well before they are sites of education. And for certain populations—students of color, working-class students, anyone on the margins—the sites of control in the school system can be incredibly restrictive, suffocating, perilous.

Statistics from a recent study showed that in South Carolina, black students made up 36 percent of the population and accounted for 60 percent of suspensions. It is disheartening, at best, that even school discipline is applied disproportionately. And what took place at Spring Valley High goes well beyond disproportion.

In the wake of such indecency, there has been a vigorous public response—shock and outrage, with many people denouncing Mr. Fields's actions. There have also been those who questioned what the young girl did to beget such brutality and sought for her to take responsibility. Oh, how we are, as a culture, enamored with this ideal of responsibility when we don't want to acknowledge the extent of an injustice or when we want to pretend that if we behave well enough, we will find the acceptance we have long been denied.

Sheriff Leon Lott defended some of his deputy's actions and called for the young girl to accept responsibility, too. The sheriff also revealed that the deputy was dating a black woman, as if through such intimate connection, Mr. Fields might be absolved of any racism or wrongdoing. Nonetheless, Ben Fields has been fired and the Department of Justice has begun an investigation. There is the faintest hope that finally, justice will be done.

And yet, we have these inescapable reminders that no form of justice after the fact can erase trauma, or bring people back to life. There are the precedents of Eric Garner, Walter Scott, Samuel DuBose, Christian Taylor, and this is a list that has no end. When black people commit or are perceived to have committed infractions, the punishment is severe—physical brutality, prison or death without due process.

There are always questions, so many questions that elude both common sense and the heart of the matter at hand. What was the girl doing before the cameras started filming? The CNN anchor Don Lemon asked this question on the air. Why didn't she comply with white authority? Why didn't she just behave, fall in line? This question came from Raven-Symoné, a co-host of *The View*, also on the air.

Time and again, in such situations, black people are asked, why don't we mind our place? To be black in America is to exist with the presumption of guilt, burdened by an implacable demand to prove our innocence. We are asked impossible questions by people who completely ignore a reality where so many of the rules we are supposed to follow are expressly designed to subjugate and work against our best interests. We ignore the reality that we cannot just follow the rules and find our way to acceptance, equality or justice. Respectability politics are a delusion.

Far too little attention is being given to who the young girl is, or that, according to the lawyer representing her, she is in foster care. When that officer saw her, sitting quietly, defiantly, she was not allowed to be human. She was not allowed to have a complex story. She was held to a standard of absolute obedience. She was not given the opportunity to explain the why of her defiance because she was a black body that needed to be disciplined by any means necessary.

Michel Foucault—the philosopher who was deeply concerned about power and how power was enforced—wrote of the panopticon, inspired by the work of Jeremy Bentham, who designed a prison where prisoners could be watched without knowing when or if they were being watched. Discipline, in such a structure, would be enforced by prisoners never knowing when the watchful eye would be turned toward them. We can certainly see how the panopticon functions in any organization predicated on hierarchies of power and the preservation of that power.

Technology has made the world a panopticon. It has widened the range of who watches and who is watched. Each day, we learn of a new injustice against the black body and in many cases, we now have pictures, videos. We have incontrovertible evidence of flagrant brutalities, though, sadly and predictably, this evidence is never enough. At some point, this evidence, these breathtaking, sickening images, will render us numb or they will break our hearts irreparably. There is no respite from the harsh reminder that our black bodies are not safe. The black bodies of those we love are not safe.

We are watchers and the watched, and we are burdened, never knowing when our best, or our most abject, moments will be preserved digitally and disseminated virally, exposing the vulnerabilities we aren't allowed to keep to ourselves.

Given how pervasive surveillance has become, I would think the black body, black people would be safer. I would think that police officers or assorted racists would think twice before acting, inappropriately, against the black body. It is a horrifying, desperate reality where such people act with impunity, undeterred by the threat of surveillance. They know they might be seen and remain empowered in their racism, their sense of dominion. They realize the nauseating truth—there are some injustices, against certain groups of people, that can be witnessed without consequence.

Originally published in the *New York Times*, October 29, 2015

Alton Sterling and When Black Lives Stop Mattering

Over the past several years, we have borne witness to grainy videos of what "protect and serve" looks like for black lives—Tamir Rice, Walter Scott, Eric Garner, Kajieme Powell, to name a few. I don't think any of us could have imagined how tiny cameras would allow us to see, time and again, injustices perpetrated, mostly against black people, by police officers. I don't think we could have imagined that video of police brutality would not translate into justice, and I don't think we could have imagined how easy it is to see too much, to become numb. And now, here we are.

There is a new name to add to this list—Alton B. Sterling, 37, killed by police officers in Baton Rouge, Louisiana. It is a bitter reality that there will always be a new name to that list. Black lives matter, and then in an instant, they don't.

Mr. Sterling was selling CDs in front of a convenience store early Tuesday morning. He was tasered and pinned down by two police officers, who the police say were responding to a call. He was shot, multiple times, in the chest and back. He died, and his death looks and feels as though he were executed.

Mr. Sterling leaves behind family and children who will forever know that their father was executed, that the image of their father's execution is now a permanent part of the American memory, that the image of their father's execution may not bring them justice. Justice, in fact, already feels tenuous. The body cameras the police officers were wearing "dangled," according to the police department's spokesman, L'Jean McKneely, so we don't know how much of the events leading to Mr. Sterling's death were captured. The Baton Rouge police department also has the convenience store surveillance video, which it is not, as of yet, releasing.

Mr. McKneely said the officers were not questioned last night because "we give officers normally a day or so to go home and think about it."

It has been nearly two years since Michael Brown's death in Ferguson, Missouri, and the rise of the Black Lives Matter movement. It has been nearly two years of activists putting themselves on the front lines as police officers continue to act against black lives with impunity. At the same time, according to *The Guardian*, there have been 560 people killed by police in the United States in 2016.

Tuesday night I heard about Mr. Sterling's death, and I felt so very tired. I had no words because I don't know what more can be said about this kind of senseless death.

I watched the cellphone video, shot by a bystander and widely available online, of the final moments of a black man's life. I watched Alton Sterling's killing, despite my better judgment. I watched even though it was voyeuristic, and in doing so I made myself complicit in the spectacle of black death. The video is a mere 48 seconds long, and it is interminable. To watch another human being shot to death is grotesque. It is horrifying, and even though I feel so resigned, so hopeless, so out of words in the face of such brutal injustice, I take some small comfort in still being able to be horrified and brought to tears.

We know what happens now because this brand of tragedy has become routine. The video of Mr. Sterling's death allows us to bear witness, but it will not necessarily bring justice. There will be protest as his family and community try to find something productive to do with sorrow and rage. Mr. Sterling's past will be laid bare, every misdeed brought to light and used as justification for police officers choosing to act as judge, jury and executioner—due process in a parking lot.

In the video, a police officer can be heard shouting that Mr. Sterling had a gun (Louisiana is an open-carry state). The National Rifle Association is likely to stay silent because the Second Amendment is rarely celebrated in these cases. The Department of Justice will investigate this case. Perhaps things are changing because the investigation was announced immediately. Charges might be brought against the two officers involved, but, as history both recent and not shows us, it is rare for police officers to be convicted in such shootings.

I don't know where we go from here because those of us who recognize the injustice are not the problem. Law enforcement, militarized and indifferent to black lives, is the problem. Law enforcement that sees black people as criminals rather than human beings with full and deserving lives is the problem. A justice system that rarely prosecutes or convicts police officers who kill innocent people in the line of duty is the problem. That this happens so often that resignation or apathy are reasonable responses is the problem.

It's overwhelming to see what we are up against, to live in a world where too many people have their fingers on the triggers of guns aimed directly at black people. I don't know what to do anymore. I don't know how to allow myself to feel grief and outrage while also thinking about change. I don't know how to believe change is possible when there is so much evidence to the contrary. I don't know how to feel that my life matters when there is so much evidence to the contrary.

The video that truly haunts me is from a news conference with Quinyetta McMillon, the mother of Alton Sterling's oldest child, a 15-year-old boy, who sobbed and cried out for his father as his mother read her statement. The grief and the magnitude of loss I heard in that boy's crying reminds me that we cannot indulge in the luxuries of apathy and resignation.

If the video of his father's death feels too familiar, the video of this child's raw and enormous grief must not. We have to bear witness and resist numbness and help the children of the black people who lose their lives to police brutality shoulder their unnatural burden.

Originally published in the *New York Times*, July 6, 2016

How to Build a Monument

———

The Great Pyramid of Giza is as miraculous and majestic as you might imagine, if not more. It was built with 2.3 million blocks of limestone and granite, reaching far into the sky, a monument to the pharaoh Khufu. I saw other pyramids in and around Cairo that were equally awe-inspiring, constructed in seemingly perfect proportions, still standing after millennia despite desert winds and the blazing sun and millions of visitors, eager to see a wonder of the world. In Luxor, we visited the Valley of the Kings, and descended several stories below ground to see tombs that are still preserved, the walls adorned with elaborate hieroglyphics—resting places for Tutankhamun, Ramesses II, Ramesses III, Amenhotep. The Temple of Hatshepsut stood at the top of a very long staircase, its columns proudly erect, because Egyptian pharaohs built such monuments to honor the deities, to honor themselves, to honor their reigns. An avenue of sphinxes once connected the Temple of Luxor and the massive complex of the Temple of Karnak, and some of those sphinxes still remain, standing guard for what those monuments represent.

In Agra, India, the Taj Mahal serves as a monument to love, built to honor a beloved wife. In Rome, the Colosseum is a monument to human brutality, gladiators fighting to the death for the merriment of the masses, at the will of bloodthirsty rulers. The Arc de Triomphe in Paris looms over the Place de l'Etoile, a monument to the French armies and the French empire. A gift from the French, the Statue of Liberty is a symbol of what were once open American borders, the promise that immigrants would find safe harbor.

Two acres in Washington, D.C., are dedicated to the Vietnam Veterans Memorial. Nearly sixty thousand names are etched into long slabs of black granite. The Memorial to the Murdered Jews of Europe in Berlin stands where the Berlin Wall once divided West and East Germany. The memorial is marked by 2,711 concrete slabs, the scope of it an overwhelming reminder of human atrocity. The first memorial to the victims of lynching opened in 2018, in Birmingham, Alabama. The National Memorial for Peace and Justice features 800 steel columns, each bearing the names of counties where black people were lynched and the names of the black lives lost to an abhorrent practice. In the museum, visitors learn, in detail, about the extent of lynching, how an entire people were terrorized by the threat of noose and limb. The Cape Coast Castle, in Ghana, still stands, allowing visitors to walk through dungeons where Africans were held before making the transatlantic crossing. There are spaces to leave memorial wreaths and tributes to the people once held in such a terrible place. At the United Nations headquarters in New York, the Ark of the Return—triangles of marble featuring a map of the slave trade, a person carved from black granite from Zimbabwe, a reflecting pool—serves as a memorial to the victims of the transatlantic slave trade.

Rumors of War is a statue created by artist Kehinde Wiley. It is a towering work of art, in all senses. A young black man with dreadlocks, wearing a hoodie and Nike sneakers, sits astride a muscular stallion. He looks strong and proud, unapologetic in his blackness. Or, at least, that's what I see. Before this statue was moved to its final home in Richmond, Virginia, it stood in Times Square, a spectacle in the center of a spectacle. My wife and I went to look at the statue, to appreciate the scale of it, to see how a black artist challenged how we think of monuments, what deserves to be remembered, immemorial.

Every culture throughout history has dedicated an unfathomable amount of resources to the preservation of lives lived and lost, monarchic reigns, elected leaders, wars and the men and women who fought in them, and the deities they worship. It is only in recent years that we have begun to memorialize atrocities and the lives sacrificed to hatred and oppression. It is only in recent years that we have acknowledged the importance of reminders of our failings as much as we remember our successes.

There are more than 1,700 monuments and other public symbols of the Confederacy still standing in the United States. They memorialize America's original sin, a war lost, lives sacrificed to white supremacy and the shame of a society more invested in human capital than freedom and

dignity. For decades, the fact of these monuments went largely unques-
tioned or questions about their place in our society were ignored. These
monuments, according to their defenders, preserve history. But that preservation comes at a cost and they are a constant reminder that some people value a history that was, for their forefathers, quite different from the
history of the people they enslaved and fought to keep enslaved.

The word *monument* finds its origins in Latin and French, deriving
from the word *monere*, to remind, but all too often, people revere monuments not because they want a reminder to avoid repeating historical
wrongs but because they want to preserve toxic ideologies, because they
want what they know of the world to remain unchallenged. In Richmond,
Virginia, Monument Avenue is lined with monuments to Robert E. Lee,
Stonewall Jackson and others. A statue of Jefferson Davis once also stood
on the avenue, but it was torn down during a protest following the police
murder of George Floyd in Minneapolis. Behind the statues of Monument Avenue, there are mansions, some more than one hundred years
old, monuments to wealth and whiteness, because when the neighborhood was created, only white people were allowed to live there and this
segregation was, for many years, codified by city ordinances. It is supposed to be a different time, but it isn't. State and city officials and local
residents continue to fight over the disposition of the remaining monuments and over what should or should not be remembered.

All across the United States and around the world, monuments to the
Confederacy, to slavery, are being torn down by people who have had
enough of racial oppression, systemic racism and the monuments that
valorize these conditions. In tearing down these monuments, activists are
declaring that some things do not deserve to be remembered and that
some memories are actively detrimental to our well-being and cultural
memory. Just as many people are decrying the removal of these monuments, prioritizing their attachment to the past over the lived realities of
people in the present. In June 2020, Donald Trump signed the "Executive Order protecting American Monuments, Memorials, and Statues,"
to prosecute anyone who "destroys, damages, vandalizes, or desecrates a
monument, memorial, or statue within the United States." The order is
also punitive, and will deny funding to municipalities that don't protect
monuments, no matter how odious the practices or people they celebrate.

Efforts to preserve monuments to racism and oppression are, hopefully, a last gasp of Confederate malignance, a last attempt to hold on to the way the world once was, where people thrived not on merit, but by the mere virtue of white skin because in a world where everyone is equal, their success would be unlikely.

In the scars left behind by these monuments, we have the opportunity to build something new. That's what this moment requires—not merely change, but a completely new way of thinking. We must finally dismantle white supremacy and create something equitable in its place.

Where do we begin? What do we do as individuals? There are no easy answers. Racism has persisted across centuries. We will not suddenly vanquish racism simply because more people are finally aware that systemic racism is real and malignant and affects every aspect of our lives. And though we need to re-imagine our understanding of race and equity, the work (white) people must do now is not nearly as impossible as it might seem, and it is certainly not as impossible as living under systems of oppression that limit every opportunity.

Yes, you can read all of the books about race and racism that are suddenly in fashion. You can donate money to nonprofits dedicated to community bail, combatting racism, and protecting civil rights. You can and should attend protests and bear witness to how aggressively, militaristically, and violently police departments across the country are dedicated to protecting the status quo. You can volunteer your time and expertise to organizations working to enfranchise voters, abolish police and prisons, and the like. You can support political candidates at the local, state, and federal levels and canvas and vote in every election. But really, these are table stakes, the kind of community-oriented work we should all be doing, because we share this world with a great many others.

This is a moment that demands the repudiation of silence in the face of this oppression. All too often, people remain silent in the face of bigotry. They are aware racism persists, that police brutality is rampant, that voters across the United States are disenfranchised, but they decide there's nothing they can do about it, so feeling bad about it is enough. Such laments are not nearly enough. One of the most important things white people, in particular, can do, is not remain silent about racism. It is important to actively and consistently acknowledge racism and its effects, call out racism when you witness it, and use your privilege to demand equity whenever and wherever you can. You have to be willing to hold yourselves, your friends and neighbors, your coworkers, your community, and your family accountable for the prejudices they hold. You have to abandon the notion of allyship, abandon the comfortable distance allyship provides, and decide you are only as free as the most marginalized members of your community.

Now is the time to do the work of being actively anti-racist, even when it is uncomfortable, even when it demands more of you than you are willing to give. It will require sacrifice and the ceding of position and power that was not earned on merit but on the back of white supremacy and black suffering. Now is also the time of changing what you value and what you believe deserves remembrance. We do not need monuments to preserve the history of the Confederacy and those who benefitted from that treason—books do that work, and well.

To build a monument is a time- and labor-intensive process. Someone decides a person or an era or event need to be memorialized. They design an obelisk or a structure or a statue. In the case of a statue, a model is made, and then a framework and then a mold and then a cast and then that cast is filled with bronze, melted at 2,000 degrees, and then the cast is removed, and the bronze is cleaned and a patina is applied and the statue is displayed in whatever way its designer deems fitting. It's all very intricate, which defies credulity when considering the horrors to which this intricacy has been applied. But that can change. We can change what we value and what deserves remembrance. We can learn to build new monuments to create a cultural memory that acknowledges the sins of the past, the realities of the present and the possibilities for the future.

Originally published in *We Present/We Transfer*, July 16, 2020

The World Expects Black Men to Make Themselves Smaller. My Brother Never Did.

———

At the end of Antoinette Chinonye Nwandu's Broadway play, *Pass Over*, I was in tears. One of the two main characters in the play, Kitch, is faced with the choice of a purgatorial existence with something material he covets, or an eternity in paradise, free from worldly suffering. What moved me was knowing how the decision Kitch needs to make is both easy and impossible.

I am not much of a crier in my actual life. When I'm on the verge of tears, I try to hold them back. My misguided stoicism is something I hold as a ridiculous, slightly self-destructive point of pride. But when I'm reading a beautiful book or I watch a poignant moment in a movie or television show or even a commercial, something tightly held will break loose inside me, and tears will stream down my face. I am grateful for brilliant art that moves me beyond the emotional walls I build around myself.

Pass Over is the story of Moses and Kitch, two young Black men who have little more than each other. In Danya Taymor's production at the August Wilson Theatre, the set is spare. There is a streetlamp, a milk crate, an abandoned tire, a steel drum. The two men, played by Jon Michael Hill and Namir Smallwood, try to provide each other with the emotional sustenance they are denied anywhere else. They banter energetically. They fantasize about a better world, in which they are not trapped, without hope, in a stark urban setting. They try to believe they can pass over to a better place.

My brother Joel Gay died two months and 11 days ago. I have missed him every day since his passing over to wherever he is now. I am in shock. I am heartbroken. I do not know how to live in this world without him. I cry when I can, but I have yet to allow myself to surrender to my sorrow. I'm scared to do so because if I start to truly cry, I don't know if I will be able to stop.

Joel and I were born only three years apart. He was my younger brother, and then the middle child when our baby brother, Michael Jr., came along. We were very close, a team. We begged our parents to name Michael Jr. Ben. Ben Gay. Get it?

For my whole life, Joel was a magnetic force who drew everyone toward him. When he was born, the nurses in the hospital were so enamored with him that they threatened to steal him. As he was growing up, my mother worried with some regularity that someone would snatch him in a grocery store or at the zoo.

He was charming and adorable and then he was handsome—and always, he knew it. He smiled with his whole face. He laughed with his whole chest. He loved with his whole heart.

When my brother died, at 43 years old, he had already lived several full lives. He had played professional soccer in Europe. He had raised his son, who is now 26, as a single father. He had a brief stint as a conscious rapper and helped organize a boycott against Taco Bell, demanding more money per bushel for the farm workers who picked tomatoes. He had run his own lawn care company.

He entered corporate America, got an M.B.A. at the University of Chicago, rose through the ranks, and became one of the youngest Black chief executives of a public company. When he died, he was the chief executive of an alternative energy company he was about to take public.

He was wildly ambitious and competitive. He loved to cook and could have been a chef. He loved cars. He loved his family, passionately. He was loud and gregarious and arrogant and generous. He was annoying and stubborn. We argued, a lot, and still he was my biggest fan. He was my mom's best friend, my dad's best friend. He was our brother's best friend. At his funeral, we met a dozen people who introduced themselves as Joel's best friend. He was my best friend.

The world was a larger, better place with Joel in it, but even he could not escape the realities with which all Black men must contend—the realities that limited possibilities for Moses and Kitch in *Pass Over*. Whenever Joel moved to a new city, he introduced himself and his son to the local police. "This is my child; take a good look at him," he would say, trying to ensure that the officers would see my nephew, this young Black man, as a human being rather than a target. He told them the makes and models of the cars that he and his son drove.

It is not likely that these gestures could prevent the tragedies he feared most—tragedies that happen daily in America, even if they don't make headlines—but I think my brother needed to feel a semblance of control in a world where so much was beyond his control.

He never made himself smaller in the ways the world expected him to. But he needed to believe that he and his child were not trapped in an impossible place.

There is no intermission in *Pass Over*, which means there is no respite from the relentless, sometimes frenetic dialogue, the actors bounding back and forth across the stage, saying "nigga" in a hundred different ways to express a hundred different emotions. It is fitting that we, the audience, are held in place for 95 minutes, much in the way that Moses and Kitch are held in their own unforgiving place.

Every so often, the characters freeze, trembling in fear, and we know why, all too well. They are being confronted by the fragility of their Black lives and the existential terror that is always hounding them.

Pass Over is absurdist, but so are the conditions of this world—the conditions my brother Joel faced, the conditions far too many of us face. In the days since I saw *Pass Over*, I have been thinking about the play's power, how it reached inside me and opened up a well of grief that continues to deepen. The show reminded me that even when I feel there is nothing more any of us can say about our collective grief for the fragility of Black life, there can be a way forward. We can also celebrate our strength and grace and uncanny wisdom.

I've been thinking about the final minutes of the play, the painful, delicate moment of watching one man pass over into a beautiful and bountiful place while one man lingers, uncertain, between this world and the next.

I am thinking too about my brother, as a Black man, as our family's bright shining star. Every day I pray that he, too, is in a beautiful and bountiful place.

Originally published in the *New York Times*, September 29, 2021

Making People Uncomfortable Can Get You Killed

———

Increasingly, it is not safe to be in public, to be human, to be fallible. I'm not quoting breathless journalism about rising crime or conservative talking points about America falling into ruin. The ruin I'm thinking of isn't in San Francisco or Chicago or at the southern border. The ruin is woven into the fabric of America. It's seeping into all of us. All across the country, supposedly good, upstanding citizens are often fatally enforcing ever-changing, arbitrary and personal norms for how we conduct ourselves.

In Kansas City, Missouri, Ralph Yarl, a Black 16-year-old, rang the wrong doorbell. He was trying to pick up his younger brothers and was simply on the wrong street, Northeast 115th Street instead of Northeast 115th Terrace, a harmless mistake. Andrew Lester, 84 and white, shot him twice and said, according to Ralph, "Don't come around here." Bleeding and injured, Ralph went to three different houses, according to a family member, before those good neighbors in a good, middle-class neighborhood helped him.

In upstate New York, a 20-year-old woman, Kaylin Gillis, was looking for a friend's house in a rural area. The driver of the car she was in turned into a driveway and the homeowner, Kevin Monahan, 65, is accused of firing twice at the car and killing Ms. Gillis.

In Illinois, William Martys was using a leaf blower in his yard. A neighbor, Ettore Lacchei, allegedly started an argument with Mr. Martys and, the police say, killed him.

Two cheerleaders were shot in a Texas parking lot after one, Heather Roth, got into the wrong car. One of her teammates, Payton Washington, was also shot. Both girls survived, with injuries.

In Cleveland, Texas, a father asked his neighbor Francisco Oropesa to stop shooting his gun on his porch because his baby was trying to sleep. Mr. Oropesa walked over to the father's house and has been charged with killing five people, including an 8-year-old boy, with an AR-15–style rifle. Two of the slain adults were found covering children, who survived.

At a Walgreens in Nashville, Mitarius Boyd suspected that Travonsha Ferguson, who was seven months pregnant, was shoplifting. Instead of calling the police, he followed Ms. Ferguson and her friend into the parking lot and, after one of the women sprayed mace in his face, according to Mr. Boyd, began firing. Ms. Ferguson was rushed to the hospital, where she had an emergency C-section and her baby was born two months early.

And sometimes there is no gun. On Monday, Jordan Neely, a Michael Jackson impersonator experiencing homelessness, was yelling and, according to some subway riders, acting aggressively on an F train in New York City. "I don't have food, I don't have a drink, I'm fed up," Mr. Neely cried out. "I don't mind going to jail and getting life in prison. I'm ready to die." Was he making people uncomfortable? I'm sure he was. But his were the words of a man in pain. He did not physically harm anyone. And the consequence for causing discomfort isn't death unless, of course, it is. A former Marine held Mr. Neely in a chokehold for several minutes, killing the man. News reports keep saying Mr. Neely died, which is a passive thing. We die of old age. We die in a car accident. We die from disease. When someone holds us in a chokehold for several minutes, something far worse has occurred.

A man actively brought about Mr. Neely's death. No one appears to have intervened during those minutes to help Mr. Neely, though two men apparently tried to help the former Marine. Did anyone ask the former Marine to release Mr. Neely from his chokehold? The people in that subway car prioritized their own discomfort and anxiety over Mr. Neely's distress. All of the people in that subway car on Monday will have to live with their apparent inaction and indifference. Now that it's too late, there are haunting, heartbreaking images of Mr. Neely, helpless and pinned, still being choked. How does something like this happen? How does this senseless, avoidable violence happen? Truly, how? We all need to ask ourselves that question until we come up with an acceptable answer.

In the immediate aftermath, the New York City mayor, Eric Adams, couldn't set politics aside and acknowledge how horrific Mr. Neely's death was. Mr. Adams said: "Any loss of life is tragic. There's a lot we don't know about what happened here." His was a bland and impotent statement, even though the sequence of events seems pretty clear and was corroborated by video, photography and a witness. And while any loss is in fact tragic, this specific loss, the death of Jordan Neely, was barely addressed. Mr. Adams didn't bother to say Mr. Neely's name and went on to equivocate about his administration's investments in mental health, a strange claim to make while allowing first responders in New York City to involuntarily commit people experiencing mental health crises.

All of these innocent people who lost their lives were in the wrong place at the wrong time. In most cases, armed assailants deputized themselves to stand their ground or enforce justice for a petty crime. Some claimed self-defense, said they were afraid, though some of their victims were unarmed women and children. We have to ask the uncomfortable questions: Why are men so afraid? Why are they so fragile that they shoot or harm first and ask questions later? Why do they believe death or injury is an appropriate response to human fallibility? Public life shared with terrified and/or entitled and/or angry and/or disaffected men is untenable.

We are at something of an impasse. The list of things that can get you killed in public is expanding every single day. Whether it's mass shootings or police brutality or random acts of violence, it only takes running into one scared man to have the worst and likely last day of your life. We can't even agree on right and wrong anymore. Instead of addressing actual problems, like homelessness and displacement, lack of physical and mental health care, food scarcity, poverty, lax gun laws and more, we bury our heads in the sand. Only when this unchecked violence comes to our doorstep do we maybe care enough to try to effect change.

There is no patience for simple mistakes or room for addressing how bigotry colors even the most innocuous interactions. There is no regard for due process. People who deem themselves judge, jury and executioner walk among us, and we have no real way of knowing when they will turn on us.

I will be thinking about Jordan Neely in particular for a long time. I will be thinking about who gets to stand his ground, who doesn't, and how, all too often, it's people in the latter group who are buried beneath that ground by those who refuse to cede dominion over it. Every single day there are news stories that are individually devastating and collectively an unequivocal condemnation of what we are becoming: a people without empathy, without any respect for the sanctity of life unless it's our own.

It's easy, on social media, to say, "I would have done something to help Mr. Neely." It's easy to imagine we would have called for help, offered him some food or money, extended him the grace and empathy we all deserve.

It's so very easy to think we are good, empathetic people. But time and time again, people like us, who think so highly of themselves, have the opportunity to stand up and do the right thing, and they don't. What on earth makes us think that, when the time comes, we will be any different?

Originally published in the *New York Times*, May 4, 2023

CIVIC
RESPONSIBILITIES

Who Gets to Be Angry?

———

I am an opinionated woman so I am often accused of being angry. This accusation is made because a woman, a black woman who is angry, is making trouble. She is daring to be dissatisfied with the status quo. She is daring to be heard.

When women are angry, we are wanting too much or complaining or wasting time or focusing on the wrong things or we are petty or shrill or strident or unbalanced or crazy or overly emotional. Race complicates anger. Black women are often characterized as angry simply for existing, as if anger is woven into our breath and our skin.

Black men, like black women, are judged harshly for their anger. The angry black man is seen as a danger, a threat, uncontrollable.

Feminists are regularly characterized as angry. At many events where I am speaking about feminism, young women ask how they can comport themselves so they aren't perceived as angry while they practice their feminism. They ask this question as if anger is an unreasonable emotion when considering the inequalities, challenges, violence and oppression women the world over face. I want to tell these young women to embrace their anger, sharpen themselves against it.

If you really want to see my anger, you would have to join me in my car, when I am driving. I am afflicted by road rage. I have deeply held opinions on the driving habits of others. When I am alone in my car, and sometimes when I have passengers, I yell at other drivers. I gesticulate wildly. I mutter terrible things about the mothers of these others. I am not proud of this but it is cathartic to release my anger. There is no fallout beyond a rise in my blood pressure.

And still, it's scary to recognize how much anger I have roiling beneath the surface of my skin and how few outlets I have for that anger, how I don't feel entitled to that anger. I keep most of my anger to myself, swallowing it as deep as I can, understanding that someday, I won't be able to swallow it anymore. I will erupt and then there will be fallout.

There are countless other moments when I get angry. Some are trivial—when the phone rings and I don't want to answer, when my first name is misspelled, when someone says they don't read. There is also the anger I harbor over far more serious things—a recent law passed in Indiana, where I live, further restricting abortion rights, and how reproductive freedom is being challenged across the country; the light sentence Brock Turner received this month in the Stanford rape case and the reality that he will receive more punishment than most people who commit similar crimes; the fractious political climate as we head into the general election.

Anger is a significant part of our cultural conversation. Sometimes, I see people log on to Twitter and ask, "What are we outraged about today?" In this, there is dismissiveness suggesting that the asker is bored with the injustices, small and great, that inspire anger within us.

In these circumstances, anger becomes an emotion that needs to be controlled, an inconvenience and an irritant. It gets confused for rage, which also has its uses.

There are consequences for both expressing and suppressing anger. In northeastern Brazil, women refer to suppressing their anger as "swallowing frogs," which contributes to "emotion-based ailments," according to L. A. Rebhun, an anthropologist who studied the connection between anger and illness in the region. The physical manifestations of anger, Professor Rebhun writes, "may also be seen as symptoms of the pain of bridging gaps between cultural expectation and personal experience in emotion, a process neither easy nor simple."

In Dallas, a place called the Anger Room is set up explicitly for customers' destructive pleasure. Clients can release their anger by taking a bat to the room. In Toronto, there is a Rage Room. One of the options is a date night package, for two. The couple that rages together, perhaps, stays together.

Beyoncé's latest album chronicles heartbreak, betrayal and the anger that rises from those experiences. In the video for the song "Hold Up," Beyoncé strolls down a city street, a placid smile on her face, as she carries a baseball bat. And then, without warning, she slams that bat against car windows, a fire hydrant, a surveillance camera. With each blow, her face falls into a mask of concentrated rage and then she's on to the next target, with ever more bounce in her step.

In her keynote speech to the National Women's Studies Association in 1981, Audre Lorde said, "Every woman has a well-stocked arsenal of anger potentially useful against those oppressions, personal and institutional, which brought that anger into being."

Politics is one arena where anger is brought into being over oppression and other matters. President Obama is often accused of being angry. He is often accused of not being angry enough. Critics have written many pieces on why Mr. Obama cannot be or be perceived as an "angry black man" for fear he might alienate white voters who are, it would seem, so fragile as to be unable to handle human emotion. At the 2015 White House Correspondents Dinner, there was a comedic bit where Mr. Obama brought on Luther, an "anger translator" who expressed the anger that the president himself could not.

In the Democratic primary this year, people flocked to Bernie Sanders because they were angry about campaign finance and excessive debt and too few opportunities to flourish. The candidate reveled in his anger, often wagging his finger and raising his voice. Together he and his supporters were angry. Their anger was celebrated, framed as passion and engagement.

Conversely, Hillary Clinton is not allowed to be angry though certainly some of her supporters are. Mrs. Clinton, once again, has shown how the rules are different for women. She cannot raise her voice without reprisal. When she appears as anything but demure, when she is passionate and sharp, she is attacked not for her ideas, but for her demeanor.

Amid all this anger, history is being made. She is the first woman who will serve as a major party's nominee for the American presidency.

The presumptive Republican nominee for president, Donald J. Trump, is the angriest from a large field of angry contenders.

Many of his supporters seem angry about so many things—a black president, their lot in life, not getting their piece of the American dream or having to share that American dream with people of color, women, gay, lesbian and transgender people. This anger is discussed with no small amount of compassion or curiosity. It is allowed to flourish. At many of Mr. Trump's rallies, this anger spills into violence.

Mr. Trump himself revels in his anger or the performance of anger. He often shoots off angry tweets, insulting anyone who doesn't submit to his petty worldview. Or he pulls out of a debate. On *Meet the Press*, in March, Mr. Trump said that his supporters were angry at the state of the world, and he was "just a messenger."

There is a medical name for excessive anger—intermittent explosive disorder. A 2006 Harvard study suggested that up to 16 million people suffered from this disorder. When the study was published, there was a vigorous debate as to whether this disorder was real—discomfort in the idea that the inexcusable could be explained.

But anger is not an inherently bad thing. Most of the time, it is a normal and even healthy human emotion. Anger allows us to express dissatisfaction. It allows us to say something is wrong. The challenge is knowing the difference between useful anger, the kind that can stir revolutions, and the useless kind that can tear us down.

Originally published in the *New York Times*, June 10, 2016

Voting with My Head and Heart

I have tried, for the duration of this election, to stay informed, without being obsessive. It hasn't been easy. The media has been frenzied, at best, particularly as they cover Donald J. Trump. Early on, cable news networks aired entire Trump events before he was even his party's nominee. They created an unhealthy demand for "news" that they were more than happy to supply. There is no escape.

People who care about this election, which is to say most people, have also become frenzied. At times, I see people reacting to the election online and I want to say, "Get ahold of yourselves." There is an almost dark, sexual energy to how people talk about the portent Donald Trump, as if they are both disgusted and excited about each new terrible revelation about the Republican candidate. I watch these people and wonder why they are surprised, how they can be surprised.

We knew everything we needed to know about Mr. Trump when he said Mexicans were rapists and when he called for barring Muslims from entering the country. We knew exactly who he was years ago when he was a reality television spectacle and we knew exactly who he was as he cycled from one marriage to the next. Each new revelation simply reminds us that Mr. Trump is exactly who he appears to be.

The closer we get to the election, the more I see people on social media rending their garments about how terrible 2016 has been and how terrible this election is, sharing tired jokes about November 8 as the end of the world. In some ways, I understand the frenzy, the panic, the obsession over this election. It is a hell of a thing to see fascism being so robustly embraced by so many Americans.

This anxiety is exhausting to watch. But regardless of this election's outcome, Tuesday will not and cannot be the end of the world. We don't have that luxury.

I am excited about Hillary Clinton as a presidential candidate and soon to be (I hope), president of the United States. I haven't written this too many times in the past year. This is not because I am apathetic. In part, I haven't had the energy to deal with the inevitable harassment that rises out of demonstrating any kind of support for Mrs. Clinton. I've also been torn. I like, admire and respect so many things about Mrs. Clinton. She is fiercely ambitious, intelligent, funny, interesting and complex. She prepares for everything she does like her life depends on it and in many ways, politically speaking, it does.

During each of the three presidential debates I marveled at the extent of Mrs. Clinton's policy knowledge and how she knew when and where to attack her opponent. I'm also thrilled to see a woman as president. Small-minded people want to call this voting with my vagina, as if there is something wrong with wanting to see a woman become president after 44 men have had a go at it. Despite the historicity of this moment, I am voting with my head, mostly, and some of my heart.

Hillary Clinton does not come without baggage, though I must confess, I cannot bring myself to give one single damn about the emails. As a woman, as a human being, I find some of Mrs. Clinton's decisions unacceptable—her vote for the war in Iraq; some of the rhetoric she used during the 1990s; her stance, for far too long, that marriage equality was best left to the states. She has made decisions that treated marginalized lives cavalierly. It is difficult to reconcile such decisions with everything I admire about Mrs. Clinton.

I also know that no one can spend a lifetime in politics and public service and emerge with clean hands or a clear conscience. This is what I tell myself so I can feel more comfortable with supporting her. I recognize the rationalization.

In truth, I am not overlooking anything. I see the whole of who Mrs. Clinton is and what she has done throughout her career. At their best, people are willing and able to grow, to change. Clinton is not the same woman she was twenty years ago, or ten years ago. Even during the primary, running against Bernie Sanders, she demonstrated an ability to move further left from many of her centrist positions. Mrs. Clinton, as she presents herself today, impresses me. I am choosing to believe she is at her best.

And to be president of the United States, of any country, means making many impossible decisions, many of which will cost people their lives. When she is president, I know Hillary Clinton will make more decisions that appall me or make me uncomfortable. There is no such thing as an ideal president who never has to make life or death decisions. I can only hope that as president, Mrs. Clinton will make those decisions with grace and compassion.

The election is imminent and for that, I am grateful. I cannot remember a longer election cycle in my lifetime, or one that has felt so disgraceful, because Mrs. Clinton is running against a man who is unworthy, in all ways, of any public office, let alone the presidency. I live in Indiana, a fairly conservative state. Mike Pence, the Republican nominee for vice president, is the state's governor so I know just how horrible, homophobic, and misogynistic he is. Governor Pence makes the threat of a Trump presidency even more of a travesty.

Whether it is Hillary Clinton or Donald Trump who is elected, we will be living not in an apocalypse, but in a new world, and each and every one of us is going to have a lot of work to do to hold the new president accountable to the needs of the people they have been elected to serve. And when I think about everyone who will suffer if Mr. Trump is elected, I am overwhelmed. I feel hopeless. I also feel ready to fight.

Originally published in the *New York Times*, November 6, 2016

Hate That Doesn't Hide
(on Trump's Presidency)

———

Angry white men holding tiki torches and shouting their throats raw chanting "blood and soil," spittle hanging from their lips. Angry white men, arms outstretched in the Nazi salute. Angry white men playing soldier, heavily armed in public. Nazi flags, Confederate flags, American flags, "Make America Great Again" hats. Bodies clashing. A slate-gray car barreling into people standing up to racism. Bodies flying.

For the past week, I have seen hate thriving in plain sight. I am disgusted. I am angry. I am worried. And I keep thinking about how different things would be if Hillary Clinton had been elected president. I was, like so many of us, wildly overconfident about her chances. Her presidency was a certainty in my mind and in my heart. And then, it wasn't.

Instead, it is 2017 and white supremacists no longer feel the need to wear hoods to hide their racism and anti-Semitism. I am a black woman and I live in a country where the president does not disavow racism. It is 2017 and we are having a national conversation about the resurgence of white supremacy, American Nazism and fascism, or perhaps more accurately, we are being reminded that this hatred has been here all along.

Throughout the 2016 election, I did not do as much as I could have done to support Mrs. Clinton's presidential bid. I contributed money to the campaign, but I didn't volunteer or try to get out the vote. I didn't write about her campaign as much as I could have. I don't think that I, as an individual, could have swayed the election in a meaningful way but I know I could have done so much more and I did not. I hold myself accountable for that. I am increasingly concerned with accountability because our country is being led by a man who believes he is accountable only to himself and enriching his coffers rather than the more than 300 million people he was so narrowly elected to lead and serve.

It pains me to think about what could have been. It is even more difficult to face the way things are. Every single morning, I am tense as I check the news, wondering what the president has tweeted overnight. Throughout the day, my shoulders tense when I see a news alert about his latest misstep or his latest provocation to North Korea or his latest insult to the media whose adulation he so desperately craves.

Between the election and the inauguration, I tried to imagine what a Trump presidency would look like. I tried to prepare for the worst. What has unfolded over the past seven months is far more terrible than I could have imagined. Advances made during the Obama era are being dismantled. I tell myself to remain hopeful but struggle to find a reason. And then I struggle to remind myself that despair is a luxury we cannot afford right now.

A week ago in Charlottesville, Virginia, white men assembled to rage for a world long lost—one where their mediocrity was good enough. These were men emboldened by a president who shares their odious beliefs.

I've watched in horror as they've been energized by his campaign and his presidency. It's possible that hate like this would have been on the rise anyway, given eight years of the Obama presidency and animus toward Hillary Clinton. But now we don't have hate on the fringe; we have it reinforced in the White House.

Most politicians, of all political persuasions, have released statements condemning racism and the violence in Charlottesville, violence that ended in the death of one person, Heather Heyer, and the injuring of many others. Even if these statements are political posturing, they must be made. Our leaders need to make crystal clear where they stand. Now, more than ever, everyone needs to be unequivocal about where they stand.

Unfortunately, far too many people are being equivocal, including, most alarmingly, the president. In the days following the Charlottesville unrest, we have seen Mr. Trump reluctant to disavow white supremacy. The president resents that he, as the leader of the United States, is rightly expected to condemn hateful acts and ideas. Mr. Trump and far too many others believe there is more than one side to the story of Charlottesville. The president thinks that leftist resistance is as culpable as far-right white supremacy. He has lamented the removal of Confederate statues, tweeting that it is "sad to see the history and culture of our great country being ripped apart with the removal of our beautiful statues and monuments," as if books and museums do not exist.

When you look at the sum of his behavior, it's obvious that Mr. Trump is actually not equivocating. He is actively demonstrating that his loyalties lie with only some of the American people.

There are other forms of equivocating. Back in November, pundits began attributing Mr. Trump's win to "economic anxiety," because they were unwilling to face the blatant racism that fueled his popularity. Look where that thinking has brought us. Everyone who says, "This is not America" or "This is not us" is being willfully ignorant of both the past and the present. We all need to acknowledge that yes, this is indeed us, the very worst of us. There are people who think it is a problem that the white supremacists from Charlottesville are being publicly identified and fired from their jobs, as if those who would eradicate all of us who are not Aryan deserve empathy. They do not. A white newscaster cries because talking about race makes her uncomfortable because discomfort is most likely the worst thing she can imagine.

We cannot afford to delude ourselves about the state of things. We cannot mollify ourselves with some ideal of neutrality or objectivity as if white supremacy deserves anything but resounding contempt. Taking down Confederate statues is a symbolic but necessary gesture, but we cannot merely dismantle these markers of America's painful past. We must work to dismantle the pernicious ideologies these statues represent. We must root out white supremacy, wherever it lurks, and call it by its name even when it makes us uncomfortable, even when the people we are calling out are those we live and work with, or consider friends and family.

We are on a precipice. What happened in Charlottesville is not the end of something but, rather, the beginning. And it is from this precipice that I am reminded of everything I did not do during the 2016 election. Hindsight reminds me that resistance must be active, and constant. Resistance is the responsibility of everyone who believes in equality and demands the eradication of racism, anti-Semitism and the hatred that empowers bigots to show their truest selves in broad daylight. I am reminding myself that I should never allow my fears to quiet me. I have a voice and I am going to use it, as loudly as I can.

Originally published in the *New York Times*, August 18, 2017

No One Is Coming to Save Us from Trump's Racism

———

I could write a passionate rebuttal extolling all the virtues of Haiti, the island my parents are from, the first free black nation in the Western Hemisphere. I could write about the beauty of the island, the music and vibrant art, the majesty of the mountains, the crystalline blue of the water surrounding her, the resilience of the Haitian people, our incredible work ethic, our faith. I could tell you about my parents, how they came to this country with so many other Haitians, how they embraced the American dream and thrived, how I and so many first-generation Haitian-Americans are products of our parents' American dreams.

Or I could tell you about the singular, oppressive narrative the media trots out when talking about Haiti, the one about an island mired in poverty and misery, the one about AIDS, the one about a country plagued by natural and man-made disasters, because these are the stories people want to hear, the stories that make Haiti into a pitiable spectacle instead of the proud, complicated country it is. I could tell you how I have spent an inordinate amount of time and energy, throughout my life, educating people about Haiti and disabusing them of the damaging, incorrect notions they have about the country of my parents' birth.

On the eve of the eighth anniversary of the January 12, 2010, earthquake that devastated Haiti, the president, in the Oval Office, is said to have wondered aloud why he should allow immigrants from "shithole countries" like Haiti, El Salvador and African nations to enter the United States. Mr. Trump has tweeted a denial that he made this statement. "He said those hate-filled things and he said them repeatedly," Senator Richard J. Durbin of Illinois, who was in the room, said Friday.

But the president has to know that even if video footage of the comment existed, there wouldn't be any political consequences for him. He has to know, like we all do, that xenophobic commentary plays well with his base, the people who were more than happy to put him in office because they could seamlessly project their racism and misogyny onto his celebrity persona. It's no wonder Fox News hosts have defended the comment.

Now, in response to the news about the reports of the vile remark, there are people saying "vote" and highlighting the importance of the 2018 midterm elections, as if American democracy is unfettered from interference and corruption. There is a lot of trite rambling about how the president isn't really reflecting American values when, in fact, he is reflecting the values of many Americans. And there are entreaties to educate the president about the truth of Haiti as if he simply suffers from ignorance.

But the president is not alone in thinking so poorly of the developing world. He didn't reveal any new racism. He, once again, revealed racism that has been there all along. It is grotesque and we must endure it for another three or seven years, given that the Republicans have a stranglehold on power right now and are more invested in holding onto that power than working for the greater good of all Americans.

What I'm supposed to do now is offer hope. I'm supposed to tell you that no president serves forever. I'm supposed to offer up words like "resist" and "fight" as if rebellious enthusiasm is enough to overcome federally, electorally sanctioned white supremacy. And I'm supposed to remind Americans, once more, of Haiti's value, as if we deserve consideration and a modicum of respect from the president of the United States only because as a people we are virtuous enough.

But I am not going to do any of that. I am tired of comfortable lies. I have lost patience with the shock supposedly well-meaning people express every time Mr. Trump says or does something terrible but well in character. I don't have any hope to offer. I am not going to turn this into a teaching moment to justify the existence of millions of Haitian or African or El Salvadoran people because of the gleeful, unchecked racism of a world leader. I am not going to make people feel better about the gilded idea of America that becomes more and more compromised and impoverished with each passing day of the Trump presidency.

This is a painful, uncomfortable moment. Instead of trying to get past this moment, we should sit with it, wrap ourselves in the sorrow, distress and humiliation of it. We need to sit with the discomfort of the president of the United States referring to several countries as "shitholes" during a meeting, a meeting that continued after his comments. No one is coming to save us. Before we can figure out how to save ourselves from this travesty, we need to sit with that, too.

Originally published in the *New York Times*, January 12, 2018

You're Disillusioned.
That's Fine. Vote Anyway.

––––––

A young woman in Milwaukee recently asked me if I had any advice for dis-illusioned young voters. She said that in a representative democracy it was hard to want to vote for, in her words, "yet another 40,000-year-old white man" who didn't look like her or have familiarity with her experiences.

Her question was genuine, and even though more women are running for Congress than in previous years and Stacey Abrams of Georgia has a chance to be the first African-American woman elected governor, I understood her overall frustration. For every beacon of progress there is a stark reminder that the status quo all too often prevails.

Young people are facing a lot of problems they had no hand in creating. Far too many of them are saddled with incredible amounts of student loan debt, working in a gig economy where job security is scarce. If they have health insurance, it is likely inadequate. Homeownership can seem out of reach. Black voters are being disenfranchised at alarming rates. Reproductive freedom is precarious. Citizenship is precarious. Climate change threatens our planet on an alarming timeline. Things are grim and politicians of all persuasions are doing very little to assuage or address the very real concerns people have about this country and their place in it.

I could have offered a warm, gentle answer but these are not warm, gentle times. Given everything that has transpired since President Trump took office, I have no patience for disillusionment. I have no patience for the audacious luxury of choosing not to vote because of that disillusionment, as if not voting is the best choice a person could make. Not voting is, in fact, the worst choice a person could make.

In 2016, nearly 40 percent of eligible voters chose not to vote. Many who showed up to vote for Barack Obama in 2008 and 2012 were apparently so underwhelmed by Hillary Clinton that they simply stayed home. And, of course, there were the voters who chose third-party candidates who had no chance of winning the presidential election but were still able to affect the outcome in key states. If and how one votes is a personal choice, but that choice has consequences.

We are reaping what has been sown from voter disillusionment and we will continue doing so until enough people recognize what is truly at stake when they don't vote. A representative democracy is flawed but it is the political system we must work within, at least for the time being. We have a responsibility to participate in this democracy, even when the politicians we vote for aren't ideal or a perfect match. Voting isn't dating. We are not promised perfect candidates. Voting requires pragmatism and critical thinking and empathy and now, more than ever, intelligent compromise.

Only 40 percent of Americans choose to vote during midterm elections, generally speaking. There has been a lot of talk about the importance of voting next Tuesday because we are desperate to change the political climate and the first step in doing that is shifting the balance of power in Congress. Politicians, their volunteers and progressive publications have been vigorously trying to get out the vote in a range of ways.

Many of these efforts have been well intended but poorly executed. One tactic has been the use of bait-and-switch on social media—sharing something innocuous like celebrity gossip or a recipe, only to direct people to a webpage about voting and voter registration. These efforts imply that one cannot care about both trivial things and the state of our democracy. This bait-and-switch approach may not be anyone's primary voter outreach strategy, but it is happening often enough to grate on my nerves. These efforts are predicated upon the belief that condescension and manipulation are the only way to reach apathetic or disillusioned voters when what we need is brutal honesty.

We deserve a better class of politicians who recognize the greater good and act in service of that greater good rather than in service of amassing more power. We deserve politicians who are held accountable for their decisions. We deserve politicians from all walks of life, not just the same old wealthy white heterosexual people who are overly represented in all branches of the government.

We also deserve to be disillusioned and disappointed with what our politicians, thus far, have offered. For the most part they have failed us spectacularly because they understand that radicalism doesn't play well even though radicalism is what we need now, more than ever. And it is certainly a travesty that universal health care and a livable minimum wage and civil rights and higher taxes on the wealthy are considered radical, but here we are.

I am going to vote on next Tuesday but I can't say I am particularly optimistic about the impact my vote will have. Between the corrupt stranglehold the Republican Party has on political power and the incompetence and cowardice of the Democrats, voting feels futile. The politicians I will vote for don't represent me and what I believe in as much as I would like them to.

Voter disillusionment makes perfect sense but it is also incredibly selfish and shortsighted. In the past week, a biracial man was charged with sending pipe bombs to prominent Democrats; reports said he drove a van covered in hateful propaganda. A white man tried to enter a black church in Louisville, Kentucky, and when he couldn't, he went to a nearby Kroger grocery store and killed two black people. On a Saturday morning in Pittsburgh, a white man entered a synagogue, shouting anti-Semitic epithets. He killed 11 Jews and injured six others. This took place in the same week in which it was reported that the Trump administration thinks it might be able to define the transgender community out of existence, and in which the president continues to use the caravan of migrants heading to the United States to stoke the xenophobic hysteria of his base.

Every single day there is a new, terrifying, preventable tragedy fomented by a president and an administration that uses hate and entitlement as political expedience. If you remain disillusioned or apathetic in this climate, you are complicit. You think your disillusionment is more important than the very real dangers marginalized people in this country live with.

Don't delude yourself about this. Don't shroud your political stance in disaffected righteousness. Open your eyes and see the direct line from the people in power to their emboldened acolytes. It is cynical to believe that when we vote we are making a choice between the lesser of two evils.

We are dealing with a presidency fueled by hate, greed and indifference. We are dealing with a press corps that can sometimes make it seem as though there are two sides to bigotry. Republican politicians share racist memes that spread false propaganda and crow "fake news" when reality interferes with their ambitions. Progressive candidates are not the lesser of two evils here; they are not anywhere on the spectrum of evil we are currently witnessing.

If you are feeling disillusioned, get over it, at least enough to vote and vote pragmatically. Tell your friends to vote. Drive people to the polls. Support candidates you believe in with your time or, if you can afford it, money. Volunteer for community organizations that address the issues you most care about. Attend town halls held by your elected officials. Hold them accountable for the decisions they make with the power you give them. Run for local office. Do something. Do anything.

Nothing will change by sitting at home for the midterms or any other election. We cannot afford disillusionment. We cannot afford to do nothing. Lives are at stake and if you don't recognize that, you are no better than those with whom you are disillusioned.

Originally published in the *New York Times*, October 30, 2018

Remember, No One Is
Coming to Save Us

———

After Donald Trump maligned the developing world in 2018, with the dismissive phrase "shithole countries," I wrote that no one was coming to save us from the president. Now, in the midst of a pandemic, we see exactly what that means.

The economy is shattered. Unemployment continues to climb, steeply. There is no coherent federal leadership. The president mocks any attempts at modeling precautionary behaviors that might save American lives. More than 100,000 Americans have died from Covid-19.

Many of us have been in some form of self-isolation for more than two months. The less fortunate continue to risk their lives because they cannot afford to shelter from the virus. People who were already living on the margins are dealing with financial stresses that the government's $1,200 "stimulus" payment cannot begin to relieve. A housing crisis is imminent. Many parts of the country are reopening prematurely. Protesters have stormed state capitols, demanding that businesses reopen. The country is starkly dividing between those who believe in science and those who don't.

Quickly produced commercials assure us that we are all in this together. Carefully curated images, scored by treacly music, say nothing of substance. Companies spend a fortune on airtime to assure consumers that they care, while they refuse to pay their employees a living wage.

Commercials celebrate essential workers and medical professionals. Commercials show how corporations have adapted to "the way we live now," with curbside pickup and drive-through service and contact-free delivery. We can spend our way to normalcy, and capitalism will hold us close, these ads would have us believe.

Some people are trying to provide the salvation the government will not. There are community-led initiatives for everything from grocery deliveries for the elderly and immunocompromised to sewing face masks for essential workers. There are online pleas for fund-raising. Buy from your independent bookstore. Get takeout or delivery from your favorite restaurant. Keep your favorite bookstore open. Buy gift cards. Pay the people who work for you, even if they can't come to work. Do as much as you can, and then do more.

These are all lovely ideas and they demonstrate good intentions, but we can only do so much. The disparities that normally fracture our culture are becoming even more pronounced as we decide, collectively, what we choose to save—what deserves to be saved.

And even during a pandemic, racism is as pernicious as ever. Covid-19 is disproportionately affecting the black community, but we can hardly take the time to sit with that horror as we are reminded, every single day, that there is no context in which black lives matter.

Breonna Taylor was killed in her Louisville, Kentucky, home by police officers looking for a man who did not even live in her building. She was 26 years old. When demonstrations erupted, seven people were shot.

Ahmaud Arbery was jogging in South Georgia when he was chased down by two armed white men who suspected him of robbery and claimed they were trying to perform a citizen's arrest. One shot and killed Mr. Arbery while a third person videotaped the encounter. No charges were filed until the video was leaked and public outrage demanded action. Mr. Arbery was 25 years old.

In Minneapolis, George Floyd was held to the ground by a police officer kneeling on his neck during an arrest. He begged for the officer to stop torturing him. Like Eric Garner, he said he couldn't breathe. Three other police officers watched and did not intervene. Mr. Floyd was 46 years old.

These black lives mattered. These black people were loved. Their losses to their friends, family, and communities, are incalculable.

Demonstrators in Minneapolis took to the street for several days, to protest the killing of Mr. Floyd. Mr. Trump—who in 2017 told police officers to be rough on people during arrests, imploring them to "please, don't be too nice"—wrote in a tweet, "When the looting starts, the shooting starts." The official White House Twitter feed reposted the president's comments. There is no rock bottom.

Christian Cooper, an avid birder, was in Central Park's Ramble when he asked a white woman, Amy Cooper, to comply with the law and leash her dog. He began filming, which only enraged Ms. Cooper further. She pulled out her phone and said she was going to call the police to tell them an African-American man was threatening her.

She called the police. She knew what she was doing. She weaponized her whiteness and fragility like so many white women before her. She began to sound more and more hysterical, even though she had to have known she was potentially sentencing a black man to death for expecting her to follow rules she did not think applied to her. It is a stroke of luck that Mr. Cooper did not become another unbearable statistic.

An unfortunate percentage of my cultural criticism over the past 11 or 12 years has focused on the senseless loss of black life. Mike Brown. Trayvon Martin. Sandra Bland. Philando Castile. Tamir Rice. Jordan Davis. Atatiana Jefferson. The Charleston Nine.

These names are the worst kind of refrain, an inescapable burden. These names are hashtags, elegies, battle cries. Still nothing changes. Racism is litigated over and over again when another video depicting another atrocity comes to light. Black people share the truth of their lives, and white people treat those truths as intellectual exercises.

They put energy into being outraged about the name "Karen," as shorthand for entitled white women rather than doing the difficult, self-reflective work of examining their own prejudices. They speculate about what murdered black people might have done that we don't know about to beget their fates, as if alleged crimes are punishable by death without a trial by jury. They demand perfection as the price for black existence while harboring no such standards for anyone else.

Some white people act as if there are two sides to racism, as if racists are people we need to reason with. They fret over the destruction of property and want everyone to just get along. They struggle to understand why black people are rioting but offer no alternatives about what a people should do about a lifetime of rage, disempowerment and injustice.

When I warned in 2018 that no one was coming to save us, I wrote that I was tired of comfortable lies. I'm even more exhausted now. Like many black people, I am furious and fed up, but that doesn't matter at all.

I write similar things about different black lives lost over and over and over. I tell myself I am done with this subject. Then something so horrific happens that I know I must say something, even though I know that the people who truly need to be moved are immovable. They don't care about black lives. They don't care about anyone's lives. They won't even wear masks to mitigate a virus for which there is no cure.

Eventually, doctors will find a coronavirus vaccine, but black people will continue to wait, despite the futility of hope, for a cure for racism. We will live with the knowledge that a hashtag is not a vaccine for white supremacy. We live with the knowledge that, still, no one is coming to save us. The rest of the world yearns to get back to normal. For black people, normal is the very thing from which we yearn to be free.

Originally published in the *New York Times*, May 30, 2020

How We Save Ourselves

Corporations finally believe black lives matter. Or they at least understand that they have to make it look like they believe black lives matter.

From Microsoft and Peloton to the National Football League—the same league whose teams shunned Colin Kaepernick after his peaceful protest—they have released carefully crafted messages affirming that they are committed to diversity and inclusion, that they stand in solidarity with their black employees. You can ask Amazon's virtual assistant Alexa if black lives matter and she will respond, "Black lives matter. I believe in racial equality."

This messaging is curious. There have been several incidents of police brutality in recent years and usually the response from corporate America is nothing like this. This time, for some reason, executives seem to have decided that their brands will be best supported by engaging in an elaborate performance of allyship.

Several companies are making significant financial contributions and other gestures. YouTube has established a $100 million fund for black creators. Walmart and its foundation have said they will spend $100 million on the creation of a racial equity center. Several companies, including Apple, Coca-Cola and Citibank, have donated to the Equal Justice Initiative. Amazon will not allow police departments to use its Rekognition software for a year. Both *Cops* and *Live PD* have been canceled by their networks. And after more than 15 years, ABC's *The Bachelor* will finally have a black bachelor, Matt James.

A great many things that were supposedly impossible have suddenly become priorities. It's a bittersweet moment because we always knew change was possible. The world just didn't want to do the work.

Each time there is a horrifying racist incident, I wonder whether things will actually be different. For a short while people say the right things. They lament racism. They mourn the black person who has died at the hands of unchecked police officers or white vigilantes. They vow to be part of the necessary change. They ask, earnestly, what they can do to create such change. And then they return to their lives. Public enthusiasm for addressing police brutality has to wait until another black life is prematurely lost to racism.

I want this time to be different. I need this time to be different. There has never been more public support for contending with systemic racism and reimagining law enforcement. The Los Angeles Police Department commission recently held a virtual public meeting where hundreds of Angelenos spoke—first for two minutes at a time, then a minute and then 30 seconds as the commission tried to accommodate everyone. It took hours.

It was cathartic to see nearly every person who took their time at the microphone castigate the police department for their violent tactics against protesters, their bloated budgets subsidized by taxpayers, their militarized tactics and their general incompetence. People were legitimately angry and demanded more from public servants. Throughout the proceedings—which the police chief, Michel Moore, attended—the commissioners looked by turns bored, indifferent, annoyed and frustrated. There was no gesture to acknowledge the public frustration. They did not behave like people who were at all willing to rethink how to do their jobs.

If you had asked me, before George Floyd's killing, if I believed in police abolition I would have said that reform is desperately needed but that abolition was a bridge too far. I lacked imagination. I could not envision a world where we did not need law enforcement as it is presently configured. I am ashamed. Now I know we don't need reform. We need something far more radical. The current system does not work. Even during protests against the current system, law enforcement officers largely behaved as they always do, with blunt force and apparent indifference to the safety of protesters. They believe they are righteous. Burn it all down and build something new in the ashes.

I want this time to be different and there are moments when I think it might be. While I don't believe the ubiquitous corporate statements on diversity are sincere, it is at least good to see that these companies are aware that something has to change. But then you look at the executive leadership of these companies. You look at their boards of directors. You look at the demographic makeup of their workforce. More often than not, they lack any real diversity. They have no black executives. Their black employees are miserable.

In the wake of some of these corporate statements, employees have pushed back. They have described "toxic" workplaces, abusive co-workers, racist founders, unchecked bigotry, pay inequities and more. We know racism is a virulent cancer—but it is increasingly clear we have grossly underestimated the extent of the rot.

Sacrificial lambs have tendered letters of resignation. They have apologized for the damaging work environments they have created and nurtured. But in most instances, the offenders will likely be replaced by people who will repeat the toxic patterns. They will continue to enjoy their wealth without being forced to truly reckon with their racist ideologies.

Something about this moment feels different, but I am not sure anyone knows how to move forward in ways that will effectively eradicate racism once and for all. I am not sure that the people who most need to do that difficult work have any incentive to change.

It is clear no one is coming to save us, but we can and will save ourselves. We will do so by relentlessly continuing to protest and remembering that the anger fueling the protests is entirely justified. We will do so by tearing down statues of Confederate soldiers, captains of slave ships, colonizers and anyone else who rose to prominence on the backs of black or Indigenous suffering.

We will save ourselves by holding people and corporations accountable for how they value black lives when they are beyond the glare of public opinion. There has to be more than crafted statements about equality. We all have to challenge ourselves. We have to consider ideas that previously seemed impossible. We have to take risks and make ourselves uncomfortable. We need to continue talking about all of the ways racism influences our lives.

We are on the precipice of change. Public opinion is, at last, shifting. But even with the force of public outrage, there are crystal-clear reminders of what we are up against. The incident report for Breonna Taylor's killing by Louisville police officers was nearly blank when it was released, nearly three months after her death. One of the officers involved has been fired but none of them have been charged with a crime, more than three months after Ms. Taylor's death. The sham of a police report was a pointed message: Police officers can get away with killing people and there's little the public can do about it.

If a change is indeed coming, we have not yet seen the shape of it—and the enemy we are facing is powerful beyond measure. Understanding this truth and persisting nonetheless is how we will save ourselves.

Originally published in the *New York Times*, June 20, 2020

I Am Shattered but Ready to Fight

Joe Biden appears poised to win the presidency, but his win will not be a landslide. And that's fine. A win is a win and the margin of that win only sweetens the victory. Democrats can and should celebrate this win if it does, indeed, come to pass.

And still, many of us are disappointed, for good reason. Republicans are likely to maintain control of the Senate, which will make enacting progressive legislation nearly impossible. Odious politicians like Mitch McConnell and Lindsey Graham were re-elected. Though Mr. Biden will probably win more votes than any previous presidential candidate, that President Trump was a contender at all is a disgrace. That Mr. Trump has received nearly 70 million votes is a disgrace. And it says a lot about this country that too many people refuse to face.

This is America. This is not an aberration. This is indeed our country and who the proverbial "we" are. The way this election has played out shouldn't be a surprise if you've been paying attention or if you understand racism and how systemic it really is. Polling can account for a great many factors, but unless they ask about the extent to which racism motivates voters—and find a way to get honest answers on this topic—they will never be able to account for this.

Some Trump voters are proud about their political affiliation. They attend his rallies. They drive around with their cars draped in Trump posters and flags and other paraphernalia. They proudly crow about America and pride and nationalism. They are the subjects of fawning profiles that aim to explain their voting tendencies as the result of "economic anxiety," as if they are tragically misunderstood. They aren't. We know exactly who they are.

And then there are the other Trump supporters, the ones who are ashamed. The ones who want to seem urbane. The ones who want to be invited to all the good parties. They lie to pollsters. They lie to family and friends. And when they fill out their ballots, they finally tell the truth. That is their right. We live in a democracy, or at least we say we do.

I expect to hear a lot of frenzied political discourse over the next several months. I imagine pundits will try to understand how the 2020 election panned out and why. Too many white liberals will obsess over early exit polls indicating that 20 percent of Black men and a significant number of the overly broad categories of Latinos and Asians voted for Mr. Trump. They'll do this instead of reckoning with how more white women voted for the president this time around and how white men remain the most significant demographic of his base. They will say that once more, Black women saved America from itself, which of course, we did, even though some things don't deserve salvation.

Many will say it was identity politics—which, in their minds means a focus by Democrats on the experiences of marginalized people, which some find distasteful—that kept Mr. Biden from winning by a larger margin. They may be right, but not for the reasons they mean. There is no greater identity politics than that of white people trying to build a firewall around what remains of their empire as this country's demographics continue to shift.

The United States is not at all united. We live in two countries. In one, people are willing to grapple with racism and bigotry. We acknowledge that women have a right to bodily autonomy, that every American has a right to vote and the right to health care and the right to a fair living wage. We understand that this is a country of abundance and that the only reason economic disparity exists is because of a continued government refusal to tax the wealthy proportionally.

The other United States is committed to defending white supremacy and patriarchy at all costs. Its citizens are the people who believe in QAnon conspiracy theories and take Mr. Trump's misinformation as gospel. They see America as a country of scarcity, where there will never be enough of anything to go around, so it is every man and woman for themselves.

They are not concerned with the collective, because they believe any success they achieve by virtue of their white privilege is achieved by virtue of merit. They see equity as oppression. They are so terrified, in fact, that as the final votes were counted in Detroit, a group of them swarmed the venue shouting, "Stop the count." In Arizona, others swarmed a venue shouting, "Count the votes." The citizens of this version of America only believe in democracy that serves their interests.

I do not know how we move forward from this moment. I am optimistic, certainly. I am excited that Kamala Harris will be the first Black woman vice president. I am excited that Mr. Biden will not lead and legislate via social media, that he is competent and that he may not lead the revolution but he will, certainly, lead the country.

I am also worried. I am worried about what Mr. Trump's court-packing will mean for voting rights, reproductive freedom and L.G.B.T.Q. civil rights. I am worried that my marriage is in danger. I am worried that the police will continue to act as if Black lives don't matter, committing extrajudicial murders with impunity. I am worried that the yawning chasms between the poor and middle class and wealthy will grow ever wider. I am worried that too many people are too comfortable in their lives to care about these problems.

I'll be honest. The past four years have shattered my faith in just about everything. I feel ridiculous saying that. I feel ridiculous that I was so confident in a Hillary Clinton victory, that I believed that if a terrible person was elected president, checks and balances would minimize the damage he could do. Since Mr. Trump's election, we have watched him and the Republican Party execute their plans systematically and relentlessly. They have dismantled democratic norms with vigor. We have seen an endless parade of horrors, from families being separated at the Mexican border, to a shattered economy, to an administration completely indifferent to a pandemic that continues to ravage the country. And the list goes on and on. Atrocity only begets more atrocity.

At the same time, the past four years have energized me. They have moved me further left from the comfort of left of center. I have become more active and engaged in my community. I find my sociopolitical stances changing toward real progressive values. I am not the same woman I was and I am grateful for that, even if I hate what brought me to this point.

For much of the 2020 election cycle, many of us wanted anyone but Donald Trump as president because literally anyone but Mr. Trump would be an improvement. The bar he set was subterranean. As the Democratic field narrowed, there was time to consider who would best serve the country, but even as we found our preferred candidates, it was clear that getting Mr. Trump out of office would only be the beginning of the work. That's where things stand. The state of this country will improve if and when Joe Biden is inaugurated as the 46th president of the United States, but a great many things will stay exactly the same unless we remain as committed to progress under his administration as we were under Mr. Trump's.

This is America, a country desperately divided, and desperately flawed. The future of this country is uncertain but it is not hopeless. I am ready to fight for that future, no matter what it holds. Are you?

Originally published in the *New York Times*, November 5, 2020

[FOR THE CULTURE]

So Fast, So Damn Furious

There is a moment in *The Fast and the Furious*, when Dominic "Dom" Toretto, played by Vin Diesel, struts, chest erect, to his classic American muscle car because he's real angry. He's wearing a T-shirt, stained with dirt and blood (long story), his face is set hard, and there is purpose in his stride because someone has to pay. A friend has been killed (another long story) and Dom is the kind of man who believes in settling scores, particularly when his friends, who are also his family, are involved. The scene exudes testosterone, American brawn, and exemplifies why the *Fast & Furious* franchise (currently comprised of six films) is so wonderful.

Let us be clear. Each movie has a fragile and generally absurd suggestion of a plot. The movies don't waste time with plausibility and it's refreshing to know that you must abandon all sense of logic to proceed. There is no pretense of character development. The acting is rarely very good and features wooden delivery, an excess of face acting and if Michelle Rodriguez is in a scene, an epic amount of lip sneering. The actors love to talk to themselves while they're driving, mostly shit-talking their opponents in a given race. They give great driving face, too, gripping steering wheels, staring at the road before them intently. At times, there are bits of dialogue so random you cannot help but laugh out loud. In the first movie, for example, Ja Rule (the once-was rapper) is racing toward the promise of a ménage a trois with two beautiful women. "Noooooo. Monica," he laments, as he loses the race.

Women are gleefully objectified in each movie. They are scantily clad set dressing, often gyrating in pairs or groups of three in settings where such gyrations make no sense, their barely encased and spectacular breasts and asses threatening to break free from whatever leather or vinyl encasement contains them. Women drape themselves across car hoods and stand behind their men and ogle the men who drive and flex their muscles in tight shirts and otherwise express machismo. If women do have speaking roles, they are, with few exceptions, the sister or love interest. They will, at some point, be imperiled because action movies generally have no idea what to do with a woman if she is not in danger.

To be fair, men and cars are objectified too. There are lots of convenient excuses for men to rip their shirts off, revealing impeccably toned abdominals. In the later movies, the bigger men are often spritzed in a delightful sheen of . . . who knows what, but it brings out their musculature in lovely ways. In all six movies, fast cars are pornographically displayed—gleaming paint, flawless chrome, powerful engines, a bewildering panoply of brand names emblazoned across the cars and their various parts—so intense is the gaze on these cars that at times, you want to look away, offer them a little privacy as they bask in their physical perfection. The sound effects are always masterful. We hear every piston firing, every gear shifting with precision and clarity. It's all very erotic in its way.

But, I am getting ahead of myself. If you are unfamiliar, the *Fast & Furious* franchise is a set of movies about street racing—an unholy but glorious combination of *West Side Story*, the myth of Robin Hood, *The Outsiders, The Karate Kid, Ocean's Eleven* and dance movies where disputes might be settled by enthusiastic dance and a whole lot of swagger. There's always a little romance, interesting locales, aggressive hip-hop soundtracks, and plots that bank heavily on loyalty (in times of crisis, street racers stick together), creating communities of choice, and realizing what you really stand for.

In the first movie, Brian O'Conner (Paul Walker) is an ambitious undercover police officer in Los Angeles who infiltrates a gang of street racers led by Dominic Toretto (Vin Diesel) to find out if they are responsible for a series of truck hijackings. Also in the gang are Mia, Dom's sister (Jordana Brewster), Letty (Michelle Rodriguez), Vince (Matt Schulze), and Jesse (Chad Lindberg). They're all misfits but under Dom's leadership, they are family and family is everything. When they're not street racing at night on streets miraculously free of traffic, they are working on cars in the garage and having backyard barbecues where they always say grace. There are rivalries with Mexicans and Asians and most beefs are settled exactly where you expect—on the street, with cars that drive very fast. They race for money and registration slips. They race for honor. Dom is a bit of a bad boy, with his bald head and bulging muscles, offering up cheesy bits of wisdom about life through racing metaphors whenever he gets the chance. He also has a past—he was in Lompoc for two years after nearly beating to death the man who killed his father during a race. The need for speed is genetic in the Toretto family. Throughout this movie, Dom makes it clear he is not going back to prison, no way. There are lots of amazing car chases and races. The movie is a gearhead's wet dream. In the end, Brian ends up letting Dom go because he has become rather fond of him. His true loyalty is to the race and the family.

The second movie is set in Miami with, save for Brian O'Conner, a completely new cast. You know how Hollywood is—if you don't lock actors into a multi-film contract, you never know if you can bring them back into the fold. There is some kind of unspoken movie rule that anything set in South Florida needs to involve the drug trade so that's what happens here. Brian is hanging out with street racers, outcast for letting Toretto go. And then, for some reason, he is recruited by the FBI and U.S. Customs! If he works with them, he'll get his good name back, etc., etc. Brian partners up with his childhood friend, Roman Pearce (Tyrese), to bring down a bad drug guy, Carter Verone (Cole Hauser). Ludacris and a magnificent crown of hair also feature heavily in the movie. Eva Mendes is an undercover agent, pretending to be Verone's girlfriend but she's also the imperiled love interest—two for one. The highlight is probably at the end when Brian and Roman drive a car onto a moving yacht at high speeds. This really happens and it is spectacular.

We head across the Pacific to Tokyo for the third installment—*Tokyo Drift*—and this movie features an entirely new cast. This is the *Karate Kid I* and *II* of the *Fast & Furious* franchise. Sean Boswell (Lucas Black, who is about as convincing as a high school student as Gabrielle Carteris in *Beverly Hills 90210*) is a street-racing troublemaker from Alabama who is sent to Tokyo to live with his military father to get him on the right track. He immediately, and I mean immediately, finds all the street racers in Tokyo. His crew includes Twinkie (Bow Wow) and Han (Sung Kang) and he develops a rivalry with a guy named DK (Brian Tee). Of course they're fighting over a girl. What's key about Tokyo is that they have this magical thing they do in their cars. They drift, which is to allow the rear end of the car to float before the front end of the car. I'm probably

not explaining it well but I don't really do cars. Regardless, Sean has
to learn to master drifting, much in the way of waxing on and waxing
off. He does eventually learn and becomes the king of Tokyo street racing. He is like Daniel-san, performing the street-racing equivalent of the
crane kick during a race against DK for the girl, for pride and honor, for
everything. Along the way, Han dies but it's a bit of a soap opera death.
He will rise again. With this movie begins the franchise's awesome habit
of having a jaw-dropping ending. Guess who shows up to race Sean now
that he's running things in Tokyo? Yes. Dominic Toretto who considers
Han family.

What's particularly charming about these movies is that they largely
give no fucks about plot continuity from one movie to the next. It is with
the fourth movie, *Fast & Furious*, basically the same name as the first
movie, that the original cast is reunited, having realized that their careers
only happen when they are associated with this franchise. We are now
five years past the first movie BUT we are before *Tokyo Drift* takes place.
Bear with me.

The international flair continues as *Fast & Furious* opens in the Dominican Republic, where Dom and his crew are hijacking fuel tankers.
Han is there, as is Letty and some new friends. The street-racing scene is
just as vibrant in the DR as it is elsewhere but we won't learn too much
about it because Dom, in a moment of conscience, leaves Letty, as she
is sleeping, for her own good. Back in Los Angeles, Brian O'Connor is,
somehow, reinstated as a law enforcement officer. Before he was a cop
but now he's an FBI agent or something. It's not really clear. Dom is
hiding out in Mexico when he gets a call from Mia—Letty has been murdered. (Don't get too upset. She may rise again.) Dom returns to L.A.,
even though he is being hunted by several agencies. He must figure out
why his love was murdered. He spends most of the movie in tank tops,
showing off his amazing arms and we are all the better for it. There's lots
of tension as Brian reconnects with Mia (his one-time lover) and Dom
(his one-time friend), but soon they are all working together against the
Braga Cartel in Mexico. There's also this hot woman, Gisele, who works
for Braga but has feelings for Dom, and she helps the heroes overcome.
At the end of the movie, Dom is sentenced to many years in prison, but
his crew busts him out of the prison bus.

Now things get really interesting. In *Fast Five*, everyone is on the lam in Rio, Brazil, cue requisite shot of the *Christ the Redeemer* statue. Mia is pregnant (which we know because, movie rule, she vomits). Vince is back and still sullen and a bit of a Judas. They are being hunted by The Rock who spends the entire movie spritzed and shiny and so swollen with muscles you cannot help but wonder when his body will break. There's a train heist. At one point, Dom and Brian jump from a car, over a gorge, into a river. There are foot races through the favelas. The Rock flexes. Dom's T-shirts get ever tighter. Through some convoluted events, they realize they have something a very powerful bad guy wants. They need to assemble a team so everyone joins in the fun—Tyrese, Ludacris, the two Dominican guys from the fourth movie, Han from the third movie, and Gisele from the fourth movie. It's like the "Quintet" in *West Side Story* only better. In the end, this mighty gang teams up with The Rock and steals a crazy amount of money and gets away with it. But wait! There's more. At the very end, The Rock is back in the United States and Eva Mendes (from the second movie?!) makes a cameo, handing The Rock a file with pictures of, wait for it, Letty. She's baaaack.

Fast & Furious 6 is much of the same only more awesome. Brian and Mia have a kid and I hate to say it, but he is not cute at all. They're all enjoying their ill-gotten gains when Dom is involved with this woman he met during *Fast Five*, a Brazilian cop because in these movies, people move in and out of law enforcement without consequence. The Rock comes calling and has evidence that Letty is alive and working with a very bad bad guy, Shaw. He needs the gang's help in exchange for full immunity. Everyone soldiers up and heads to London to figure out what's going on and to catch the bad guy and his crew of criminal street racers. Ludacris is back, as is Tyrese, Han and Gisele, the latter two of whom are a couple now. Gina Carano, the lady MMA fighter, stars as a law enforcement person working with The Rock and is, toward the end of the movie, involved in a twist. There is also some sadness when Gisele dies and then, this is what brought me to tears, at the very end, we see the scene from *Tokyo Drift*, where Han dies, only from a different perspective and it turns out that the driver of the car who crashes into Han is Shaw's brother played by Jason Strathan. Can you believe it? Amazing.

It would be easy to dismiss these movies as pop confections. They are rather silly. During *Fast & Furious 6*, the gang is driving around London in extremely expensive cars, and they are talking to each other via walkie talkies you could probably buy at Wal-Mart. No one involved in the production seems to think this is a problem but there it is. For all the attention that goes into the cars, other details are blithely overlooked.

There is something that usually goes unacknowledged in these movies—multicultural casting. A Taiwanese director, Justin Lin, has helmed the movies since *Tokyo Drift*, and that is also noteworthy. In every movie, there is a range of ethnicities on the screen. People of color are involved in speaking roles and people of color are not merely the bad guys. This isn't to say the franchise doesn't make missteps or reductive choices. In *2 Fast 2 Furious*, for example, the movie confuses Haitians and Jamaicans in a rather lame, avoidable way. Still, it is refreshing to see movies where the actors have some melanin. It is sad that this is refreshing.

In an interview with ComingSoon.net, Sung Kang, who plays Han, said, "Prior to *Tokyo Drift*, the iconic perception of Asians in Hollywood films has been either the Kung Fu guy, the Yakuza guy or some technical genius. It used to be such a joke, to be laughed at rather than with. I've gotten to travel and meet people all over the world who embrace Han. He's the kind of guy that I would like to emulate in terms of his values. He's just a guy you want to hang out with. The Asian thing totally disappears."

I suspect this desire to have race disappear is something familiar to many actors of color who want to be able to inhabit roles that go beyond the rigid, race-based caricatures we encounter in film (and television and literature and life) over and over again. Great movies also offer the audience an opportunity to disappear. The lights go down and we disappear into these bright and beautiful images, ten feet high. We fall into different times and places. We are allowed to step away from our own lives for a time. The loveliest thing about the *Fast & Furious* franchise is that both actors and viewers get to disappear together, and oh what a time we have.

Originally published in *The Toast*, July 10, 2013

Nickel and Dimed (Mitchell Jackson's *The Residue Years*)

———

In Mitchell S. Jackson's powerful debut novel, *The Residue Years*, we know how things will end for Champ Thomas and his mother, Grace, before we know how they get there. In the prologue—one of the few I've read that is organic to the story that follows—a mother is visiting her son in prison. This imbues what follows with a sense of hopelessness that becomes ever sharper in contrast to the novel itself, which is, in its way, full of impossible hope.

Told in chapters that alternate between Champ and Grace, *The Residue Years* describes a black family in Portland, Oregon, trying hard to remain a family. Grace is just out of rehab, hoping to stay straight and get her kids back, to make up for all the wrong she's done. Her eldest, Champ, who recognizes his own sharp intelligence, is in college and living with a girlfriend he loves and disappoints in near equal measure. Champ's two younger brothers live with their father and have started to distance themselves from Grace in the way of children let down one time too many. For both Grace and Champ, bringing the family back together might offer a way to something better.

The Residue Years is also about cycles of poverty and addiction, and as such it offers a stark look at the ravages of drugs in black urban neighborhoods. Champ slings crack to support his family, unapologetic because it brings in money and he has responsibilities. He also has a dream: He wants to buy the house where he remembers being happiest, even though a new family lives there now and the house is not for sale. Grace gets a legitimate job, but she's never far from the influences that have always held her back. There's just too much temptation in too many places, and most of the time she has to face that temptation alone. The beating heart of this novel is a journey toward a home that is always just beyond grasp no matter how fiercely Grace and Champ reach. Their story is as moving as it is unbearable.

Jackson's prose has a spoken-word cadence, the language flying off the page with percussive energy, as when Champ takes his brothers to the barbershop: "KJ's ambivalent about his cut. Looks to me, with his shoulders hiked. My bro is always demurring, always deferring. But since it's a 0.00 percent of reclaiming a vacated seat, it won't be no assurance from intimate distance today. Give him a low one-lengther, I say from my perch. Dude's averse to cuts."

There is warmth and wit, and a hard-won wisdom about the intersection of race and poverty in America. Before Grace finds work, she has to contend with a complicated past that includes time in prison; most employers aren't interested in "complicated." When she does get a job, she has to pay court fees and fines and feed herself, all on a fast-food worker's wages. There is no way up and no way out.

Champ, meanwhile, has always known the limits of his options. He played basketball in high school but wasn't quite good enough to make it to the next level—he couldn't make a name for himself, or even a nickname. "My word," he says, "a nickname is a christening, meaning you got a shot, meaning they think you can go, which is one chance more than most of us, so no wonder the chosen are all there is to speak of. No wonder when, for most, hoop's about our only shot to be better and bigger than the rest, to secure a life that counts." That Champ keeps trying to have a life that counts despite the odds is one more way this novel treads so finely between hope and despair.

One of the most affecting of Jackson's choices comes by way of the blank forms he intersperses with the prose: a drug diversion contract, new member registration for a church, a petition for child custody, a police report. These forms are presented without context, but they reveal how the very institutions meant to serve often fail us instead.

The Residue Years is an autobiographical novel, and at times Jackson has so much empathy for his characters that he understandably sacrifices plot. He demonstrates more devotion to the truth than to fiction. We know Grace and Champ inside out. We see all their failings and the desperation of their hopes. Though that is in many ways the point of this novel, the story stagnates in scenes that seem written to satisfy the writer's need to remember more than the reader's need to know.

It would be easy to suggest that *The Residue Years* is "about" race, since it revolves around black people and their lives. Yet if that assumption is reductive—the novel also takes a raw, hard look at poverty, after all, and how it holds people so firmly in the very places they want to escape—it's not entirely wrong, either. In his advanced speech class, Champ gives a presentation about the disproportionate criminal penalties for crack-related drug offenses. After a classmate suggests that not everything is about race, Champ answers: "You're right, not everything's about race. But what if this is?"

Originally published in the *New York Times*, August 16, 2013

Why the Beach Is a Bummer

It is summer, and so, we are repeatedly reminded, it is time for the beach—beach bodies, beach reads, fruity beach drinks in tall glasses festooned with tiny paper umbrellas and fruits skewered on tiny plastic swords. This is an ideal beach of hot sun, warm sand, crystal-clear water that leaves your skin salted. But it is all too often a mirage.

I have known beaches.

When I was a child, my parents took my brothers and me to Port-au-Prince during the summer so we could get to know the country of our ancestors. Because Haiti is an island, the beach is everywhere. Haitians are particular, even snobby about beaches. We scoff at the beaches of other Caribbean islands or Hawaii (let us not speak of continental American "beaches") because nowhere in the world, we know with certainty, is the water warmer and clearer. Nowhere is the sand whiter or more willing to embrace our warm flesh.

In Haiti, beach bodies are simply bodies, and beach reads are simply books, because the beach is all around you. Here in the United States, it is similar for those who live on the coasts. The beach is five miles away from my parents' Florida home. They have lived there for more than 15 years. They have been to the beach once, to take guests who were visiting.

But for the rest of us, the beach exerts a different kind of gravitational pull. Sixty-one percent of Americans don't live anywhere near a beach. We spend a surprising amount of time hearing about this place we will hardly ever see. We watch commercials, TV shows and movies in which nubile young women and their strapping male counterparts frolic on sand, their hair golden and sun-streaked. Long walks on the beach are the supposed holy grail of a romantic evening. The beach becomes a kind of utopia—the place where all our dreams come true.

I have known beaches, but I have no particular fondness for them. I don't like sand in my crevices. I don't like sand at all. I don't enjoy all that sunshine and heat without the benefit of climate control. I don't enjoy other people at the beach—sticky children, young people with firm bodies and scanty bathing suits, those of less firm body staring forlornly at this spectacle. People bring pets, and I am not an animal person. No, I do not want to pet your dog.

After 10 minutes, I find myself bored. What are we supposed to do at the beach? I'm black, and so I understand sunbathing as a concept but less so as an activity. How long am I supposed to lie in the sun? When do I turn myself over like roasting meat on a spit? How often do I apply this sunscreen you speak of?

I don't like bathing suits. There is so little material involved and they ride up in places where there should be no riding. They are not flattering for many body types because a beach body is a very specific, slender, toned and tan body. The rest of us, if we dare show up at the beach, should probably don caftans, neck to toe. Wearing a bathing suit on a beach would leave me exposed in ways that terrify me: no clothing to hide behind, so much of my flesh spilling, available for mockery or, as this modern age demands, amateur photography in which I end up as the punch line on some website that masks cruelty with so-called humor. I'm not that brave.

There is the water, lapping gently on the shore, but, honestly, it's not that much fun to get into it. Sometimes there are creatures and slimy lengths of seaweed and sharp things at the bottom. Unlike the swimming pool, there is no chlorine at the beach, and I am quite certain that people are using the ocean as their vast personal toilet. It is an unfathomable stretch of water that holds too much potential for treachery. And sharks.

It's no better up on the sand. Beach seating is uncomfortable, particularly when you're tall. There my feet are, hanging over the edge of the chaise. Or I'm in some kind of lawn chair, my parts sticking to polyester in ways that will leave firmly indented patterns. Reading at the beach is an ordeal—trying to find a comfortable position, keeping sand out of the book and sun out of my eyes, managing the pages if there is a strong breeze. Soon enough, my sunglasses start sliding down my face.

Once, I drove down to Key West, which is, basically, New Orleans at the beach: loud, grimy, abundant in alcohol. I saw the southernmost city in the continental United States and waited in a line of tourists to hug the marker and have my picture taken. I stepped carefully onto those strange undulations of sand. I thought, *This is pretty and all, but I could die without ever having this experience again.* The beach is a place lovelier in theory than practice.

Summer itself is also lovelier in theory than practice, despite the best efforts of splashy magazines trying to hype us up. "Get ready for summer," they say, when they should be saying, "Prepare for inconsistent weather, humidity, disappointment and dreams deferred."

I always have grand plans for myself each summer. I teach, and throughout the academic year, my colleagues and I wax wistful about all the things we're going to do when the spring semester ends. We will read, and it will be luxurious, because we will be reading for ourselves. We will travel, and not to attend a conference. And, of course, we will diligently prepare for our fall courses. I have, thus far, spent my summer watching an inordinate amount of *Barefoot Contessa* on the Food Network.

It will never be what we want it to be, and yet we cannot help but hold on to this vision of summer, of the beach, of contentment. Despite my better judgment, I am also vulnerable to this fantasy, to so much trembling want. It is an unattainable idyll that we never quite reach, but somehow, it remains enough.

Originally published in the *New York Times*, July 26, 2014

Discomfort Zone
(*The Unspeakable* by
Meghan Daum)

In the song "Poetic Justice," Kendrick Lamar raps, "You're in the mood for empathy, there's blood in my pen." This is how we might consider the essay—blood in the pen of the essayist, inking the personal to bring about an empathetic response. When it comes to the personal essay, we want so much and there is something cannibalistic about our desire. We want essayists to splay themselves bare. We want to see how much they are willing to bleed for us. This desire introduces an interesting tension for essay writers. How much should they bleed, and how much blood should they save for themselves?

This tension is readily apparent in Meghan Daum's new collection, *The Unspeakable*. Daum bleeds, but only so much as she delves into subjects that are, she says, unspeakable for one reason or another: reluctance to have children, bearing witness to her mother's hard death without the extravagant demonstrations of mourning we might expect, an aversion to cooking and foodie culture.

Like the pieces in her influential essay collection *My Misspent Youth*, these essays tread a fine line between self-deprecation and reveling in difference. Because of this frankness, you might think that by the end of the collection, you would have a visceral sense who this writer is, but this is not the case. In the introduction, Daum writes of her ambivalence toward "mining my own life for material. . . . In the end, the work I always come back to, the work that seems best remembered and draws the strongest reactions, is the work in which the 'outside world' forms a vital partnership with that I narrator." The work for which she is most remembered is the work in which she bleeds.

Overall, this collection is formidable, lucid and persuasive. Daum writes with confidence and an elegant defiance of expectation. She reveals the most unspeakable parts of herself or what she perceives as unspeakable or what she assumes the reader will perceive as unspeakable. A question emerges repeatedly: Are the topics Daum writes about actually unspeakable or are they simply topics people respond to in complex, unpredictable ways?

There is a bravado in claiming to voice the inexpressible. "I am speaking truths few others have the courage to share," is what the writer seems to say. Or, "Look at me! I am willing to show the least culturally palatable parts of myself."

In one of the strongest essays, "Matricide," Daum writes of being at her mother's side as her mother died a painful death. This is a story we've seen before—dutiful daughter holding vigil at a parent's deathbed, a sacred time of mourning and reconciliation. "Matricide," however, is not that kind of essay. Daum writes explicitly against such expectations, expressing impatience with her mother's dying and the relief she felt when her mother finally died. Her mother remarked that she felt nothing when her own mother died the same week she learned she had cancer. In each of these revelations, there is the sense that Daum is making an intensifying confession, with each new essay, showing the ways in which her writing might be considered unspeakable. Mostly, though, Daum comes off as merely human, a person caught in horrifying circumstances for which there can be no appropriate emotional response. Her account reads more as liberating than unpalatable. She shows that there is no singular way to bear loss.

Another difficult subject she explores over the course of several essays is ambivalence toward marriage and other human connection. Daum is married now but makes clear she did not see herself as the marrying kind, until she did. The repetition of this theme is curious, as if she were trying to convince either herself or the reader of how she feels about love, or perhaps she is trying to acknowledge the contradiction of actions and words. In "The Dog Exception," where she discusses her fondness for dogs, Daum writes, "I suppose what I'm really saying is that I can't connect with people, or that I don't want to, or that I'm unwilling or unable to do the work required to be someone for whom the idea of having a human loved one beside me at my deathbed is a source of comfort rather than ambivalence." And yet, Daum doesn't seem especially ambivalent about these things. She tries to connect with children by mentoring, then by participating in foster care advocacy. When she gets pregnant, she plans on carrying the fetus to term but then miscarries. She considers adoption when her husband expresses the desire to have a child. When she falls ill and becomes temporarily unable to speak, an experience she chronicles in "Diary of a Coma," she doesn't seem particularly ambivalent about having her husband by her side.

This is another tension of the personal essay: We are invited, by the very nature of the medium, to judge the lived experiences of others. We are encouraged to seek out contradictions whether or not they exist.

And then there is the piece "Honorary Dyke." "There was a period in my life, roughly between the ages of 32 and 35, when pretty much anyone who saw me would have assumed I was a lesbian," Daum writes. "I had very short, almost spiky hair, owned three pairs of Chuck Taylor tennis shoes and wore lots of cargo pants with tank tops and silver jewelry. . . . I had a toe ring. I drove a Subaru station wagon." She calls herself "'an aspirational lesbian,' otherwise known as the basically hetero broad for whom the more glamorous expressions of dykery hold a distinct if perpetually enigmatic allure."

I suppose this is the kind of essay where we are supposed to chuckle because it's charming and humorous, but mostly it reads as tone-deaf, with a straight woman sending up a caricature of lesbianism that suits her purposes without examining the appropriation going on. Given the rigorous and frank self-examination in the rest of the collection, this essay falls far short of the others.

There is no doubt Daum is a brilliant, incisive essayist. I would follow her words anywhere. As she returns to the question of what is unspeakable, she comes across as a woman who has made peace with the best and worst parts of herself. And maybe that is what is unspeakable in our culture—admitting to mere fallibility, humanity.

Originally published in the *New York Times*, December 10, 2014

Bridled Vows
(Jenny Offill's *Dept. of Speculation*)

———

As a Finnish proverb reportedly has it, love is a flower that turns into fruit at marriage. In contemporary fiction, though, that fruit is often spoiled, and its faintly reeking rot gives purpose to a great many novels exploring the notion that staying true to one person for the rest of your life and raising children (or, sometimes, not) are difficult, complex, unknowable endeavors. This is the mythology and often enough the truth of marriage, and novelists are forever reaching for the right words to capture it.

Jenny Offill's second novel, *Dept. of Speculation*, charts the course of a marriage through curious, often shimmering fragments of prose. A writer lives in Brooklyn. A writer lives in Brooklyn and falls in love. A writer in Brooklyn marries and has a child. A married writer in Brooklyn lives, and then there are bedbugs. The novel is, at times, reminiscent of Renata Adler's *Speedboat* with a less bitter edge. Seemingly significant information is doled out in inscrutable doses. Each fragment is satisfying or not, and exists unto itself but also, clearly, as part of something bigger. *Dept. of Speculation* moves quickly, but it is also joyously demanding because you will want to keep trying to understand the why of each fragment and how it fits with the others.

The narrator offers observations like: "The Buddhists say there are 121 states of consciousness. Of these, only three involve misery or suffering. Most of us spend our time moving back and forth between these three." There is gravity to the mere idea of Buddhism. We're supposed to do something with this information, right? There is meaning here, whether about marriage or love or life or all of the above, but the precise nature of that meaning is never fully revealed. Yet Offill is a smart writer with a canny sense of pacing; just when you want to abandon the fragmented puzzle pieces of the novel, she reveals a moment of breathtaking tenderness. Here for instance is the narrator remembering the early days of her relationship: "I bought a warmer coat with many ingenious pockets. You put your hands in all of them." Details like this cast welcome light on the couple's history and intimacy.

Offill builds a story out of these fragments, observations and other mental detritus. There is a sister and a philosopher friend. There is the narrator and the man at the center of the novel, the man she falls in love with, the man she marries, the man she has a child with, the man who ultimately fails her. Over the course of their marriage there are jobs and dinners with friends and sleepless nights. No modern Brooklyn love story would be complete without bedbugs, so there is also that urban tragedy. There is the looming threat of an unfinished second novel that plagues both narrator and reader. What is this novel? Why hasn't it been written? This particular plot point feels very self-referential—a wink and a nod to writers who deal with the quiet but insistent pressure of the next thing after the memory of the first thing has nearly faded.

Dept. of Speculation is especially engaging when it describes new motherhood—the stunned joy and loneliness and fatigue of it, the new orientation of the narrator's world around an impossibly small but demanding creature. And just when you think you understand the novel's cadence, Offill offers up a stunning line like: "But the smell of her hair. The way she clasped her hand around my fingers. This was like medicine. For once, I didn't have to think. The animal was ascendant." There is a primal energy in these passages, the tension of a modern woman giving in to the raw urge of motherhood.

From this raw energy rises the most engaging person in the novel. From her infancy onward, the unnamed daughter who is precocious without being cloying, moderate with her affection, deliberate in her ways, is by far the most intriguing person in the ongoing drama. Then, sadly, she drifts out of the story because she is older, because the marriage is older, because the story, inevitably, must grow in a different direction.

Or this is the story of a me and a you and then a she and a him and finally a you, a me, an us, as Offill deftly moves the novel forward with elegant shifts of point of view. First, we are part of the marriage and then we are studying the marriage from a distance as things begin to fall apart. There is an infidelity and an excruciating period of indecision and self-doubt as the wife, as she is now known, tries to assess her role in the marriage coming apart, and as she determines the right and proper shape for her anger.

The wife's pain and sorrow are rendered through a wryer brand of observation as she becomes the betrayed. It is easy to feel for her because she is a desperately interesting character. Each newly disclosed flaw only makes her more compelling. In fact, we know everything about the wife and how she thinks and feels and moves through the world. It is much more difficult to feel anything about the marriage because the husband is so secondary a character. He is an accessory and a bit player in the wife's meditations.

When we do learn anything about the you, the husband, it is by way of the wife setting herself up for fallibility by depicting him as infallible. "He is famously kind, my husband. . . . He's from Ohio. This means he never forgets to thank the bus driver or pushes in front at the baggage claim." And then: "This is another way in which he is an admirable person. If he notices something is broken, he will try to fix it. He won't just think about how unbearable it is that things keep breaking, that you can never . . . outrun entropy." It all seems too deliberate, setting the husband up in this way.

Of course he falls because he has been placed, quite grandly, on a pedestal for the wife to admire him more than actually be married to him. But maybe that is what happens in love and marriage. We admire from a distance, and we look away when we get too close and see what is actually there.

As the husband and wife try to repair their relationship, he often seems petulant and repulsively indistinct while the wife becomes ever more complicated. For better or worse, this is not so much a book about their marriage; it is a book about the wife's marriage. It would be interesting to read the other story to this marriage, to know more of the husband, the father—but Offill still makes it seem as if the wife's version of the marriage is story enough and, perhaps, the only story that matters. The book calls to mind another proverb, this one from Madagascar: Marriage is not a tight knot, but a slip knot.

Originally published in the *New York Times*, February 7, 2014

Food TV's Sadistic Glee

I am competitive. I try to keep this to myself, but oh, in my heart of hearts, I want to win anything that can be won. As a child, I needed to earn the highest grades and offer, when called upon, the most astute answers, the better to impress teacher. Yes, I was that girl. I have a national Scrabble ranking, though it is not impressive. When I sit across from other word nerds, I want to destroy them. I feel competitive when driving on the interstate, when following the career arcs of other writers, when reading a book and the Kindle tells me I have eight hours left. That is a throwing down of the gauntlet. I determine to finish in six.

When we compete, we try to prove we are excellent. When we win, we say, "I have mastered this endeavor, and I am excellent." The rush is seductive. I am not alone in craving that rush, and perhaps that is why contests have become the mainstay of so many cultural pursuits that don't seem conducive to them. Spelling bees and poker and bridge tournaments—nothing too surprising. But then we start to get further afield—eating, arm wrestling, Quidditch, running with the bulls, even rock-paper-scissors championships. No matter how exotic or mundane the arena, someone wants to be the best.

It is perhaps inevitable that we have ended up here, in a robust age of cooking television, privy to a lineup of increasingly complex tests that will reveal once and for all who is the best chef in the land. These shows feed the insatiable cultural appetite for reality television while offering more than a parade of pretty people through potentially humiliating or harrowing circumstances. We want a spectacle, but sometimes we want it imbued with a sense of purpose. Food is also delicious, and we get a masochistic thrill watching it lovingly prepared but knowing we are unlikely ever to taste such delights.

This madness began 20-odd years ago when *Iron Chef* debuted in Japan in 1993 and was later picked up by the Food Network and aired in the United States, at first replete with dubbing reminiscent of Godzilla movies, then as an Americanized knockoff. The premise was both simple and elaborate. A man named Chairman Kaga enjoyed hosting battles in a "kitchen stadium" decked out with modern equipment and a full pantry. The iron chefs, masters of their craft, were challenged in each episode by upstart chefs of varying renown. Contestants were tasked with using a mystery ingredient to prepare the most impressive dishes they could to determine "whose cuisine reigns supreme." One more twist—the chefs had an hour. Nothing brings out the thrill of competition like an artificial time constraint.

This doesn't sound like a promising premise, but the show's play-by-play commentary and slow-motion shots of, say, food dropped into a fryer made it seem like something real was at stake. It was always interesting to see what each chef would do with ingredients that have been over the years, at times, bewildering—Asyura oyster, blue-foot chicken. Judges exhaustively narrated their experience eating the dishes. At home, we watched this delectation and wanted more.

In the years since, televised competitive cooking has become a bustling industry. Much of the current interest was spurred by the debut, in 2006, of Bravo's *Top Chef*. Each season, a gaggle of chefs converge with knives sharpened in an American city (New Orleans, New York, Miami, Chicago, Seattle). The contestants live together—cloistered, as so many reality-television participants are. But for the most part, *Top Chef* is about cooking. Episodes start with a "quick-fire" challenge, often with a celebrity guest judge. Contestants, or chef-testants if you will, have to create the perfect omelet or the perfect hamburger or the perfect amuse-bouche using convenience-mart ingredients like pork rinds and a prepackaged ham-and-cheese sandwich. Quick-fire winners earn not only the flush of victory but also an advantage in the subsequent elimination challenge, whether it is first choice of ingredients or extra prep time.

The elimination round is the show's centerpiece. The chef-testants prepare a meal for a celebrity, a healthy but delicious lunch for schoolchildren, or hors d'oeuvres for festivalgoers. As with *Iron Chef*, *Top Chef* makes it seem like something greater than prize money and career opportunities is being fought for. This is, you might say, about culinary honor.

Top Chef has succeeded because it is reality television with a veneer of mannered restraint. Certainly, drama arises among the chefs. But food is the point, and pornographically so. In addition to seeing each dish prepared in the show's crucible, we see it beautifully plated and watch the judges eat and wax rhapsodically (or not) about its merits.

Not all cooking-competition shows are so well behaved. Brash British chef Gordon Ramsay reigns over *Hell's Kitchen*, which originated in the U.K. The prize is, purportedly, a head-chef position at a fine restaurant. The format is curious. Early in the season, the contestants are divided into teams and given one job—to manage a successful dinner service. Spoiler alert: They rarely do. Ramsay is something of a kitchen tyrant, lording it over the contestants as they try to prepare beef Wellington and soufflés and other dishes. It's fun to hear Ramsay shouting, "I need three risotto, please," in his gruff and staccato voice while the contestants fail, miserably, at tasks they have long been doing professionally, beyond the glare of reality television.

Though other networks try their hand at competitive cooking shows, the Food Network is still at the forefront. In his recent book *From Scratch*, Allen Salkin charts the network's rise to prominence. By the late aughts, its personality-driven shows like *Emeril Live* and *Molto Mario* were proving expensive to produce and waning in ratings. In one of the book's more charming anecdotes, Salkin reveals the origins of an entry into the competitive genre, *Chopped*, whose backstory is stranger than you might think. The show was pitched with the setup of a "tycoon" planning to throw a dinner party in his castle. Salkin writes, "His butler, a snooty John Cleese type, would find four sous chefs who would compete in the castle kitchen for the privilege of cooking the dinner. The competition covered three rounds: an appetizer, a main course, and a dessert. After each round, one chef would be eliminated by a panel of judges. The food of each eliminated chef would be scraped into a dog bowl and fed, on camera, to the butler's ravenous Chihuahua."

Alas, during the taping, the dog, Pico, was a problem. If he had been fed throughout the day, he would get sick. The strange elements didn't come together—too much affect. What did work was the four contestants taking everything so seriously—"These chefs [were] dying to play this game and compete and prove they made the right choices in their lives," said Linda Lea, a Food Network producer. What gripped the audience was the chefs in their pursuit to be excellent, to be the best.

I am always mesmerized by *Chopped*, now in its 20th season—Food Network seasons are notoriously abbreviated so that multiple seasons can appear in a calendar year. At the beginning of each course, we feel a giddy moment of anticipation as the chefs grapple with the secret basket of ingredients they are given and instructed to highlight. In one early episode's opening round, the chefs had to work with baby octopus, bok choy, oyster sauce, and smoked paprika. They moved on to duck breast, green onions, ginger, and honey. Finally, the two chefs left standing wrangled prunes, animal crackers, and cream cheese into a dessert. There is a sadistic glee in the composition of many of the baskets, which become puzzles that must be solved in 20 minutes—a culinary Rubik's Cube.

The judges, renowned chefs, take the proceedings seriously. From their deliberation table, they offer commentary and wisdom as the competing chefs toil over hot stoves. As time winds down, a judge will often say, "Just get it on the plate," or, "Grind it out." Though they will decide the chefs' fates, they make it seem like they want nothing but the best for the chef-testants.

Chopped has spawned redemption episodes in which losing chef-testants return and try to, well, redeem themselves. Besides a now-traditional celebrity edition of the show, a new *Chopped* cookbook has arrived. The book encourages people to "use what you've got to cook something great" and "focuses on ingredients most Americans tend to buy every week at the supermarket." The recipes and tips treat preparing dinner like a more realistic version of working with basket ingredients. We are armed, the book implies, with the potential for greatness by using this cookbook and supplies in our kitchens. We no longer have to lust for food we cannot have. We can satiate ourselves. The middle classes, at least, have new ways to think about food and unprecedented opportunities to consume better food.

Competitive cooking shows have become increasingly and intriguingly convoluted as the market crowds. In *Food Court Wars*, two teams vie for a year's lease in a food court. *Guy's Grocery Games* sends chefs racing through aisles of food products. *Cutthroat Kitchen*, hosted by Food Network mainstay Alton Brown, eggs chefs on to bid for nefarious obstacles they can bestow upon fellow competitors; things quickly get out of hand. In *Sweet Genius*, pastry chefs enjoy their moment, with strange and flummoxing ingredients sent to the chefs on a conveyor belt. *Worst Cooks in America* pits against each other people who have no business being in a kitchen. The entire United States is the stage for *The Great Food Truck Race*, in which entrepreneurial-wannabe teams compete to win their own food truck. Let us not forget *Extreme Chef*, in which contestants cook MREs in the galley of a Coast Guard cutter, or in a desert using the indigenous tools of Native Americans, or on a mountain after trekking up with supplies to prepare a meal.

What is it about food television that captures our imagination? While we are in an age of competitive cooking, we are also in the age of slow food and locally sourced, organic ingredients. The middle classes, at least, have new ways to think about food and unprecedented opportunities to consume better food.

Food is not simply sustenance; it is a significant part of a growing cultural conversation, albeit a privileged and fanciful one. In addition to watching people compete, we feel like if we watch these shows, we might absorb some culinary excellence.

In one season of *Top Chef*, a contestant talked about preparing a velouté, a soup or sauce made of chicken, veal, or fish stock and cream and thickened with butter and flour. I loved the sound of "velouté," so sensuous off the tongue, and even though I am a vegetarian, I became obsessed with the idea, deploying the word whenever I could. I found vegetarian velouté recipes and used the technique to prepare sauces. I cannot say I achieved any kind of greatness, but I certainly expanded my repertoire.

I cannot help but feel these shows speak to a need, a yearning for that which we dare not eat. There's no denying that we have a fraught relationship to food. We have these bodies, and they must be fed. Our bodies, however, can only be fed so much before they become unruly. Beyond these shows, we are inundated by commercials for diet products and sensible snacks. We read about weight loss in glossy magazines. We fret over cellulite and count calories. Perhaps we watch these shows to attempt to satisfy a hunger that never will be satisfied. Perhaps we watch these shows to consume beautiful food without consequence for our delicately human bodies.

Originally published in *American Prospect*, April 24, 2014

The Marriage Plot

Boy meets girl. Boy and girl fall in love. Boy and girl marry, etc., etc., etc. Or. Boy (Girl) meets 25 girls (boys). Boy and girl perform falling in love in front of video cameras, producers and millions of television viewers. It is spring, the feverish time when people fall in love, when people who have fallen in love promise their lives to one another—blushing brides, nervous grooms, extravagant weddings, compressed versions of the overproduced rituals of television shows like *The Bachelor* and *The Bachelorette*.

Since 2002, these two shows have offered a grotesquerie of the courtship ritual that is predicated on the fragile premise that "the one" is waiting among a carefully selected group of entrepreneurs, pharmaceutical reps, dental hygienists and personal trainers.

I have never dreamed of being a princess. I have not longed for Prince Charming. But I do long for something resembling a happily ever after. I am supposed to be above such flights of fantasy, but I am not. I am enamored of fairy tales.

In "Aschenputtel," or Cinderella, by the Brothers Grimm, the daughter of a wealthy remarried man is subject to the cruel whims of her stepmother and stepsisters. When the king throws a ball, a white dove brings Cinderella a gown and slippers so she can attend the ball. For three nights, wearing ever more beautiful gowns, Cinderella dances with the prince. He falls in love, but on the third night, she flees, leaving behind a golden slipper. The prince comes to her home bearing the slipper. The stepmother counsels one daughter to cut off her toes so her foot might fit in the slipper. This deception is revealed. The second sister has cut off part of her heel to fit into the slipper, but her deception, too, is revealed. Then the prince learns of Cinderella, hidden away in the kitchen, and her foot slides perfectly into the slipper. They marry while the stepsisters are blinded by doves who strike them in the eyes.

In both darker and lighter versions of fairy tales, a woman's suffering is demanded in exchange for true love and happily ever after. She must be trapped in a tower or poisoned by an apple or forced to spin straw into gold. She must wait for the hand of a man who is fooled not once but twice before he finds her. Throughout any given season of *The Bachelor*, the women exclaim that the experience is like a fairy tale. They suffer the machinations of reality television, pursuing—along with several other women, often inebriated—the promise of happily ever after. Instead of bleeding from the foot to fit a golden slipper, they bleed their dignity, one episode at a time.

The show encourages us to believe in love until we shouldn't: The chemistry isn't there or the time isn't right or he simply isn't that into her. The ending of this approximation of a relationship is as banal as it is humiliating. When each contestant leaves, eyes red, lips trembling, mascara streaking, she is embraced by the soft leather seat of a limousine. Many of the young women, in their early to mid-20s, plaintively say, "I'm never going to find anyone"—a lament that is a bit hard to take from someone who would have trouble renting a car.

I am 39. I am single. I am a black woman. I have too many advanced degrees. Many a news story tells me finding true love is likely a hopeless proposition. Now is the time when I need to believe in fairy tales. People are impossible, but I am clawing for ways to find someone with whom to be impossible. I know how damaging fairy tales are for women, how much sacrifice is demanded for an all-too-fragile promise of love, but still I watch *The Bachelor* and *The Bachelorette*. I suspend my disbelief and common sense. I mute my feminism. I buy into the notion that a man or woman can find love among 25 tanned and extremely fit potential suitors, in a mere matter of weeks, as long as the courtship is, unlike the revolution, televised. Maybe true love isn't out there for me, but I can sublimate my loneliness with the notion that true love is out there for someone.

The Bachelor harkens back to Puritan times, when courtships were supervised by parents and other invested parties to secure wealth, land, social standing. Love was not a necessary condition of marriage. Instead, Puritans focused on more rational considerations. Though these rational considerations are different on *The Bachelor*, they are there—is this person attractive? Can they form basic sentences? Are they willing to sacrifice themselves to the spectacle? But now it's television producers who work to make the proper match.

During the colonial era, courting couples were bundled together, fully dressed, in individual cloth sacks tied at the neck with a bundling board between them. These couples could whisper sweet nothings to each other but couldn't satisfy any other desire. Beneath the glare of cameras and the manipulative intrusions of producers, the couples on *The Bachelor* and *The Bachelorette* are similarly bundled until one of the last episodes, where couples can visit a "fantasy suite." The cameras disappear. The next morning, the men and women stare into the camera and say things like, "We talked all night," or "It was perfect." The rest of us know they finally had sex.

Last season, *The Bachelor* was, however, a fairy tale interrupted. Two women refused to be arranged. Sharleen Joynt decided that though she was intensely attracted to Juan Pablo, the Bachelor, he didn't stimulate her intellectually, and she left the show. Andi Dorfman, who will be the next Bachelorette as that show begins again next week, was sent with Juan Pablo into the fantasy suite. The morning after, she went off script, saying: "The fantasy suite turned into a nightmare. I saw a side to him that I didn't really like, and the whole night was just a disaster." She, too, left the show. Juan Pablo himself refused to be Prince Charming, resisting, despite pressure from the show's host, to say that he loved the woman he chose. Finally there were cracks in the fairy tale facade.

Romantic comedies and romance novels dish up the same beautiful lies. Couples start out ambivalent or disliking each other or there is unrequited emotion lurking in one heart, waiting to be uncovered by the other. And then the couple fall in love somehow, and there are obstacles, but these things can and will be overcome because true love is always possible when we suffer and sacrifice. Eventually, inevitably, there is a bold, desperately romantic declaration of love followed by a happily ever after. These moments are addictive, bittersweet, strangely satisfying. They fill a hollowness carved by the ways in which our own romantic lives fall ever so short of the beautiful lies. We know better, of course. We rail against these shows and romantic comedies and romance novels and the overwrought consumerism of Valentine's Day. We say, "This is not how love works." And mostly, that isn't how love works. Love is a messy and ragged thing. For many of us, it is endlessly elusive.

And so we'll be watching next Monday as the newest Bachelorette— who has been through the exquisitely staged courtship routine and knows her lines—says she's ready for love and knows The One is out there, offering up the trite pablum of Hallmark love. We will watch, mocking the spectacle, secretly trying to fill the ways we are hollow. We are not as cynical as we pretend to be. We continue to date and fall disastrously in love and marry and divorce and try again despite overwhelming evidence that it is a hell of a thing to stay with one person for the rest of your life. Few among us want to die alone, holding that hollow space inside us. The real shame of *The Bachelor* and *The Bachelorette*, of the absurd theater of romantic comedies, of the sweeping passion of romance novels, is that they know where we are most tender, and they aim right for that place.

Originally published in the *New York Times*, May 10, 2014

Warning Signs (*The Sacrifice* by Joyce Carol Oates)

———

Writing difference is a challenge, particularly in fiction. How do men write women and vice versa? How do writers of one race or ethnicity write about people of another race or ethnicity? More important, how do writers tackle difference without reducing their characters to caricatures or stereotypes? Some handle the challenge with aplomb. Bill Cheng's *Southern Cross the Dog* and Louise Erdrich's *The Round House* come to mind. Others fail: At one point in Kathryn Stockett's *The Help*, a black woman compares her skin color with that of a cockroach. To write difference well demands empathy, an ability to respect the humanity of those you mean to represent.

In late November 1987, Tawana Brawley was found in her upstate New York hometown, covered in racist and misogynist slurs, feces in her hair. The teenager said she had been kidnapped and raped by several white men, including police officers and (in a detail she added later) an assistant district attorney. The horrifying story quickly generated national headlines.

Al Sharpton and two lawyers, Alton Maddox and C. Vernon Mason, began to represent the young woman and "manage" her interests. There were holes in Brawley's story, though, and the case quickly inflamed racial tensions. (Granted, anything that reminds people racism exists tends to "inflame racial tensions.") Nearly a year later, a grand jury determined Brawley had lied. The case remains divisive to this day because it touches on so many fraught issues: race, class, sexual violence and the winners and losers in America's justice system.

Joyce Carol Oates's new novel, *The Sacrifice*, is a fictional retelling of the Brawley story, set in the invented Red Rock neighborhood of Pascayne, New Jersey, and based so heavily on the facts of the actual case that you could think of it as true-crime fan fiction. The novel opens with Ednetta Frye frantically searching for her daughter in the streets of Red Rock. From there, it traverses multiple points of view to describe how a community reacts to tragedy even as the truth remains elusive. At the center of the constellation of characters is Sybilla Frye, the young woman found bloody and bruised, degraded in an abandoned factory.

There is also Ada Furst, a substitute teacher who finds the brutalized Sybilla; Ines Iglesias, the "Hispanic American" detective assigned to the case; Anis Schutt, Sybilla's stepfather, who beat his first wife to death; the twin brothers Marus Cornelius and Byron Randolph Mudrick, a minister and a lawyer who come to represent Sybilla's interests; Jerold Zahn, the young man accused of being one of the rapists; and the Black Prince, a Muslim community leader who later takes up Sybilla's cause. As the novel unfolds, it becomes clear that nearly all of the characters sacrifice something—faith, hope, dignity, truth, justice.

There are strong moments. As a stand-in for Sharpton, the Rev. Marus Mudrick is flamboyantly inspired, particularly when Ednetta meets him for the first time: "She had never seen, at close quarters, so suavely handsome a man, so elegantly masculine a man; she was conscious of his dazzling-white smile, his burnished, caramel-colored skin, the fine-trimmed mustache on his upper lip. Reverend Mudrick wore a three-piece suit of a dark, soft wool, with a waistcoat in a lighter fabric, a white silk shirt and a rich, resplendent salmon-colored silk tie." His character is impeccably drawn in how he speaks, comports himself and orchestrates the spectacle of outrage.

Oates doesn't lack for ambition. Her narrative builds carefully and patiently, revealing how this kind of morality play can occur. She covers a great deal of sociological ground—domestic violence, colorism in the black community, class issues both inside the black community and between the black and white populations of Pascayne. In one perceptive scene, Anis Schutt is pulled over by a police cruiser, and Oates demonstrates great insight into the reality of driving while black. "There were two choices," she writes: "silent, or deferential. Silent might be mistaken by the cops for sullen, dangerous. Deferential might be mistaken for mockery."

Through Ada Furst, Oates also offers a brief interpretive history of the civil rights movement, falling back on a heavy-handed, somewhat condescending didacticism: "Ada recalled the great excitement in Red Rock when the bill had finally been passed. Lyndon Johnson had been everyone's hero at the time. Memories were strong of John F. Kennedy who'd been assassinated for championing black people. Then, Reverend King Jr.—of course. Robert Kennedy, Malcolm X—assassinated for their beliefs in social justice."

The problems in this novel, however, are legion. Again and again Oates comes frustratingly close to creating in-depth portraits only to back away. These characters have so much yearning—for love, fulfillment, acceptance, reprieve from suffering—that demands to be explored and is instead ignored. There is little sense of closure for the numerous plot threads, no sense of deliberation in how these story lines are abandoned. The awkward attempt at political statement is so blatant as to detract from the storytelling. And Oates has a distracting quirk of offering certain words and phrases parenthetically, though to what end remains unclear.

Then there are the physical descriptions; this novel contains a lot of dark skin and nappy hair. Oates is particularly preoccupied with Ednetta Frye's heavy breathing and high blood pressure. Cumulatively, these descriptions leave the reader with a distinct impression not of the characters but of the writer who created them. The n-word is used flagrantly, as if this were a Quentin Tarantino screenplay, often without plausible context.

There is also the baffling use of the word "nigra" as scrawled on Sybilla's chest, a word that would not have been part of the vernacular in New Jersey in the 1980s, or ever, for persons black or white.

That, however, is not this novel's most significant problem. Writers can and should write across difference, so long as they do so respectfully, intelligently, with some degree of accuracy. They may not fully succeed, but a good-faith effort and a demonstration of empathy are generally all that is required. There is little such empathy in *The Sacrifice*. Too often, difference is treated as caricature, as the speculations of someone who understands the black or working-class experience only through what might be gleaned from an encyclopedia.

Some of the black characters speak in a dialect vaguely resembling

African-American Vernacular English, but inconsistently and seemingly without syntactic rules—although A.A.V.E. has, in fact, both a grammar and a phonology. This is most glaring when Ednetta Frye speaks. She does not pronounce the short "i" (or, occasionally, the rest of the vowels), yet there are lines of dialogue where the dialect is not applied consistently even within the same sentence. Here she is, for instance, complaining to Sergeant Iglesias: "My daughter's health come first, before anythin else. You got this girl to tell you somethin could get her killed, and you better not misuse it, or S'b'lla, I'm warnin you—Off'cer." This inconsistency becomes increasingly egregious and then it becomes deeply offensive.

The lack of empathy is not just a social problem but a literary one, and this novel's biggest failing is its utter disregard for nuance. Oates approaches difference like a creative experiment, without giving enough consideration to the experiment's impact. By the end of the novel, the narrative offers an explanation for how Sybilla came to be so battered when Ada Furst discovered her, how the teenager invented so damaging a story with such unfathomable repercussions, how a fractured community fractured even further. This resolution should offer satisfaction; there is pleasure in fiction that provides answers where in reality there can be none. Alas, Oates handles critical issues so irresponsibly, with so little empathy as to make the ambiguity and mess of reality ever so soothing.

Originally published in the *New York Times*, January 30, 2015

Wise Crack (*Delicious Foods* by James Hannaham)

———

When crack cocaine enters a story, we usually brace ourselves for a downfall. The tales of those who have fallen prey to the drug are so familiar that they have taught even nonusers to consider themselves experts. Many speak knowingly of the crack addict—gaunt, unkempt, willing to do anything for the next fix. In James Hannaham's second novel, *Delicious Foods*, crack figures heavily in two ways. Darlene Hardison, a young widow, is an addict, and Scotty, who narrates a good deal of the novel, is crack personified (that's right: Crack is one of the novel's narrators). This is a welcome change to the standard, purely abject crack narrative: Hannaham circumvents the usual pity and loathing that permeate most addiction stories and instead investigates the source of crack's power—how it cajoles its users into surrendering, how it speaks.

When the novel opens, Eddie, seventeen, is on the run in what he thinks is Louisiana, though he isn't entirely sure. He has left the farm where he spent much of his childhood, and he worries he is being chased. His hands have been cut off, and he's doing his damnedest to get by with a stolen car and $184. This gripping, and disorienting, opening raises many questions, most notably: How did Eddie come to such a pass? Hannaham's engaging novel flashes back in time to answer these questions in surprising ways.

Eddie's parents, Darlene and Nat, are African American students who meet at Grambling State University after the Vietnam War. Nat is dating Hazel, one of Darlene's sorority sisters, when he and Darlene begin an affair. It is an intoxicating time: "Their secret dalliance inflated her—it practically pulled her skin taut with joy." On a weekend when they think Hazel is at a basketball game, they steal away to a bed-and-breakfast in

Shreveport to finally consummate their relationship. All is blissful until Hazel discovers them. They are ostracized, mostly Darlene, though Nat, too, endures his fair share of petty torments and physical violence from people they once called friends.

Things get so bad that Darlene and Nat transfer to Centenary College, in Shreveport. Because of the difficulties they have endured, the two become inextricably bound to each other. "We're practically the same person now," Darlene explains. After college, they settle in Ovis, Louisiana, where Darlene gives birth to Eddie. They open Mount Hope Grocery and build a life for themselves. Nat becomes interested in political action and is embraced, if somewhat warily, by the townspeople. Hannaham writes, "For the most part they admired Nat's determination to mobilize the community, his fund-raising, his voter-registration drives, but they did not expect rapid change."

Just before Eddie turns six, two policemen show up at the Hardison home. Nat has been murdered. In the wake of this news, Darlene succumbs to a grief from which she cannot emerge. At first, she tries to lead a semblance of the life she led with Nat, but it quickly falls apart. Darlene and Eddie move to Houston, where she starts smoking crack and takes to the streets as a prostitute to support her habit. She descends into addiction and ultimately abandons Eddie, who immerses himself in Houston's underworld, searching for his mother. Darlene, meanwhile, winds up back in Louisiana. There she is forced into what can only be described as indentured servitude on a farm called Delicious Foods, where crack and liquor are readily available to keep the workforce pliant. Through a strange sequence of events, Eddie makes his way to Delicious Foods himself. He becomes part of his mother's life once again, though Darlene remains more devoted to her addiction than anything else.

Delicious Foods captures what it was like to be black in the South at the end of the past century. Hannaham's prose is gloriously dense and full of elegant observations that might go unmade by a lesser writer. There is great warmth in this novel that tackles darkness. Darlene's behavior may appall, but the author reveals how circumstances guided her fate. He also creates full-bodied characters. Even the minor figures are drawn with subtle details. Sparkplug McKeon, for instance, is "the most frankly angry man for miles."

The novel is most affecting when we see the world from Eddie's perspective, as he attempts to make sense of his bewildering experiences. When Darlene takes up with Sextus, the owner of Delicious Foods, the young Eddie "drew conclusions on his own from hearing their labored breathing and Sextus's feral grunts through the door, their low voices and whispers, their frequent invocations of the Lord. At first he tried to convince himself that they were merely praying together."

Hannaham's decision to give a voice to crack—in the character Scotty—occasions some lively and inventive writing. Scotty has swagger and a sly sense of humor, and when he narrates he holds your attention. Describing Texas, he says: "Texas was stupid, I'm sorry. Fat sunburned gluttons and tacky mansions everywhere, glitzy cars that be the size of a pachyderm, a thrift store and a pawn shop for every five motherfuckers." The character is complex, both tender and ruthless. That said, it is incredibly distracting to realize that great swaths of the narration emanate not from a person but from an anthropomorphized drug. Disbelief can only be suspended so much. The novel's rushed conclusion, too, challenges belief: When Eddie finds his way to a safe, almost bucolic existence, it feels as if Hannaham knew he had to wrap up the novel but did not quite know how to exit the engrossing world he had built.

These missteps, however, do little to detract from what is, on the whole, a grand, empathetic, and funny novel about addiction, labor exploitation, and love. Hannaham tells a familiar story in a most unfamiliar way. *Delicious Foods* should be read for its bold narrative risks, as well as the heart and humor of its author's prose.

Originally published in *Bookforum*, April/May 2015

The Oscars and Hollywood's Race Problem

When we talk about diversity, or the lack thereof, we refer to it as "a problem." This or that industry, organization or group has a gender problem or a race problem or some other kind of diversity-related problem. We identify the problem and discuss it, exhaustively, often contentiously, because the problem is significant, pervasive, and for those of us who are most affected, the problem is personal.

Another year, another set of Oscar nominations. For the second year in a row, no black actors have been nominated. This profound absence is compounded by the Academy of Motion Picture Arts and Sciences' robust history of overlooking the work of actors, writers, directors and other film professionals who are people of color.

Hollywood has a race problem. Hollywood has always had a race problem. The movie industry continues to ignore audiences of color, to its own detriment, given the box office success of movies that do feature diverse casts. It continues to ignore the simple fact that people of color want to see their lives reflected in the movies they watch. Representation is not a lot to ask.

I love movies unabashedly. I always have. The cinematic spectacle grabs hold of me every time. Han Solo frozen in carbonite and Princess Leia choking Jabba the Hutt with the chain binding her to him. The defiance of Private Trip in pursuit of dignity in *Glory*. Julia Roberts as Vivian Ward in *Pretty Woman* triumphantly returning to the Rodeo Drive boutique that snubbed her, laden with shopping bags from other stores—big mistake, huge. Monica Wright-McCall, at center court, while her husband and daughter cheer her on in *Love and Basketball*. The ensemble of *Furious 7*, parachuting, in cars, from a cargo plane.

When I am at the movies, I lose myself. There is electricity running through my body. When I saw *The Hunger Games* I wanted to jump up and shout because I couldn't contain the emotion I was feeling. During *Whiplash* I was speechless. Nostalgia and then sorrow overwhelmed me when I watched *The Best Man Holiday*, not once but three times. I am awed by what it takes to make a movie, so many people and practices that have to come together. Movies, the best and worst of them, offer me indelible memories and so much pleasure. They offer escape. They are an art form to which I, as a writer, aspire.

That aspiration is thwarted, though, because movies don't often feature people who look like me. I am not interested in writing movies about a sylph looking for love, living in New York in an improbably large apartment with a lot of natural light who never seems to spend much time at an actual job. I am not interested in writing movies about a white man who is on some kind of journey to find himself or avenge a wrong, whether in Brooklyn or the wilds of Montana and South Dakota. That there seems to be no place for people who look like me in movie making doesn't keep me from writing or working, but I am constantly aware of the iron ceiling above me.

As of 2012, 94 percent of academy voters were white and 77 percent of those voters were men. The demographics of who makes movies, writes movies, edits movies, produces movies and stars in movies are equally stark. According to a 2014 report by the University of California, Los Angeles, on diversity in Hollywood, only 10.5 percent of lead actors in movies from 2011 were people of color and only 7.6 percent of movies from that same year were written by people of color.

When this year's Oscar nominations were released, I wasn't surprised. I was tired. I was, despite my fatigue, disappointed to see Ryan Coogler overlooked as best director and Michael B. Jordan overlooked for best actor for their work in *Creed*. I was frustrated that even if these men had been nominated, the Oscar nominations would still have been unbearably white.

Yet again, people of color were told, both implicitly and explicitly, that our stories and ways of seeing the world are not as valuable. We were told we should be satisfied with the scraps of recognition received in years past.

There is, perhaps, some hope. A little more than a week after the all-white slate of nominees was unveiled, the academy's governing board announced Friday that it was going to make changes that might address the problem. It said it was committed to doubling the number of women and academy members of color by 2020. Members will have their voting status reviewed every 10 years, and that status could be revoked if a member hasn't been active in the industry within that decade. These are not immediate solutions and they may do little to improve matters, but at least the academy is acknowledging the problem. Meanwhile, we still must face Hollywood's race problem as it currently stands.

In the debate that has followed the 2016 Oscar nominations, there is the usual outrage, disgust and, in some parts, indifference or thinly veiled contempt. Robert Redford, from the Sundance festival, said: "I'm not focused on that part. To me, it's about the work, and whatever reward comes from that, that's great. But I don't think about it." Mr. Redford, of course, already has his Oscar and he doesn't think about "it" because he has the luxury of not needing to.

Charlotte Rampling, who is nominated for a best actress Oscar this year, suggested that all this talk of Hollywood and diversity is racist against white people. "But do we have to take from this that there should be lots of minorities everywhere?" she asked. Let that sit for a minute. Hear what she is saying.

Michael Caine also had some insight, asking black actors to be patient because, well, it took him a long time to win his first Oscar. He also noted: "In the end you can't vote for an actor because he's black. You can't say, 'I'm going to vote for him, he's not very good, but he's black, I'll vote for him.'" Mr. Caine trotted out that old canard that the desire for diversity is the desire for the elevation of mediocrity.

Here, we have three veterans of the industry who appear to be positioning their white skin as the norm, as what deserves merit before anyone else receives consideration, as a marker of people whose experiences should be represented.

In the aftermath of the nomination announcements, the filmmaker Spike Lee and the actor Jada Pinkett Smith and her husband, Will Smith, have all stated that they plan not to attend the awards ceremony next month in protest.

The thing about a boycott is that there needs to be something at stake. I am not entirely clear what's at stake if we skip the Oscars. The root of the problem is not the academy, which selects the Oscar nominees, though certainly we should turn our critical eye to those voters who seem to favor white filmmakers and who tend to reward only a kind of "diverse" movie that centers struggle as the mainstay in the black experience. They are just one part of a much larger, wholly diseased, industry.

The root of the problem is that there just isn't enough filmmaking by people of color. There isn't enough work in the pipeline. And not only are black actors and filmmakers overlooked by the academy, so are artists of other races and ethnicities. As often as we have conversations about this problem, the conversation remains desperately narrow. There are a great many of us demanding a rightful place in the filmmaking world while the burden of keeping "problem" conversations alive, and the burden of providing solutions, also falls to us.

Actors and filmmakers of color can and should take the stands they choose, but white people in the movie industry need to step up and spend less time complacently reveling in their privilege. White actors and filmmakers need to do more than offer a few thoughtful words in interviews. They need to unequivocally acknowledge the very real diversity problems that continue to go unsolved. They, too, need to stay home from the Oscars. They need to turn down projects that are monochromatic both in front of and behind the camera. They need to take on this problem as their own.

If we're going to boycott the Oscars, we also need to boycott the movie studios determined to ignore the box office success of movies featuring people of color. We need to boycott the people who are so reluctant to produce movies made by people of color. We need to boycott this system that refuses to acknowledge life beyond the white experience as rule and not exception. As a movie lover, I take no pleasure in the prospect of staking out such a hard line so that people of color might be heard and ultimately represented on the silver screen, but Hollywood has left us with little choice.

Originally published in the *New York Times*, January 22, 2016

Black Lives Imagined
(Jodi Picoult's *Small Great Things*)

———

In a very earnest author's note at the end of her latest novel, *Small Great Things*, Jodi Picoult says that she has long wanted to write about American racism. Picoult is savvy enough to make her position as "white and class-privileged" known from the start. She details the rigorous research she did, the people she talked to, including women of color and skinheads. Of the former, she said: "I hoped to invite these women into a process, and in return they gave me a gift: They shared their experiences of what it really feels like to be black." There is also a lot of introspection about her presumed audience (white people) and her own racism. She ends the note acknowledging that talking about racism is difficult but that "we who are white need to have this discussion among ourselves. Because then, even more of us will overhear and—I hope—the conversation will spread."

Picoult certainly seems to have the best of intentions. The question is whether good intentions translate into a good novel. *Small Great Things* is, in most ways, a classic Jodi Picoult novel—tackling contemporary social issues, creating interesting, relatable characters and presenting a gripping courtroom drama.

Ruth Jefferson, a black woman with a teenage son, has been a labor and delivery nurse for more than 20 years when the white supremacists Turk and Brittany Bauer come to her maternity ward for the delivery of Brittany's first child, a boy named Davis. Turk demands that Ruth have no interaction with the baby—but when the ward is short-handed, Ruth finds herself alone with Davis just as he stops breathing. In that moment, Ruth has to decide whether she should heed her humanity and her oath as a nurse or follow the orders she has received to stay away from the Bauer baby. In the end, Ruth does both, but cannot prevent serious consequences. The parents, as you might expect, need someone to blame. In short order, Ruth's nursing license is suspended. She is charged with felony crimes, and her fate lies in the hands of the public defender Kennedy McQuarrie, a white woman.

Picoult knows how to tell an interesting story, and the novel moves briskly. This is a writer who understands her characters inside and out. She knows her story equally well. In terms of research, Picoult has put in the work—even too much work at times, as if she is saying, "Look at everything I know about everything I'm writing here." Still, this preparation and eagerness to please don't really detract. I'd rather read a writer who knows too much about the story she is telling than a writer who knows not enough.

Small Great Things particularly shines when Picoult writes from Turk Bauer's point of view. She makes this man with loathsome ideologies flawed but human. He is a white supremacist, but he is also a husband and father. We see his anger and impotence, and as the story unfolds, we see how he learned to hate, how he met and fell in love with Brittany, how avenging his son becomes his singular motivation. At times, Turk's story feels like a history of the modern white supremacy movement, but given the current political climate it is quite prescient and worthwhile.

Then there is Kennedy, Ruth's public defender, married to a surgeon who (of course) seems to be the perfect man. They have one child, a daughter who is (of course) adorable and precocious. Kennedy is harried, but (of course) a loving and well-loved wife and mother. By the end of the novel, she becomes a proxy for well-meaning white folk who don't realize the extent of their racism until they are forced to confront it. Kennedy's evolution quickly becomes too contrived and convenient. There is even a moment in her closing arguments during which Kennedy says: "When I started working on this case, ladies and gentlemen, I didn't see myself as a racist. Now I realize I am." Girl, I guess.

When it comes to race itself, the novel stumbles. Its least believable character is Ruth. Her blackness is clinical, overarticulated. I certainly appreciate the research Picoult did and the conversations she had, but research does not necessarily translate to authenticity. Ruth and her sister, Adisa, were raised in Harlem by a single mother who works as a maid for a wealthy white family. Ruth is light-skinned and Adisa darker.

(Née Rachel, Adisa had an awakening in her 20s and changed her name to get in touch with her African roots.) Now Adisa is the militant one while Ruth is more open to integration. The more we see of Ruth and her family, the more their characterization feels like black-people bingo—as if Picoult is working through a checklist of issues in an attempt to say everything about race in one book. Colorism, professional discrimination, segregation, the challenges of black ambition, microaggressions, the welfare system, negotiating predominantly white spaces, the boundaries of authentic blackness and, of course, race and the justice system: Bingo! There are references to Trayvon Martin's killing and the tennis player James Blake's mistaken arrest (though Blake, inexplicably, becomes "Malik Thaddon"). There is a stand-in for Al Sharpton, one Wallace Mercy: "His wild white hair stands on end, like he's been electrocuted. His fist is raised in solidarity with whatever apparent injustice he's currently championing." Bingo!

It all starts to feel excessive and desperately didactic. This rises, I suspect, out of Picoult's keen awareness that she is writing mostly for a white audience, which needs a more nuanced understanding of the black experience. And therein lies the true challenge of writing across difference, or of writing a political novel—if the politics overcomes the prose, then it becomes something other than a novel.

During Ruth's trial, it's clear that the courtroom is where Picoult feels most comfortable. We are treated to pages and pages of legal discovery and testimony. At times, it starts to feel like reading court transcripts—but to be fair, they are very interesting court transcripts. Turk and Brittany Bauer show up, and Brittany, racked with grief, makes the occasional outburst from the gallery. Ruth's son starts to struggle with his mother's precarious position and the revelations of the trial. There are more legal maneuvers. And then there is the ending, with a twist that is so unexpected and so over-the-top that it undermines what is, on the whole, a compelling and well-intended novel. Truly, the twist still has me shaking my head because I understand the why of it while recognizing that Picoult has crossed a bridge too far. From there, the ending is breathlessly rushed, with revelations, resolutions and epiphanies.

It is, in the end, the author's note that leaves me feeling generous toward *Small Great Things* despite its shortcomings. Picoult wanted to write about race in contemporary America, and she does. The novel is messy, but so is our racial climate. I give Picoult a lot of credit for trying, and for supporting her attempt with rigorous research, good intentions and an awareness of her fallibility. Picoult's flawed novel will most likely be well received by her intended audience. I trust that the next time she writes about race—and I do hope there is a next time—she'll write about it in ways that will also be compelling for the rest of us.

Originally published in the *New York Times*, October 11, 2016

I Don't Want to Watch
Slavery Fan Fiction

———

Many fiction writers have tried, to varying degrees of success, to reimagine slavery or create alternate histories where the Civil War never happened or never ended, or the Confederacy won.

Most recently, in the novel *Underground Airlines*, Ben H. Winters created an alternate history where slavery still exists in four states, there was no Civil War and segregation is the order of the day throughout the United States. I suppose it's an interesting premise, but as is often the case with interesting premises, at what cost?

It has been more than 150 years since the Civil War ended, but it often feels like some people are still living in the antebellum era. In parts of the United States and, as evidenced by Donald Trump's visit to Poland recently, the world, the Confederate flag is still proudly flown. This month, Ku Klux Klansmen marched in Charlottesville, Virginia, to protest the removal of a Robert E. Lee statue from a city park. They were not the first nor will they be the last to resist acknowledging that the Confederacy lost the Civil War.

At the National Museum of African American History and Culture in Washington, in May, a noose was found in an exhibition about segregation. That was one of three nooses found in the city within a few months. There was a noose found hanging from a tree in Philadelphia. There have also been noose-related incidents in Maryland, Louisiana, North Carolina and Florida—quiet, insidious acts of violence, reminders that racial hatred is alive and well.

Each time I see a reimagining of the Civil War that largely replicates what actually happened, I wonder why people are expending the energy to imagine that slavery continues to thrive when we are still dealing with the vestiges of slavery in very tangible ways. Those vestiges are visible in incarceration rates for black people, a wildly segregated country, disparities in pay and mortality rates and the ever-precarious nature of black life in a world where it can often seem as if police officers take those lives with impunity.

HBO last week announced it was willing to expend this energy with a series from the *Game of Thrones* creators David Benioff and D. B. Weiss. In the show, *Confederate*, the South does, indeed, secede from the Union, the Mason-Dixon line is a demilitarized zone and slavery is the law of the land below it. Nichelle Tramble Spellman and Malcolm Spellman, black television writers and producers, are also attached to the project. They have an incredible body of work behind them and will no doubt bring their considerable expertise to this show.

When I first read about *Confederate*, however, I felt exhausted, simply because I have long been exhausted by slavery narratives. That's a personal preference, not a metric by which art should or should not be created. There are works that do capture my interest, that make me think, that remind me of why there are still stories from that era to be told. Octavia E. Butler's *Kindred* and Colson Whitehead's *The Underground Railroad* come to mind. It is probably no accident that these are novels by black writers who found a way to reimagine history in speculative fiction without making slavery into an intellectual exercise rather than plainly showing it as the grossly oppressive institution it was.

My exhaustion with the idea of *Confederate* is multiplied by the realization that this show is the brainchild of two white men who oversee a show that has few people of color to speak of and where sexual violence is often gratuitous and treated as no big deal. I shudder to imagine the enslaved black body in their creative hands. And when I think about the number of people who gave this project the green light, the number of people who thought this was a great idea, my weariness grows exponentially.

This show's premise highlights the limits of the imagination in a world where oppression thrives. These creators can imagine a world where the Confederacy won the Civil War and black people are still enslaved, but they can't or aren't interested in imagining a world where, say, things went in a completely different direction after the Civil War and, say, white people are enslaved. Or a world where slavery never happened at all. What would happen in a show where American Indians won the conflicts in which they were embroiled as the British and French and other European nations colonized this country? What would happen if Mexicans won the Mexican-American War and Texas and California were still part of Mexico?

It is curious that time and again, when people create alternate histories, they are largely replicating a history we already know, and intimately. They are replicating histories where whiteness thrives and people of color remain oppressed.

Confederate is slavery fan fiction, as the writer Pilot Viruet put it, and it will probably look beautiful—low light, sweeping cinematography, exquisite costuming. The dialogue will be crisp and the narrative tensions utterly compelling. HBO spares no expense on its prestige dramas.

I have no doubt that in *Confederate*, the painful history of slavery will be reimagined with aggressive competence. The showrunners will say all the right things in the countless interviews they do. People will watch, life will go on, and we will still not know what could have been in a world where white people imagine their own oppression rather than how they suffer from the oppression of others.

As a writer, I never wish to put constraints upon creativity nor do I think anything is off limits to someone simply because of who they are. Mr. Benioff and Mr. Weiss are indeed white and they have as much a right to create this reimagining of slavery as anyone. That's what I'm supposed to say, but it is not at all how I feel.

Creativity without constraint comes with responsibility. We do not make art in a vacuum isolated from sociopolitical context. We live in a starkly divided country with a president who is shamefully ill-equipped to bridge that divide. I cannot help worrying that there are people, emboldened by this administration, who will watch a show like *Confederate* and see it as inspiration, rather than a cautionary tale.

Given the nearly unfathomable incompetence and unabashed racism of Donald Trump's administration, I tend to think of time in terms of how many days we have been without Barack Obama as president—186, as of Monday.

There are many critiques that can be made about Mr. Obama as president, but for two terms, he served this country well. He was competent and intelligent. He made progress on several fronts. Though he made decisions with which I disagreed, I never worried that he was incapable of serving as president. I never worried that he was incapable of understanding what he did not know and doing what was necessary to address such knowledge gaps. Overall, I found him extraordinary in demeanor, charm, eloquence and his ability to make America feel like a place where change was possible.

We have lost all that. Or, rather, we have the memory of all that and are forced to face the horrifying absence of everything Mr. Obama and his administration offered. And worse yet, with each day that Mr. Trump serves as president, we face the imminent danger of all manner of bad history repeating itself while we watch it on TV.

Originally published in the *New York Times*, July 25, 2017

Mockingbird Reconsidered

To Kill a Mockingbird is a book for which a great many people harbor reverence and nostalgia. I am not one of those people. Jean Louise "Scout" Finch, the narrator of Harper Lee's coming-of-age novel set in the Depression-era South, tells the story of how her lawyer father, Atticus, defended Tom Robinson, a black man who has been falsely accused of raping a white woman in the fictional Alabama town of Maycomb. By the end of the novel, Robinson has been murdered while trying to escape prison. Scout has lost her innocence; for the first time, she truly understands the racial dynamics of her environment.

I don't find *To Kill a Mockingbird* to be particularly engaging. There are moments throughout the narrative that are exquisitely drawn, and I appreciate Lee's dry wit and intelligence. On the novel's first page, she writes, "Being Southerners, it was a source of shame to some members of the family that we had no recorded ancestors on either side of the Battle of Hastings." That one line says so much about the Finch family, the South and its ongoing relationship to the past. Scout is a memorable character, but such depth rarely extends to the others. Atticus is written as the platonic ideal of a father and crusader for justice. The black characters—Robinson and the family's housekeeper, Calpurnia—are mostly there as figures onto which the white people around them can project various thoughts and feelings. They are narrative devices, not fully realized human beings.

The "n word" is used liberally throughout and there are some breathtaking instances of both casual and outright racism. The book is a "product of its time," sure, so let me just say that said time and the people who lived in it were plain terrible. As for the story, I can take it or leave it. Perhaps I am ambivalent because I am black. I am not the target audience. I don't need to read about a young white girl understanding the perniciousness of racism to actually understand the perniciousness of racism. I have ample firsthand experience.

Which brings us to *Why* To Kill a Mockingbird *Matters*, by Tom Santopietro, whose title makes the bold claim that Lee's classic has endured over the past 58 years because it offers a message that stands the test of time. The book's continued popularity, and the success of the author's only other published work, *Go Set a Watchman*, certainly support this claim. Santopietro's book, however, does not.

The title is misleading. I expected this text to offer a complex and sustained argument about the merits of the novel itself. Instead, much of the book is given over to a biography of Nelle Harper Lee and an extremely detailed history of the making of the 1962 movie. Some light literary analysis is thrown in for good measure. Never does this book take chances or make a persuasive argument for why *To Kill a Mockingbird* matters to anyone but white people who inexplicably still do not understand the ills of racism, and seemingly need this book to show them the light.

Santopietro has certainly done his homework, and he applies the rigor of his knowledge admirably. I came away from the book knowing a great deal more about Harper Lee. He writes lovingly of her hometown, Monroeville, Alabama, and her upbringing, convincingly identifying the connective tissue between Lee's life and the most significant elements of her novel. The context in which she wrote and sold it is just as finely detailed, as is the book's critical reception upon release. I enjoyed his insights into Lee's painstaking process of composition and revision—the time and commitment it took. One of the most striking revelations was the ferocity of Lee's ambition: She was very invested in the success of both her book and the movie.

Most of Santopietro's work is given over to that movie—so much so that I began to wonder if this book was intended to be a cultural history of the adaptation alone. Santopietro has previously written books about other beloved film adaptations, including *The Sound of Music* and *The Godfather*; here, he details everything from the producers, the screenwriter, the cast and the set decorators to how the film was received by the critics, the public and Lee herself. He is passionate about Gregory Peck as just the right kind of leading man to step into the role of Atticus, and shares a great deal about the process of selecting the child actors to play Scout; her brother, Jem; and their friend Dill. Santopietro goes so far as to elaborate on the lives of everyone involved in the film for years after its release. All of this material is vaguely interesting, but the author fails to explain how it supports his argument that *To Kill a Mockingbird* matters.

On top of that, the book's structure is strange. There are all kinds of digressions in each chapter, some of which feel more like information dumps than components of a cohesive narrative. Nor is there a clear progression between them: The 11th chapter is about the merits of the movie as an adaptation, and the 13th is about Harper Lee's private nature, but the 12th asks the question: "Is *To Kill a Mockingbird* Racist?" (My answer to that question is yes.) These organizational choices—and the one or two jarring Stephen Sondheim quotations he cites—are bewildering. As much as I admire the exhaustive research, not a lot of care seems to have been put into how it is conveyed.

Not until the last few chapters does Santopietro finally try to make a definitive case for the importance of this seminal American novel. He offers statistics about the book's commercial success: "Translated into 40 languages, the novel sells approximately 750,000 copies every year," he writes. "In total, some 40 million copies have been sold worldwide since 1960, and at the time of Harper Lee's death in 2016, her annual royalties remained in excess of three million dollars." Few other books have sold so robustly for so long. *Mockingbird* is also required reading "in over 70 percent of American high schools." These numbers are impressive indeed, but ubiquity and quality are not the same thing (and neither one is necessarily the same thing as importance).

Santopietro also notes that we're still living in a world where ethnic prejudice abounds, not just toward black people but Mexicans, Syrian refugees and others. The author is not ignorant of the racial zeitgeist, but it is odd that he thinks Lee's novel speaks to it adequately. He boldly claims, "*Mockingbird* succeeds in a basic task of literature: the expansion of worldviews by means of exposure to differing communities and cultures." In that it tells the story of a wrongfully accused incarcerated black man, he is correct, but it is important to question just what kind of exposure the text offers. Given the shallowness of the black characters—how they are vehicles for Scout's story instead of their own—we as readers should raise the bar higher than mere "exposure."

Santopietro saves his keenest observation for the final pages of *Why To Kill a Mockingbird Matters*, in which he acknowledges the power of nostalgia: "The continued heartfelt response to *Mockingbird* now seems inextricably tied up in Harper Lee's ability to underscore a sense of community sorely lacking today." He goes on to discuss how people spend too much time in isolation with their electronic devices, as neighborhoods, communities and communication disintegrate. He acknowledges how much the culture has changed since the book's publication in 1960, but laments the proliferation of "dark and damaged characters" on television and in film. What he conveys most powerfully is a yearning for a simpler time—a uniquely white yearning, because it is white people to whom history has been kindest. It is white people who seem to long for the safety of cloistered communities where everyone knows one another, where people know their place and are assured of what their lives may hold. Clearly, Santopietro identifies more with Scout, Jem and Dill than with, say, Boo Radley, the town recluse who probably wouldn't yearn for that simpler time when the townspeople regarded him with open distance and mistrust.

And then the author illustrates why it is hard to take this book seriously: "The United States found in *To Kill a Mockingbird* was unquestionably a more racist, oppressive America, deaf to the desires and hopes of women, homosexuals, minorities and nearly anyone who did not fit the prevailing definition of 'normal.'" This statement is technically true, but it overlooks the serious racial tensions our nation still faces. Santopietro does make brief mentions of President Trump and his lack of leadership during the Charlottesville riots, as well as of the responses (or lack thereof) of black people to *Mockingbird*, but these asides feel tacked on and unexplored. The groundwork for *Why To Kill a Mockingbird Matters* is astute, but the intellectual analyses are not, and the book suffers for it.

Originally published in the *New York Times*, June 18, 2018

Can I Enjoy Art but Denounce the Artist?

———

Growing up, I loved *The Cosby Show*. My brothers and I were allowed only an hour of television a week, so it meant something to spend part of that time with Bill Cosby and his television family. As a middle-class black girl, I was affirmed to see something of my life reflected back to me. Such representation was elusive and necessary and incredibly meaningful. The impact Cosby had on me cannot be overstated.

As I got older and began to hear stories about Cosby's penchant for sexual assault, I wanted to look away. It didn't seem possible that the man who brought us Cliff Huxtable could also be a sexual predator. But I try to believe people when they say how they suffered. I know what it takes to come forward as a victim of sexual violence, and that when the perpetrator is famous, it takes everything, with so little to be gained. As the extent of his predation was laid bare, the sheer number of women Cosby victimized staggered me nearly as much as some people's willingness to still consider his artistic legacy, despite the damage he did.

Every time I think of Cosby's work, I remember the women he victimized and how their silence was trapped by the gilded cage of his fame. To me, Cosby's artistic legacy is rendered meaningless in the face of the pain he caused. It has to be. He once created great art, and then he destroyed his great art. The responsibility for that destruction is his and his alone. We are free to lament it, but not at the expense of his victims.

Toward the end of 2017, a dam of silence broke and women and men began coming forward in unprecedented numbers, giving voice to how they were assaulted, harassed, intimidated, silenced, and otherwise demeaned by powerful creative men. A great many legacies have been rendered meaningless by these testimonies even though the debate about whether that should be the case inexplicably continues.

We can no longer worship at the altar of creative genius while ignoring the price all too often paid for that genius. In truth, we should have learned this lesson long ago, but we have a cultural fascination with creative and powerful men who are also "mercurial" or "volatile," with men who behave badly.

These men are given wide berth. Their prominence grants them a certain amount of immunity. We forgive their trespasses because they create such brilliant work, because they are so charismatic, because there is such an allure to people who defy cultural conventions, who dare to do whatever they want. Whether we're talking about Bill Cosby or Woody Allen or Roman Polanski or Johnny Depp or Kevin Spacey or Harvey Weinstein or Russell Simmons or any man who has built his success on the backs of women and men whose suffering was ignored for the sake of that success, it's time to say that there is no artistic work, no legacy so great that we choose to look the other way.

I no longer struggle with artistic legacies. It is not difficult to dismiss the work of predators and angry men because agonizing over a predator's legacy would mean there is some price I am willing to let victims pay for the sake of good art, when the truth is no half hour of television is so excellent that anyone's suffering is recompense. Instead, I remember how many women's careers were ruined; I think of those who gave up their dreams because some "genius" decided indulging his thirst for power and control mattered more than her ambition and dignity. I remember all the silence, decades and decades of enforced silence, intimidation, and manipulation, that enabled bad men to flourish. When I do that, it's quite easy for me to think nothing of the supposedly great art of bad men.

There are all kinds of creative people who are brilliant and original and enigmatic and capable of treating others with respect. There is no scarcity of creative genius, and that is the artistic work we can and should turn to instead.

Originally published in *Marie Claire*, February 6, 2018

The *Roseanne* Reboot Is Funny.
I'm Not Going to Keep Watching.

——————

It can be very difficult to separate the art from the artist. In the case of Roseanne Barr and her critically acclaimed television show based on her life, it is nearly impossible. I wasn't going to watch the reboot because I find Ms. Barr noxious, transphobic, racist and small-minded. Whatever charm and intelligence she brought to the first nine seasons of her show, a show I very much loved, are absolutely absent in her current persona, particularly as it manifests on Twitter. She is a supporter of Donald Trump, vocalizing her thoughts about making America great, claiming that with her vote, she was trying to shake things up. She tweets conspiracy theories, rails against feminism and shares Islamophobic opinions.

Where once she was edgy and provocative, she is now absurd and offensive. Her views are muddled and incoherent. She is more invested in banal and shallow provocation than engaging with sociopolitical issues in a thoughtful manner. No amount of mental gymnastics can make what Roseanne Barr has said and done in recent years palatable.

Nonetheless, I was curious about what Roseanne Conner, her famous television alter ego, has been up to. The original *Roseanne* was a smart, hilarious and groundbreaking show that covered a lot of important ground in prime-time television. I wanted to see how the Conners were doing 20 years later.

What I found is that the tensions in the TV show—which more than 18 million people watched, a network TV high since 2014—are the same tensions that shape this current political climate. Roseanne the character voted for Donald Trump because he talked about "jobs." For that she sacrificed so many other things. The promise of jobs and the myth of the white working class as the only people struggling in this country, which animates so much of our present political moment, are right there, in this sitcom.

In many ways, the first two episodes of the *Roseanne* reboot are excellent. It is difficult to admit, but nearly everything about the production is competent. There is the familiarity of the Conner house, still well-worn, the iconic couch taking center stage in the family room. The original cast returned and their faces are pleasantly familiar—though not as aged as they could be, given the benefits of wealth, good skin-care regimens and, perhaps, medical intervention.

Darlene, the middle daughter, has moved back home with her two children, Harris and Mark, the latter of whom is gender nonconforming. D.J., the Conner son, was in the Army and has recently returned home from a tour in Syria. His wife, we learn indirectly, is still in the military, serving abroad, and D.J. is raising their daughter, who is black, while she is away. Roseanne and her sister, Jackie, played by Laurie Metcalf, have been estranged for a year because of the 2016 election, and when Jackie shows up, she's wearing a "Nasty Woman" T-shirt and a pink pussy hat. Of course she is.

The Conners are still dealing with many of the economic struggles they have always faced. Darlene has lost her job. Roseanne and Dan are getting older and, like many Americans, cannot afford adequate health care as they try to share various medications. Becky, the oldest Conner child, is going to become a surrogate and sell her eggs to make $50,000. Darlene's son, Mark, is being bullied at school for his gender presentation. The show isn't shying away from difficult topics, and that is both what works and doesn't. The Conners are portrayed as a typical working-class family and their problems are relatable, but it also feels as though the show is working through a checklist of "real issues" it wants to address, to demonstrate how the Conners are a modern American family.

The presence of D.J.'s daughter, Mary, is particularly awkward. When she appears, one of these things is clearly not like the other, but the show makes no mention of it as if to suggest how at ease the Conners are with difference. But Mary has no lines and very little camera time. We are given little information as to how she became part of the Conner family and what life for her is like in a small, predominantly white Illinois town where everyone, seemingly, voted for Donald Trump. Young Mary is just there, a placeholder, tokenized and straining the limits of credulity.

When a lot of the mainstream media talks about the working class, there is a tendency to romanticize, to idealize them as the most authentic Americans. They are "real" and their problems are "real" problems, as if everyone else is dealing with artificial obstacles. We see this in some of the breathless media coverage of Trump voters and in a lot of the online chatter about the *Roseanne* reboot. What often goes unsaid is that when the working class is defined in our cultural imagination, we are talking about white people, even though the real American working class is made up of people from many races and ethnicities.

During a Television Critics Association panel promoting the show, Ms. Barr said, "It was working-class people who elected Trump."

This myth persists, but it is only a myth. Forty-one percent of voters earning less than $50,000 voted for Mr. Trump while 53 percent voted for Hillary Clinton. Forty-nine percent of voters earning between $50,000 and $100,000 voted for Mr. Trump while 47 percent voted for Mrs. Clinton. The median income of these voters was $72,000, while the median income of Hillary Clinton voters was $61,000. A significant number of middle-class and wealthy white people contributed to Trump's election.

In the show, during an exchange about their political disagreement, Roseanne tells Jackie one of the reasons she voted for Mr. Trump is because he "talked about jobs." And that was all the political ideology we got. If we are to believe the circumstances of this character's life, a few vague words about "jobs" was more than enough to compel Roseanne, with inadequate health care, with vulnerable grandchildren, and struggling to make ends meet, to vote for Mr. Trump.

How do you reach people who make dangerous political choices grounded in self-interest? When Roseanne and Jackie finally reconcile, Roseanne never apologizes or concedes. She merely tells Jackie, "I forgive you," and Jackie acknowledges how hard that was for Roseanne. Clearly, we cannot reach people who make dangerous, myopic political choices. We concede, as Jackie does, or we resist, as hopefully the rest of us will.

In my book *Bad Feminist*, published in 2014, I wrote about giving myself permission to be flawed but feminist. I wrote about how sometimes I consume problematic pop culture, knowing I shouldn't, knowing how harmful that pop culture can be. I still believe there is room for that, for having principles and enjoying things that challenge those principles. But in the ensuing years, I've also been thinking about accountability and the repercussions of our choices. I've been thinking about how nothing will change if we keep consuming problematic pop culture without demanding anything better.

As I watched the first two episodes of the *Roseanne* reboot, I thought again about accountability. I laughed, yes, and enjoyed seeing the Conner family back on my screen. My first reaction was that the show was excellent. But I could not set aside what I know of Roseanne Barr and how toxic and dangerous her current public persona is. I could not overlook how the Conner family came together to support Mark as he was bullied at school for his gender presentation, after voting for a president who actively works against the transgender community. They voted for a president who doesn't think the black life of their granddaughter matters. They act as if love can protect the most vulnerable members of their family from the repercussions of their political choices. It cannot.

This fictional family, and the show's very real creator, are further normalizing Trump and his warped, harmful political ideologies. There are times when we can consume problematic pop culture, but this is not one of those times. I saw the first two episodes of the *Roseanne* reboot, but that's all I am going to watch. It's a small line to draw, but it's a start.

Originally published in the *New York Times*, March 29, 2018

Roseanne Is Gone, but the Culture That Gave Her a Show Isn't

On Twitter on Tuesday, Roseanne Barr wrote that if "muslim brotherhood & planet of the apes had a baby = vj." The message referred to President Barack Obama's former senior adviser Valerie Jarrett, and in it Ms. Barr traded on age-old racist ideas about black people and primates. Then she shared some incorrect nonsense about Chelsea Clinton marrying into the Soros family.

It was the kind of thing Roseanne Barr has been doing online for years. This time, however, the backlash was immediate and vigorous. Ms. Barr apologized for her "joke" that wasn't really a joke and said she was leaving Twitter as if Twitter were responsible for her racist behavior. That apology was not enough. ICM Partners, her agents, stopped representing her. The comedian Wanda Sykes, who was a consulting producer on the reboot of *Roseanne*, announced that she was quitting the show. Within a matter of hours, ABC canceled the new *Roseanne* and the original show's reruns were pulled from TV Land, CMT and the Paramount Network.

For once, a major network did the right thing. But before it did the right thing, it did the wrong thing. It is not new information that Roseanne Barr makes racist, Islamophobic and misogynistic statements and is happy to peddle all manner of dangerous conspiracy theories. ABC knew this when it greenlighted the *Roseanne* reboot. ABC knew this when it quickly renewed the reboot for a second season, buoyed, no doubt, by the show's strong ratings.

The cast, the writers and the producers knew what Ms. Barr stood for when they agreed to work on the show. Everyone involved made a decision to support the show despite its co-creator's racism. They decided that their career ambitions, or desire to return to network television, or financial interests would best be served by looking the other way. It was only when Ms. Barr became an immediate liability that everyone involved finally looked at her racism and dealt with it directly.

I watched and enjoyed the first two episodes of the *Roseanne* reboot but I could not continue watching, given everything Ms. Barr represents. I also watched the original version of *Roseanne* when it aired. I remember the Conner family as working class and solidly invested in the greater good of their community. They seemed to be liberals, which is antithetical to the Roseanne in the reboot, who is a working-class Trump supporter. Certainly, the Conner family may have changed political affiliations and become Republicans and there would be nothing wrong with that.

The problem is that Donald Trump is a toxic president who amassed his power through the provocation of hate. He has behaved as if conservatism and racism are synonymous when, in fact, they are not. The problem is that having a major character on a prominent television show as a Trump supporter normalizes racism and misogyny and xenophobia.

President Trump often seems like a living embodiment of Ms. Barr's Twitter feed, and many of his most vocal supporters revel in that. They revel in the freedom and the permission to be racist. The reboot contributed to a cultural moment that makes white people feel exceedingly comfortable and entitled as they police black bodies in public spaces.

I have, as of late, been thinking a lot about such policing and how, historically, black people have negotiated white entitlement to their bodies. The *Negro Motorist Green Book* was an annual guidebook curated during the Jim Crow era to let black people know where they could safely find gas, food and lodging while traveling across the United States by car. The *Green Book* was created out of necessity, and though it ceased publication in 1966, recent events have made it clear that there is still a need for some kind of guidebook detailing where it is safe to be black. Recent events have made it clear that such a guidebook would be a very slender volume indeed.

Lolade Siyonbola, a black Yale graduate student, was napping in her dorm's common room when a white woman came upon her, told Ms. Siyonbola she couldn't sleep there and called the police. Ms. Siyonbola then had to prove she had a right to be in her dorm, on her college campus.

In Southern California, three black women were checking out of an Airbnb rental and loading their luggage into the car when they were suddenly surrounded by police cars. A white woman had seen three black people with luggage, assumed they were criminals, and because the women didn't smile or wave at the white woman, she called the police on them.

Three black teenagers in St. Louis shopping for a prom at a Nordstrom's Rack were followed by two store employees throughout their time there. When the teenagers left the store with their purchases, the police were waiting.

Five black women were golfing in Pennsylvania when the police were called because the women were, purportedly, golfing too slowly.

Some black people were having a barbecue in an Oakland, California, public space and a white woman called the police on them for using a charcoal grill.

In Philadelphia last month, two black men waiting for a business meeting with a third person in a Starbucks were arrested for sitting in a Starbucks while black.

In each of these encounters, white people took it upon themselves to police black bodies in public spaces. They felt entitled to do so because of racism, which they used to delineate the borders of what they arbitrarily determined as acceptable behavior for black people. They felt this entitlement because that's what racism does—it allows one group of people to feel superior to and imagine dominion over another.

On the same day that Ms. Barr sent her vile tweet, Starbucks closed all its American stores for a few hours of training about racial bias, as part of its campaign to rehabilitate the company's image and ensure that what happened in Philadelphia doesn't happen again.

When asked to comment about Ms. Barr's tweet, Ms. Jarrett, the former Obama adviser, said, "This should be a teaching moment." It was a dignified statement to be sure, but one wonders just how many teaching moments we need for white people to no longer feel entitled to comment on or police black bodies. And how much longer will we choose to consume pop culture that encourages such policing, either implicitly or explicitly?

Ms. Barr was free to speak her mind, but she was not free from consequences. Now that she is reaping those consequences, many people are praising ABC and its swift action. But there is no nobility in what anyone involved in *Roseanne* has done at any point during the reboot's trajectory. Certainly, I empathize with all of the people who are now out of work, particularly those in the trades—the grips, best boys, camera people, production assistants and others who are not famous faces. But I also question what kind of empathy the decision makers had for the targets of Ms. Barr's hateful rhetoric as they supported this show and her. They seemingly had none. Even at the recent network upfronts, ABC executives were joking about Ms. Barr's Twitter feed.

Channing Dungey, the president of ABC Entertainment, said in a statement, "Roseanne's Twitter statement is abhorrent, repugnant and inconsistent with our values, and we have decided to cancel her show." Bob Iger, the chairman and chief executive of Disney, ABCs parent company, said, "There was only one thing to do here, and that was the right thing." The cast member and producer Sara Gilbert lamented the show's demise and said, "Roseanne's recent comments about Valerie Jarrett, and so much more, are abhorrent and do not reflect the beliefs of our cast and crew or anyone associated with the show."

All of these statements sound conscientious and righteous. These statements make it seem as if ABC is invested in doing the right thing. The statements make it seem as if the cast and crew are nothing like the show's star. These statements are but part of an elaborate and lucrative illusion. ABC is the same network that shelved an episode of *Blackish* because it addressed the N.F.L. anthem protests.

I am more interested in the statement ABC could have made by never making the reboot in the first place.

Originally published in the *New York Times*, May 29, 2018

Insatiable Is Lazy, Insulting from Start to Finish

The recently premiered Netflix show *Insatiable* could have been good television. Presumably intended to be a satirical, socially trenchant high school comedy, it concerns a viciously bullied, formerly overweight young woman who undergoes a dramatic reversal of fortune. As someone who was bullied in elementary school and junior high, I have a real soft spot for stories about the underdog who evolves and embodies success as the best revenge. So many of us yearned to avenge our tormentors—implicitly by becoming the beautiful, accomplished people we always hoped we would, and explicitly by ensuring that terrible things would befall those who harmed us. I was naturally primed to enjoy this show.

When the trailer for *Insatiable* premiered in July 2018, there was an immediate backlash to its fatphobia. A change.org petition asking Netflix to cancel the show now has more than 233,000 signatures. I was asked to sign, but I didn't, because not releasing *Insatiable* wouldn't address the underlying issues. I also didn't sign the petition because creators are allowed to make bad, irresponsible, problematic art.

And I held the faint hope that perhaps the trailer was not indicative of the show as a whole. Alas, it is. In fact, it's even worse and more problematic, if not dangerous, than I thought.

Insatiable is predicated on a lazy, insulting premise. Patty Bladell, the show's protagonist, is, at the beginning of the pilot, "television fat," which is to say she is only as fat as the show's creator can imagine a young woman being without completely horrifying audience sensibilities. Patty is barely even Lane Bryant fat, probably a size 18/20. The actress who plays her, Debby Ryan, wears a chin prosthetic and a lumpy stomach pillow, but it's not at all convincing. She looks like a thin woman in a fat suit, and it's grating that the show didn't even try to make Patty a convincing fat girl.

And within the episode's first ten minutes, every stereotype of a fat girl is on full display. We see Patty being teased and harassed by her classmates. During gym class, she passes out because she hasn't eaten in days, and it's supposed to be funny, I guess, but it isn't. The reality is that so many women and girls regularly starve themselves toward thinness that is ever elusive. Patty talks about being "at home stuffing another hole," while lamenting her lack of a love life, and we see her gorging on food.

Patty has a best friend, Nonnie (Kimmy Shields), who is hopelessly in love with her, and an alcoholic single mother, who is sometimes a good parent but mostly not, and she has food to fill the voids in her life. After she awkwardly asks out a boy she has a crush on and he turns her down, Patty sits on the curb in front of a convenience store eating a chocolate bar. A homeless man (Daniel Thomas May) approaches her, insults her weight, and punches Patty in the face, thereby breaking her jaw. After having her jaw wired shut for three months, Patty has lost 70 pounds, and she is smoking hot. The ugly duckling has become a skinny swan. An act of violence is framed as the best thing to ever happen to Patty.

Then it gets even grotesquely darker. Before she can enjoy her new body and new life, Patty has to go to court because she is facing assault charges for her altercation with the homeless guy. Enter Bob Armstrong (Dallas Roberts), a lawyer and pageant coach, who takes her case because he's trying to redeem himself after being accused of molesting Dixie Sinclair (Irene Choi), one of the young women he coaches. There's nothing funnier, you see, than sexual assault humor.

Before long, Bob realizes that the true path to redemption lies in making Patty a beauty queen, and Patty realizes that her true path to redemption lies in becoming a beauty queen. Girl, I guess. In addition to the pedophilia accusation Bob Armstrong faces, there's also a statutory rape plotline involving his son, Brick (Michael Provost), who has an affair with Regina Sinclair (Arden Myrin), Dixie's mother. The show is dangerously cavalier about topics where deep consideration would be more appropriate.

As the season unfolds, there is no shortage of plot. There is no excess this show won't indulge. There are all kinds of absurd twists and turns as

Patty adjusts to her new self. Bob is also dealing with changes that include trouble in his marriage, trouble with Brick, and trouble with his nemesis, Bob Barnard (Christopher Gorham), who eventually becomes his lover. By the end of the season, *Insatiable* devolves into sheer lunacy. There are so many plot points that not only defy credulity, they invite questions that are never answered. There are so many production issues and inconsistencies. In one car scene, you can tell it's a rental car because the props department didn't bother removing the "No Smoking" sticker from the dashboard. If the show was good, I wouldn't have noticed this detail, but the show is not good.

The writers of *Insatiable* have never met a stereotype they don't love, whether they're portraying fatness or queerness or Blackness or pretty much anything else. Every lame, insulting fat joke or trope you can imagine makes its way into every episode. During the third episode, Patty's safe place is a crawfish eating competition, because of course it is.

I concede that there are funny jokes in every episode, though I cannot recall any of them. Most of the cast does the best they can with the impoverished material they have been given. But the show is trying to be too many things—comedy, drama, satire, farce—and it does none of these things well. Mostly, the show is mean and petty and not in an interesting way.

Marginalized people mostly populate the landscape to contribute to Patty's emotional growth. Nonnie, one of the show's most interesting characters, is relegated to one of the most tired tropes of all time, the lovelorn gay girl who unrequitedly pines for her straight best friend. The show carelessly mines her pain for laughs, creating several cringeworthy moments. Nonnie eventually finds another love interest, Dee (Ashley D. Kelley), whose casting is inexplicable in that she is supposed to be a college student but looks much older. In every scene, Dee doesn't look like she could plausibly be Nonnie's girlfriend. The miscasting is distracting to the point of madness.

Dee is mostly there to serve as a Magical Negro, helping Nonnie embrace her sexuality, and offering sassy wisdom as needed. At one point, Dee says, "Being skinny don't mean shit if you're ugly on the inside." It's a nice, albeit trite, sentiment, but it's hard to take that seriously in a show that says, repeatedly, that "skinny is magic."

This show is supposed to be about desire, about insatiable desire, about wanting so much, wanting too much. But Patty doesn't seem particularly insatiable. It is everyone around her that is insatiable. Bob Armstrong desperately wants to coach a winning pageant queen, and he wants to stay married to his wife, and he also wants to be with his lover Bob Barnard. Bob's wife, Coralee (Alyssa Milano), yearns to be a respected society lady, and she wants a career of her own, and she wants her husband, and she lusts after Bob Barnard. Nonnie simply wants Patty to love her, to see her, to hear her.

As for Patty, though, even after 12 episodes, it's not really clear what she wants. Instead, she flails about, wreaking havoc, engaging in many of the behaviors she was once subjected to. She is all id and narcissism, but the show would have us believe her comportment is acceptable because once, she suffered the greatest of all tragedies—being fat.

Since the show's debut, the creator, Lauren Gussis has given several interviews explaining the genesis of the show. She has offered her bona fides as well as those of the show's writers, telling the *Hollywood Reporter* that her writers' room included "men and women who have had eating disorders." She shares that she has dealt with many of the issues Patty deals with in the show. That's well and good. But there is a difference between understanding disordered eating and understanding and portraying fatness and weight loss with nuance. Gussis doesn't seem to realize this. I contacted Netflix to ask if there were any fat writers in the *Insatiable* writers' room, but they have not responded.

Insatiable's greatest sin is that it suffers from a profound lack of imagination. The show cannot imagine that a straight man could truly love pageants and mentoring young women and be secure in his masculinity, or that a young lesbian could love herself enough to not fall in love with her straight best friend, or that a fat girl could be happy, healthy, and thriving without losing weight. Never does this show dare to imagine that maybe it was everyone else who had the problem when Patty was fat, not Patty herself. The show cannot imagine that perhaps, the most profound way Patty could seek vengeance would be to love herself at any size, to be seen by a love interest as lovable at any size, to see herself as beautiful because of rather than despite her fat body.

In the second episode, Patty thinks she has killed the homeless man who broke her jaw after going with him to his hotel room where she, for some bizarre reason, has gone to have sex with him as an act of vengeance. Why is this vengeance? Who knows? As she tries to find a way out of her predicament, she laments, "My life just started," and it is one of the most frustrating and painful moments of the entire series, because it reveals so much about how the show's creators, and how this world sees fatness as a problem, an obstacle to overcome. This is not entertainment. It is incredibly damaging.

There are countless missed opportunities for *Insatiable* to explore fatness, parental neglect, social ostracism, coming of age, and what it is like to be invisible, to have your most important needs and desires go unsatisfied. I suppose, in the end, this show's failures leave us desperately insatiable, too, and in that, the show's name is rather apt.

Originally published in Refinery29, August 23, 2018

The Legacy of Toni Morrison

Toni Morrison was unparalleled. She will always be so. A novelist, essayist, woman and sage, she was a genius of uncommon grace. This is not hyperbolic. It is, simply, fact.

I was on a flight from Paris to New York when a friend messaged me about Ms. Morrison's passing and I was stunned, saddened and overwhelmed with gratitude for the blessings of her work. I knew she was in her 80s, but I hoped she might be the first immortal among us.

Nonetheless, it was heartening to see the immediate and effusive outpouring of respect and affection for her unimpeachable legacy. It was also a relief to know she was one of the greats lucky enough to be appreciated while she lived.

For the past couple of months, I have been slowly reading her collected essays and speeches, *The Source of Self-Regard*. I want to savor her work—her prescient and clear-eyed distillations of power, how it is wielded, and who must bend or be broken in the face of it.

Many of the pieces were written well before the Trump era, but perfectly capture the current moment: the rise of fascism as "marketing for power" and the truth that the "danger of losing our humanity must be met with more humanity."

As I've been reading *The Source of Self-Regard*, I have also been looking for the right, so very elusive, words to respond to President Trump's embrace of white nationalism; the government's unacceptable family separation program and internment camps; the politicians doing nothing but thinking and praying in the face of gun violence; women's ever-precarious access to reproductive rights and bodily autonomy; and everything else that is so overwhelming and terrible in this country.

For the most vulnerable among us, there is a great deal at stake, and silence in the face of all this injustice is not acceptable. Then I read Toni Morrison and think, "Until I can write like that, I should say nothing."

In 2015, I interviewed Ms. Morrison for an airline magazine, of all things. She was kind, gracious, charming, witty. It was easy to be awestruck. But throughout our conversation, I felt that I was speaking not to a god, but rather to a woman of uncanny genius, absolutely mortal and as such, so very impressive. What I remember most from our conversation was how important her ambition still was to her, how, in her words, "I don't think I could do without it."

I end nearly every interview with the question, "What do you like most about your writing?" Writers often equivocate and dance around the question, afraid to admit they think well of themselves and their work. With Ms. Morrison, there was no hesitation or equivocation. She said she appreciated her ability to "say more and write less," and her "desire to give the reader space."

From that moment, I became more comfortable with my own ambition. I aspired to say more and write less. Sometimes I have failed in this endeavor, sometimes I have succeeded.

Everything I am and ever will be as a black woman who writes begins with the work of Toni Morrison. My words have been shaped by all of her work, but especially *The Bluest Eye*, *The Song of Solomon*, *Sula* and most especially, *Beloved*. Pecola Breedlove. Macon Dead III. Sula Peace. Sethe. Indelible characters and indelible stories.

When I read each of Ms. Morrison's novels for the first time, I saw far more than a reflection of what it means to live in a black woman's body. I saw majesty and infinite possibility. I saw a writer wielding her craft masterfully, being bold and audacious, avoiding the facile choices despite the risks in doing so. In a conversation with Hilton Als for a profile in the *New Yorker*, Ms. Morrison said: "I can accept the labels because being a black woman writer is not a shallow place but a rich place to write from. It doesn't limit my imagination; it expands it. It's richer than being a white male writer because I know more and I've experienced more."

Ms. Morrison taught me and an entire generation of black writers to recognize that we are rich places to write from. She showed us that we must matter first to ourselves if we hope to matter to anyone else. She demonstrated that there is no shame in writing that is both work and a necessary political act.

She taught me that you can write about black girls and black women, unapologetically, and say necessary, meaningful things about our lives in a world that often tells us that our lives do not matter. She consistently centered blackness in her narratives, but not an idealized version of it.

Instead, she wrote, for black people in the truest ways she could. She was of us and wrote for us nuanced, complicated, authentic and honest representations of our culture, our lives, our triumphs, our sufferings, our failures. She demonstrated the importance of raising our voices and challenging power structures that harm vulnerable peoples.

Her brilliant books, stories, essays and speeches are certainly a significant part of her legacy. The many accolades she accumulated will always be a part of her story.

But, perhaps, her greatest legacy will be the direct lineage between her and so many black writers who are following in her footsteps as they create their own legacies. She broadened the scope of what I thought was possible for myself as a writer and a woman. I can never repay that gift.

When someone with as much staggering talent as Toni Morrison dies, it is easy to want to deify them, to remember them as supernatural. It is particularly easy to do that with Ms. Morrison because her writing is so powerful. She wrote impeccable sentences. She imparted wisdom in ways that seemed effortless. She commanded attention and demanded respect. She told incredible, passionate, resonant stories. Her immense legacy will be discussed in perpetuity and her body of work will endure forever.

But to attribute her brilliance to some higher power would be a disservice to the very real life she lived, how hard she worked and how often she had to break through glass ceilings so that others could follow.

I often think about how Morrison wrote her debut novel, *The Bluest Eye*, in stolen moments, while working full-time as an editor and raising her two sons as a single mother. It is this kind of truth that reminds us that she actively put in the work of being a writer, even in circumstances that would have stifled lesser people.

There is a picture of Toni Morrison from the 1970s, her Afro crowning her face, and she wears a silky camisole dress. She is dancing, her face bright and beaming, arms akimbo. She looks joyful, beautifully human.

The best way we can honor Toni Morrison's legacy is to remember her as the astonishing and brilliant and very human woman she was. It is her humanity that made her so extraordinary.

Originally published in the *New York Times*, August 9, 2019

After Chadwick Boseman's Iconic Black Panther, Should King T'Challa Be Recast?

———

The actor Chadwick Boseman's death, from cancer in August 2020, was a breathtaking shock. With his performance as Marvel's Black Panther, Mr. Boseman became a towering figure, particularly for Black people, who rarely get to see themselves depicted as heroes on the screen.

As T'Challa, bearer of the mantle of Black Panther, Mr. Boseman expanded our cultural imaginations. He was the king of Wakanda, an uncolonized Black nation and the most technologically advanced country in the world. He made it seem as if anything was possible. An excellent actor playing an excellent role, Mr. Boseman was so intertwined with his superhero persona that many proclaimed no one else could ever step into the role of T'Challa—that no one should.

And indeed Kevin Feige, the president of Marvel Studios, announced in 2020 that out of respect for Mr. Boseman, Marvel would not recast the role. In Hollywood, however, only intellectual property is truly sacred, and the franchise must go on. Marvel will release the sequel *Black Panther: Wakanda Forever* in November, with Ryan Coogler returning as director.

The film's teaser trailer, released last month at Comic-Con International in San Diego, is dazzling but cryptic. It focuses on the women characters who surrounded Black Panther in the first film: his girlfriend, Nakia; mother, Ramonda; sister, Shuri; and the warrior Okoye, his bodyguard. Meanwhile, T'Challa is represented only in what looks like a memorial mural. While the franchise must go on, this beloved character appears unlikely to venture into that future, even if Black Panther lives on.

In the character's mythology, King T'Challa inherited the title of Black Panther from a line of ancestors, along with powers derived from a magical herb—so it's logically possible that it would be passed along to someone else if T'Challa died. At the end of the trailer, there is a brief, partial glimpse of a black-costumed figure—legs lunging forward, a right arm extending into five lethal claws—giving fans the impression that someone else will become the Black Panther. (The trailer set off a flurry of internet speculation about who that character is.)

Upon the trailer's release, the hashtag #recastTChalla emerged on social media, with fans arguing that the role of T'Challa should be played by another actor, much in the same way that white superheroes have been recast again and again, whether it's Batman or Wonder Woman or Spider-Man or Magneto. Mr. Boseman's loss was a tragedy, the advocates for recasting said, but should that mean the end of this iconic Black character, when the character still had so much story left to tell?

A petition with more than 60,000 signatures asks Marvel "NOT to use the tragic passing of Chadwick Boseman as a plot device in their fictional storytelling" and "for the portrayal of T'Challa to be allowed to continue" in the Marvel Cinematic Universe. "If Marvel Studios removes T'Challa, it would be at the expense of the audiences (especially Black boys and men) who saw themselves in him," the petition on Change.org argues.

This might seem like just another attempt to influence Hollywood's storytelling from an increasingly demanding fandom, but there is a sharp yearning driving the movement to recast King T'Challa—a yearning to hold onto what Chadwick Boseman represented. Especially among Black fans, there is a genuine fear that without T'Challa, the Black Panther story line could lose its sense of power and possibility. I hear the pain thrumming beneath calls to recast T'Challa. I empathize with it.

Superhero fandoms are complicated beasts. Fans are passionate and are also often inflexibly opinionated about how their beloved stories should be told. (I saw this firsthand when I co-wrote a comic book series set in the world of Wakanda, with Ta-Nehisi Coates.)

In recent years, filmmakers have increasingly performed what's known as "fan service"—making creative choices that acknowledge or acquiesce to the desires of fans. At its best, fan service is charming. It allows fans to feel seen and heard. It allows them to believe they have a small hand in a huge creative endeavor. At its worst, fan service can be exploitative, sexist or racist. Very often, it panders, making a movie or show feel as though it has no distinct point of view or creative vision, that the creators' desperation for public approval has trumped good storytelling or creative ambition.

There was no choice Marvel and Mr. Coogler could have made that would please everyone. If they recast King T'Challa, many would have thought it too soon after Mr. Boseman's death. If they simply disappeared him for a movie by inventing a reason to place him on a mission somewhere, his absence would have been a distraction. Killing him off, as they appear to have done, has already angered some.

And, unfortunately, whichever character, and actor, takes on the mantle of Black Panther next will bear the brunt of fans' doubts, disappointment and derision—particularly if the new Black Panther will be, as some have speculated, a woman. Heaven forbid! (We've seen this time and again, most notably in the *Star Wars* franchise, where actors of color have endured unconscionable harassment for contradicting certain fans' notions of who can be heroic in our imagined, interstellar futures.)

For the time being, the filmmakers made the best decision they could. It would be deeply unfair to expect any actor, however talented, to step into the massive shoes Mr. Boseman left behind. The new King T'Challa would forever compete with our memory of the original. The successor would be expected to somehow channel Mr. Boseman's swagger and gravitas, to replace the irreplaceable. And when the actor who plays the new king inevitably disappointed audiences for not actually being Mr. Boseman, he would become the target of intense ire. We should not ask anyone to be placed in that line of fire.

The #RecastTChalla movement seems well-intentioned. But the fundamental issue isn't whether or not a role in one movie should be recast; it's about what representation demands. *Black Panther*, in 2018, bore the weight of outsized fan expectations, as a groundbreaking Black superhero leading a major film. That is an unreasonable burden to place on one character, on one actor, on one film. Black people—men and boys as mentioned in the petition, but also women and girls—should have more than one superhero to enjoy and see themselves in. So should people of other races and ethnicities, cultures and identities. We should not be asking

Marvel to recast T'Challa; we should be asking it to expand the roster of heroes. We have to think bigger and demand more.

Whatever happens in the next *Black Panther* movie, the #RecastTChalla proponents may ultimately get their wish. In recent years, Marvel has introduced us to the multiverse, which allows for multiple realities to coexist (and for infinite extensions of its intellectual property). In the multiverse, there may be realities where T'Challa is alive and well and saving the world as Black Panther. We may still see some of those stories.

In the meantime, we, too, can be more expansive in our imaginings. T'Challa doesn't have to be the only hero we look up to. However incremental, we have seen progress in recent years. Marvel's Spider-Verse includes the Black and Puerto Rican Brooklyn teenager Miles Morales as Spider-Man; the Muslim superhero Kamala Khan is on Disney+ as Ms. Marvel; Captain America passed on his shield to the Falcon, a Black hero played by Anthony Mackie. We now have Shang-Chi and America Chavez, and at DC, Nubia and Cyborg. Outside of Marvel and DC, a new crop of creators—Ava DuVernay, Mindy Kaling, Michaela Coel and Shonda Rhimes among them—are exploring rich new universes and frontiers of human heroism. We can also see, if we look for it, that there are heroes walking among us—people in our communities who are doing incredible things every single day.

In November, we will likely meet a new Black Panther, who will once again shoulder the unreasonable burden of representation. If we are lucky, this actor will also entertain us and inspire us and ignite our imaginations. I cannot think of a better way to honor Chadwick Boseman's on-screen legacy.

Originally published in the *New York Times*, August 6, 2022

How to Collect Art

———

Finding your way into art collecting is a lot like stumbling into an elaborate dance routine with a partner who expects you to anticipate their every move even though you are unfamiliar with the choreography. It can be awkward and far more challenging than you might imagine, but still, you want to master the steps.

My parents have been collecting Haitian art my entire life. I grew up around vibrant depictions of Haitian life and culture, mostly oil on canvas, often large in scale. My great-aunt Carmel owned a gallery in Port-au-Prince, and when we visited during the summers, she would let us roam the gallery freely, marveling at the paintings and the sculpture. But I was never exposed to the business of art. And then I got older and majored in English and eventually became a writing professor, so art collecting seemed well beyond my reach. I certainly enjoyed art in museums and galleries, but I never considered that I could own art. I understood the price points of art as either forty-dollar posters or multimillion-dollar Basquiats sold at a frenzied auction.

And then I met my wife, Debbie, who has been a collector for more than twenty years. Everywhere you look in her, now our, house, there is art, whether it's originals or prints or interesting objects. Once we knew each other better, I asked how she built her collection, and she shared how she started with just one $500 piece that she could barely afford in the 1990s. From there she bought art she was drawn to that was within her means. Then as now, she is very distinct in her tastes. She likes experimental art and anything with typography. Sometimes, she refers to our home as "The House of Type," because everywhere you look there is art with words demanding to be read. She prioritizes women and queer artists but has a truly diverse range of artists in her collection. There is always something interesting to look at and contemplate. As I started spending more time in our home, I was reminded of the pleasures of living with art, of a life suffused with it in myriad ways.

My own collection started innocently enough. One evening Debbie introduced me to the website Artsy. I started browsing and a couple hours later, a monster was born. Art news! Artist features! Auctions! The very first piece I bought was (I think) Kahlil Robert Irving's *Music Memorial in Film [(Greeting Screening Chained) Daily Ritual & tribute (TERROR)]* (2019), a collage on industrial ceramic tile. Then I started exploring other art-related sites and discovering new artists and appreciating the work they made. When we're in New York, we live in Chelsea, so everywhere I look there are galleries and although in Los Angeles, where we also live, the galleries are a bit farther afield, the art they offer is just as urgent and exciting.

The guiding principle of my collection has been to find art I want to live with. Certainly, I have specific collecting interests. I'm drawn to the work of Black artists, women, LGBTQ artists, and people who live at the intersections of those identities. I love collage and mixed-media work, figurative art, textiles. And although I have these interests, I don't limit myself. When I find something I love, and that is within my means, I try to bring it into my collection.

When avid art collectors offer advice on building a collection, they encourage you to buy what you love. That is indeed valuable advice, and not as simplistic as you might assume. Really what they're saying is, buy art you care about and have a connection to instead of looking at art merely as an investment or a means of accruing social capital. But there is a lot of advice that is never shared, perhaps because the advice givers assume that budding collectors already understand how the art world works. I was rather naïve when all this started: I assumed that if something was for sale and I wanted to buy it, a simple transaction would ensue. But rarely is that the case. Many of the practices of acquiring art are . . . confounding if you're an outsider. It can be intimidating to walk into the hushed void of an art gallery. They are, generally, spartan affairs, the better to appreciate the art within, I suppose. A young person or two dressed all in black might be working at something architectural resembling a desk. If you're lucky, there is a small stack of reading material, and if you're very, very lucky, there is a price list. Mostly you're left to your own devices, particularly if you aren't legible as an art collector.

At art fairs, held in cavernous spaces with high ceilings, you can wander from booth to booth, taking in presentations of work, sometimes from a single artist, sometimes from a selection of a gallery's artists. There are a lot of people with chic glasses and expensive designer accessories milling about, trying to outdo one another in expressing, loudly, their opinions on what they see and how bored they are with the whole scene. And again, if you aren't legible as a collector, you are practically invisible.

There is nothing like seeing art in person, being able to look at the craftsmanship, construction methods, brushstrokes, the texture of layers of paint on canvas, but there is also something to be said for the simplicity of looking at art online, from the comfort of wherever you are, without the awkwardness of having to navigate the social mores of the art world. Over the past few years, I have developed a real fondness for galleries that are not coy with information about the art and artists they represent. Though I generally abhor being on mailing lists, the one exception is galleries, because their emails are clear in purpose and when they send installation previews, most of the information you might be seeking is available in a handy PDF or online viewing room.

Every community has its rules, both spoken and unspoken, and to collect art requires understanding that. Not all galleries are created equal. There are the smaller galleries and the galleries that are vanity projects and the galleries with a mission, and then there are the megagalleries, the Death Stars if you will, representing blue chip artists with branches in the world's most glamorous cities. There are the small collectors who just want to own a piece or two of original art and there are the people who view art as an investment rather than a joy to live with, and of course there are all kinds of collectors in between.

When it comes to buying art, not every collector pays the same price. Not every collector gets to acquire the work they covet. You can negotiate the sale price a bit, but that can be tricky, since unless the gallery absorbs the discount from its steep percentage, the artist will receive less money for their valuable labor and art. But before you even get to the negotiating stage, you have to contend with the reality that just because something is for sale does not mean you can buy it. Gallerists, generally, are representing their artists' and their own best interest, which means they sometimes want to place that work with "important" collections or museums and other institutions.

If a gallery has no relationship with you, which seems like it would be the case most of the time, they might ask you to share more information about yourself. What they're really seeking is a better understanding of your collection and its provenance, to see if you're a worthy (by their arbitrary standards) steward of the work. Once, a gallerist asked me to tell her a bit more about myself. This was before I understood how things worked so I dashed off a spicy email with an extensive biography and, as you might expect, never heard back. Another time, when I wanted to buy a specific piece from an artist whose work I love, the gallery told me they reserve his pieces for customers with whom they have an ongoing relationship. They offered instead to sell me another piece of art by a different artist I didn't know, which is to say, they wanted me to buy something I did not want in order, maybe, someday, to have the opportunity to buy a piece of art I actually did want.

By now I've learned that there are reasons for some of these practices. Artists understandably want some control over where their work goes and what happens to it. They want to protect their work from being sold on the secondary market too soon. They want to protect their standing in the art world. And galleries want to protect their artists, too. But in a world predicated on prestige that is also susceptible to the biases we all live with in one way or another, some collectors are dismissed out of hand. At the Frieze Los Angeles VIP preview in 2020, Los Angeles artist Genevieve Gaignard wore a beige dress with the words "sell to black collectors" emblazoned on the back. This was not an act of self-promotion; it was a way of instigating a conversation about access to art. Translating that conversation into change, though, has been elusive.

Originally published in *Gagosian Quarterly*, Winter 2022

[MAN PROBLEMS]

Why Are Most Father's Day Gifts So Terrible?

———

This year I wanted to get my father the perfect Father's Day gift. I know him well, but he is difficult to shop for: He has most everything a man could want or need, which, as far as he is concerned, involves the clothes on his back and a roof over his head. He is not impressed by frivolity or waste. He loves reading—and he's become the most ardent fan of my writing—but doesn't really have hobbies. And this year, in my search for the perfect Father's Day gift, I noticed a problem even greater than my own dad's austerity. Turning to the internet as I began my quest, I was stunned by how terrible most Father's Day gifts are.

There are some general categories of masculinity celebrated around Father's Day—barbecue paraphernalia, beer- and whiskey-related merchandise, affirmation-based gifts bestowing the honor of "World's Greatest Dad," lawn-care accessories, and electronic gadgets. Neckwear is ubiquitous, as are shaving accessories, golf equipment, watches, wallets, and items in the shape of briefcases, including, I kid you not, a briefcase barbecue grill and a briefcase containing barbecue accessories—some kind of triumphantly boring synthesis of Father's Day gift ideas.

Fathers, to judge by the gifts suggested for them, are manly folk who wear ties because they work at important jobs. They excel at fathering and spend their free time grilling, drinking, mowing the lawn, and fiddling with newfangled technologies. They do not have a diverse range of interests, or discernible interior, emotional lives.

This narrowness becomes even more apparent when we consider how intensely motherhood figures in our cultural imagination—motherhood is so frequently proclaimed the most important job in the world that

it can begin to feel almost cultlike. While dads are stereotypically remote, mothers are assumed to know us inside and out, and we hope we
know them to a similar extent. Though Mother's Day gift guides are also
fraught with cliché, they generally offer a broader, more distinct range of
choices. Mother's Day gifts acknowledge that mothers have interior lives
and emotional relationships. They acknowledge that there is more than
one way to be a mother.

In fact, the list of our cultural expectations for men is nearly as long
as the one for women. They have to be providers and protectors. They
have to be strong and emotionally impermeable. They have to offer moral
guidance. There is little room, amidst such expectations, for most men to
simply be human, or to be seen and understood. I suspect this situation
arises, in part, because of the persistence and pervasiveness of so-called
traditional domestic gender roles—the happy housewife keeping things
together on the home front while the man puts in his eight hours and
comes home to a stiff drink and well-behaved children who keep quiet
so Daddy can rest.

My father was and is a very present father. He was there most nights
at the dinner table, interested in our young lives. He helped my brothers
and me with school projects. This one time, he and I built a suspension
bridge out of balsa wood! He coached our soccer teams. But he was also a
mystery. He traveled a lot and was gone all day, only to return around six,
tall and lanky, his suit hanging loosely as he set his briefcase down and
opened his arms to my brothers and me. We knew him in a far different,
often more distant way than we knew our mother. I know we gave him a
lot of ties, beer mugs, and barbecue tongs as Father's Day presents, along
with homemade cards boasting, as you might imagine, how he was the
world's greatest dad. Now that I am older and, I hope, wiser, I know my
father differently. I see him and understand him more clearly. I recognize
what he missed out on by working as hard as he did to support our family.

Thankfully, the role of fathers is changing. According to a report
from Pew Research, "fathers' time with children rose from 2.5 hours
per week in 1965 to seven hours per week in 2011, nearly a threefold
increase. During the same period, fathers' time spent doing household
chores has more than doubled (from an average of about four hours per
week to about 10 hours)." Clearly, there's a lot of room for improvement,

but fathers are, increasingly, co-parents instead of occasional parents. If we expand how we think of fathers, and how we choose to celebrate them, if we took more time to see them as people with the same emotional, interior lives as our mothers, I would hope even more men would get onboard with expanding their roles in their domestic lives.

I ended up buying my father a fancy pen. I learned to read and, in turn, write, while sitting on his lap as he read the newspaper, secretly reading along. He and my mom gave me my first typewriter. One way or another, my father's hand is always covering mine when I write. With this woefully inadequate token of my appreciation for him as a father and a human being, I am offering up one small moment where my father might feel seen, where my hand might cover his.

Originally published in *The Cut*, June 13, 2014

Nate Parker and the
Limits of Empathy

———

As I get older, I try to have more empathy for other people, for the ways we fail one another. I often fall short. Today, I am struggling to have empathy for Nate Parker, a man experiencing the height of his career while being forced to reckon with his past.

Mr. Parker wrote, directed, produced and stars in the movie *The Birth of a Nation*, which chronicles the life of Nat Turner and the slave rebellion he led in Virginia in 1831. The story the movie tells is important, and to see a movie like this getting mainstream attention is equally significant.

The Birth of a Nation made a big splash when it had its premiere at the Sundance Film Festival and was purchased by Fox Searchlight for $17.5 million. As the movie's publicity machine roars to life in advance of the October release, there is renewed interest in Mr. Parker and his history with sexual assault. There are renewed questions about whether we can or should separate the artist from his art. I am reminded that I cannot.

In 1999, Mr. Parker and his roommate Jean McGianni Celestin were accused of raping a young woman while they were students and wrestlers at Penn State University. (They said that the sex was consensual.) There was a third man, Tamerlane Kangas, who chose not to participate in the incident. At the trial two years later, Mr. Kangas said, according to court transcripts, "I didn't believe that four people at one time was—you know, it didn't seem right."

What happened in 1999 is a familiar story: college athletes, alcohol, a vulnerable woman and allegations of sexual assault. The unnamed woman pressed charges against Mr. Parker and Mr. Celestin, claiming she was drunk, unconscious and unable to consent to sex.

The victim said that she was harassed and intimidated on campus by Mr. Parker, Mr. Celestin and their supporters. She twice attempted suicide, according to court records. She dropped out of school. The 2001 trial took three days. That the rape case even went to trial is a rarity. Mr. Parker was acquitted, based partly on testimony that he and the victim had previously had consensual sex. Mr. Celestin was convicted of sexual assault and sentenced to prison, but the conviction was eventually overturned. The victim, who sued Penn State because she said the university did not protect her from the harassment she endured after filing charges, received a settlement of $17,500.

Both Mr. Parker and Mr. Celestin now have families and successful careers. They remain friends and collaborators. The victim, well, she committed suicide in 2012 and left behind a young son. She can no longer speak for herself.

Mr. Parker is being forced to publicly reckon with his past, and he is doing a lousy job. I want to have empathy for him, but everything he says and does troubles me. You see, what happened in 1999 was a "painful moment" in his life. Most of what he has to say about that "painful moment" involves how he felt, how he was affected. The solipsism is staggering.

In an interview with Deadline.com, the entertainment news site, Mr. Parker said: "I've got five daughters and a lovely wife. My mom lives here with me; I brought her here. I've got four younger sisters." He offers up the women in his life as incontrovertible evidence of goodness or, perhaps, redemption. But no matter how much he wishes it to be so, his women cannot erase his past. He went so far as to bring his 6-year-old daughter to an interview where he knew he would be questioned about the circumstances surrounding the rape trial—a strange, manipulative and even cynical choice. To this day, he believes he did nothing wrong, though he also says he has "grown" and is a "changed" man.

I have my own history with sexual violence, so I cannot consider such stories with impartiality, though I do try. It is my gut instinct to believe the victim because there is nothing at all to be gained by going public with a rape accusation except the humiliations of the justice system and public scorn. Only an estimated 2 to 10 percent of rape accusations are false. And to have sex with a woman who said she was blackout drunk, to do so with a friend—that is a crime, whether the justice system agrees or not.

When it comes to sexual violence, I do not know what justice looks like; no one does. According to the Rape, Abuse and Incest National Network, out of every 1,000 rapes, 344 will be reported to the police, 63 of those reports will lead to an arrest, 13 cases will be referred to a prosecutor, seven of those cases will lead to a felony conviction and six of those perpetrators will serve prison time. They will serve that time in a broken system that incarcerates without offering offenders any kind of real rehabilitation.

And how long does someone pay for their bad decisions, or their crimes? It has been 17 years since whatever took place at Penn State. As Mr. Parker keeps pointing out, he was cleared of the charges. Do we take him at his word that he is a changed man, that he should be forgiven? Do we dare dismiss Mr. Parker and Mr. Celestin's actions as youthful indiscretions?

On August 16, Mr. Parker posted a statement on Facebook, an inadequate act of contrition. "I write to you all devastated," he began. He referred to himself, several times, as a "man of faith." He expressed sorrow for the victim's death, which he said he had heretofore been unaware of. He affirmed his belief in women's rights. On the surface, the statement seems heartfelt enough, but it also feels hollow, like a parroting of what Nate Parker thinks he is supposed to say to redeem himself.

He would have us believe that he made bad decisions at 19, and has learned from them. We have all made our fair share of bad decisions. There is a canyon of difference, however, between bad decisions and allegations of rape. I also wonder how much Mr. Parker has really changed when he continues to befriend the man with whom he shared what he terms one of the most painful moments in his life. Mr. Celestin shares a story credit on *The Birth of a Nation*, a detail that continues to stun me.

I've enjoyed Mr. Parker's work as an actor over the years—his role in *The Great Debaters*, his strong turn in *Beyond the Lights*. I have not enjoyed some of his statements about masculinity that read like homophobia, such as the interview in which he reportedly said he would never play a gay man to "preserve the black man," whatever that means. As with most artists, I was forced to reconcile his talent with his flaws.

We've long had to face that bad men can create good art. Some people have no problem separating the creation from the creator. I am not one of those people, nor do I want to be. I recognize that people are complex and cannot be solely defined by their worst deeds, but I can no longer watch *The Cosby Show*, for example, without thinking of the numerous sexual assault accusations against Bill Cosby. Suddenly, his jokes are far less funny.

I cannot separate the art and the artist, just as I cannot separate my blackness and my continuing desire for more representation of the black experience in film from my womanhood, my feminism, my own history of sexual violence, my humanity.

The Birth of a Nation is being billed as an important movie—something we must see, a story that demands to be heard. I have not yet seen the movie, and now I won't. Just as I cannot compartmentalize the various markers of my identity, I cannot value a movie, no matter how good or "important" it might be, over the dignity of a woman whose story should be seen as just as important, a woman who is no longer alive to speak for herself, or benefit from any measure of justice. No amount of empathy could make that possible.

Originally published in the *New York Times*, August 19, 2016

Dear Men: It's You Too

Statistics about the scope of sexual violence are always chilling, but even such accountings do little to capture the true breadth and scope of harassment and assault women face. In feminist discourse we talk about rape culture, but the people we most need to reach—the men who are the cause of the problem and the women who feel moved to excuse them—are often resistant to the idea that rape culture even exists.

Women are being hysterical, they say. Women are being humorless. Women are being oversensitive. Women should just dress or behave or feel differently.

Skeptics are willing to perform all kinds of mental acrobatics to avoid facing the very stark realities of living in this world as a woman.

And then, a man like Harvey Weinstein, famous but utterly common, is revealed as a sexual predator. Or, more accurately, the open secret stops being a secret and makes the news. The details are grotesque and absurd (who among us will ever look at a bathrobe the same again?). More women are emboldened and share their own experiences with the predator du jour or another of his ilk. They share these experiences because all of us know that this moment demands our testimony: Here is the burden I have carried. Here is the burden all women have carried.

But we're tired of carrying it. We've done enough. It's time for men to step up.

I confess I am sick of thinking about sexual violence, both personally and publicly. I've talked about and written about and responded to tweets about it for years. I am filthy with the subject, and yet I know this work must be done so that someday we can banish the phrase "rape culture" from our vernacular because it will have become an antiquated concept. I do not dream of utopia, but I do dare to dream of something better than this world we are currently living in.

We are a long way from that better world, in part because so many seemingly well-intentioned people buy into the precepts of rape culture. So many people want to believe there are only a few bad men. So many people want to believe they don't know any bad men. So many people do not realize they are bad men. So many people want to believe sexual harassment is only a Hollywood problem or a Silicon Valley problem when, in fact, sexual harassment happens in every single industry. There is no escaping the inappropriate attentions and intentions of men.

These same people buy into the myth that there are ways women can avoid sexual violence and harassment—if we act nicer or drink less or dress less provocatively or smile or show a little gratitude or, or, or—because boys will be boys, because men are so fragile, so frenzied with sexual need that they cannot simply control themselves and their baser impulses.

Some people insinuate that women themselves can stave off attacks. They insist we can wear modest clothes or be grateful for unconventional looks, or that we can avoid "asking for it" by "presenting all the sensuality and the sexuality," as Donna Karan has said. With each of these betrayals, the burden we all carry grows heavier.

What this reasoning does not grapple with—and it is a perennial rejoinder to discussions of sexual assault and women's vulnerability—is that no one escapes unwanted male attention because they don't meet certain beauty standards or because they don't dress a certain way. They escape because they are lucky.

Sexual violence is about power. There is a sexual component, yes, but mostly it's about someone exerting his or her will over another and deriving pleasure and satisfaction from that exertion. We cannot forget this, or the women and men who have been harassed or assaulted but aren't "conventionally attractive" will be ignored, silenced, or worse, disbelieved.

And then there are the ways that women diminish their experiences as "not that bad." Because it was just a cat call. It was just a man grabbing me. It was just a man shoving me up against a wall. It was just a man raping me. He didn't have a weapon. He stopped following me after

10 blocks. He didn't leave many bruises. He didn't kill me, therefore it is not that bad. Nothing I deal with in this country compares with what women in other parts of the world deal with. We offer up this refrain over and over because that is what we need to tell ourselves, because if we were to face how bad it really is, we might not be able to shoulder the burden for one moment longer.

In the wake of the Weinstein allegations, a list appeared online, an anonymous accounting of men in media who have committed a range of infractions from sleazy DMs to rape. And just as quickly as the list appeared, it disappeared. I saw the list. A couple of people didn't belong on it simply because their behaviors weren't sexual in nature, but some of them were men whose behavior called for a warning and who deserved public shame. Even where I live, outside the media bubble, in a small town in Indiana, I had already heard some of the stories that were shared.

There are a great many open secrets about bad men.

As the list circulated, there was a lot of hand-wringing about libel and the ethics of anonymous disclosure. There was so much concern for the "good men," who, I guess we're supposed to believe, would be harmed by the mere existence of an accounting of alleged bad men. There was concern that the "milder" infractions would be conflated with the more serious ones, as if women lack the capacity for critical thinking and discernment about behaviors that are or are not appropriate in professional contexts. More energy was spent worrying about how men were affected than worrying about the pain women have suffered. Women were not trusted to create a tangible artifact of their experiences so that they might have more to rely upon than the whisper networks women have long cultivated to warn one another about the bad men they encounter.

Meanwhile, there was a hashtag, #metoo—a chorus of women and some men sharing their experiences of sexual harassment and assault. Me too, me too, me too. I thought about participating but I was just too tired. I have nothing more to say about my history of violence beyond saying I have been hurt, almost too many times to count. I have been hurt enough that some terrible things no longer even register as pain.

We already know victims' stories. Women testify about their hurt, publicly and privately, all the time. When this happens, men, in particular, act shocked and surprised that sexual violence is so pervasive because they are afforded the luxury of oblivion. And then they start to panic because not all men are predators and they don't want to be lumped in with the bad men and they make women's pain all about themselves. They choose not to face that enough men are predators that women engage in all sorts of protective behaviors and strategies so that they might stop adding to their testimony. And then there are the men who act so overwhelmed, who ask, "What can I possibly do?"

The answer is simple.

Men can start putting in some of the work women have long done in offering testimony. They can come forward and say "me too" while sharing how they have hurt women in ways great and small. They can testify about how they have cornered women in narrow office hallways or made lewd comments to co-workers or refused to take no for an answer or worn a woman down by guilting her into sex and on and on and on. It would equally be a balm if men spoke up about the times when they witnessed violence or harassment and looked the other way or laughed it off or secretly thought a woman was asking for it. It's time for men to start answering for themselves because women cannot possibly solve this problem they had no hand in creating.

Originally published in the *New York Times*, October 19, 2017

Louis C.K. and the Men Who Think Justice Takes as Long as They Want It To

The #MeToo movement has existed for more than a decade, since the activist Tarana Burke coined the phrase, and it was popularized in 2017, as men such as Harvey Weinstein, Mario Batali, Matt Lauer, Kevin Spacey, Louis C.K. and Charlie Rose were called to account for reported instances of sexual harassment, assault and, in some cases, rape. For the past several months the court of public opinion has litigated the misdeeds of these men. Some have lost their jobs. Harvey Weinstein is facing criminal charges. They have fallen from grace, but they have had mighty soft landings.

Their victims, however, have been disbelieved. They have had to withstand accusations that they are seeking attention. Justice has been grandly elusive. The public discourse has been more about whether the #MeToo movement has gone too far than it has been about reckoning with the alarming prevalence of sexual predation in every circumstance imaginable.

In November of 2017, the comedian Louis C.K. admitted to exposing his penis and masturbating in front of women without their consent, then disappeared from public eye until this month. On Sunday night, he returned to the stage at the Comedy Cellar in New York. Apparently, he found a new way of forcing himself on an unsuspecting audience. He performed for about 15 minutes and received a standing ovation a mere nine months after the confirmation of his disgraceful behavior.

Other disgraced, once powerful men also appear to be plotting their comebacks. Matt Lauer told people that he's going to re-enter the public sphere. Stories have circulated about potential comeback vehicles for Charlie Rose and Mario Batali.

In each instance, it has been less than a year since the allegations against these men surfaced, and in each instance, the men have done little in the way of public contrition. When they have apologized, they have done so with carefully worded, legally vetted statements. They have deflected responsibility. They have demonstrated that they don't really think they've done anything wrong. And worse, people have asked for the #MeToo movement to provide a path to redemption for these men, as if it is the primary responsibility of the victimized to help their victimizers find redemption.

"Should a man pay for his misdeeds for the rest of his life?" This is always the question raised when we talk about justice in the case of harassment and rape allegations against public figures. How long should a man who has faced no legal and few financial consequences for such actions pay the price?

In June of 2018, I spoke with the poet and activist Aja Monet about my recent anthology on rape culture, *Not That Bad*, and what justice might look like for victims of sexual violence. We talked about restorative justice, where victims and offenders work together to reconcile crime and suffering, as a means of achieving rehabilitation for the offender and justice for the offended.

I appreciate the idea of restorative justice—that it might be possible to achieve justice through discussing the assault I experienced with the perpetrators and that I might be involved in determining an appropriate punishment for their crime. Restorative justice might afford me the agency they took from me. But I also appreciate the idea of those men spending some time in a prison cell, as problematic as the carceral system is, to think long and hard about the ways in which they violated me. I would like them to face material consequences for their actions because I have been doing so for 30 years. There is a part of me that wants them to endure what I endured. There is a part of me that is not interested in restoration. That part of me is interested in vengeance.

And this is what is so difficult about justice and sexual violence—the repercussions of the crime can last a lifetime. Satisfying justice may not be possible, but we can certainly do better given that all too often, victims of sexual harassment and violence receive no justice at all.

We spend so little energy thinking about justice for victims and so much energy thinking about the men who perpetrate sexual harassment and violence. We worry about what will become of them in the wake of their mistakes. We don't worry as much about those who have suffered at their hands. It is easier, for far too many people, to empathize with predators than it is to empathize with prey.

I have to believe there is a path to redemption for people who have done wrong, but nine months of self-imposed exile in financial comfort is not a point along that path. It is far too soon for any of the men who have faced the marginal consequences born of the #MeToo movement to think about redemption. People love a comeback narrative, and all too often they yearn for this narrative at the expense of victims who are only beginning to reconcile with their suffering.

Take Louis C.K. Not only did he expose himself to and masturbate in front of female comics; the actions of people in his employ reportedly worked to impede his victims' careers. Still, he has remained in control of the narrative. He gets to break the rules, and then he gets to establish rules of his own when he must answer for his misdeeds.

How long should a man like Louis C.K. pay for what he did? At least as long as he worked to silence the women he assaulted and at least as long as he allowed them to doubt themselves and suffer in the wake of his predation and at least as long as the comedy world protected him even though there were very loud whispers about his behavior for decades.

He should pay until he demonstrates some measure of understanding of what he has done wrong and the extent of the harm he has caused. He should attempt to financially compensate his victims for all the work they did not get to do because of his efforts to silence them. He should facilitate their getting the professional opportunities they should have been able to take advantage of all these years. He should finance their mental health care as long as they may need it. He should donate to nonprofit organizations that work with sexual harassment and assault victims. He should publicly admit what he did and why it was wrong without excuses and legalese and deflection. Every perpetrator of sexual harassment and violence should follow suit.

We need to figure out what justice looks like in the court of public opinion, not for the sake of the offenders, but for the sake of victims. It is painful to know Louis C.K. simply strolled into a comedy club and did a set as if he hadn't admitted to masturbating in front of women, as if for sport.

It is painful to witness the familiar narrative of transgressions coming to light, the perpetrator maybe facing opprobrium and before long, plotting a "comeback" where all is seemingly forgiven. It is painful that these men think they are so vital to the culture that the public wants them to come back. Whatever private acts of contrition these men, and a few women, might make to their victims demands a corresponding public act of contrition, one offered genuinely, rather than to save face or appease the crowd. Until then, they don't deserve restorative justice or redemption. That is the price they must pay for the wrong they have done.

Originally published in the *New York Times*, August 29, 2018

I Thought Men Might
Do Better Than This

———

I watch a lot of *Law & Order: Special Victims Unit*. Many women I know do too. I've seen nearly every episode from 19 seasons, most of them several times. I will watch a dozen episodes of the show back-to-back, no matter how many times I've seen them. At times, it troubles me, my ongoing willingness to consume this show and the disturbing story lines about sexual assault and the terrible ways of the world, but there is something so very satisfying about watching it. The victims don't always find justice, but they are, more often than not, believed by the S.V.U. detectives. Their stories are heard and respected. Justice may be elusive, but on the show, it exists within the realm of possibility.

In the real world, such is not the case. Despite everything we know about the prevalence of sexual assault and harassment, women are still not believed. Their experiences are still minimized. And the male perpetrators of these crimes are given all manner of leniency.

Over the past several weeks, we've heard from men who transgressed and fell from grace. In "Exile" by John Hockenberry, which appeared in *Harper's*, the writer is mournful for the life he lost after he was accused, by multiple women, of sexual harassment. He is aggressively self-pitying throughout his essay, airing any number of grievances about the injustice of how he has been misunderstood. And then he declares that romance is dead as if sexual harassment in the workplace is some kind of grand romantic overture that modern women who dare to stand up for themselves have forsaken.

Jian Ghomeshi, the former CBC radio host accused of sexual assault and harassment, also wrote an essay utterly lacking in self-awareness. In "Reflections from a Hashtag," published in the *New York Review of*

Books, Mr. Ghomeshi takes an almost pithy tone as he reflects on his life since he was accused of various crimes and sexual misdemeanors. (He was acquitted of sexual assault charges in 2016.) He presents himself as the misunderstood hero of his own narrative, the rational man in an irrational world.

And those are essays in publications I once held in high regard. Even more impoverished accounts have been published elsewhere, men writing about how their lives have been derailed with no clear understanding of the lives they have derailed with their actions.

Starkly lacking in these accounts is any accountability or genuine recognition of the wrong done. They display entitlement and rage and contempt for being seen for who they truly are. The people who publish such pieces treat the perpetrators of sexual misconduct as intellectual curiosities. They reserve their empathy for these broken men, for themselves, rather than for women because, as a culture, we expect women to suffer. We gild women's suffering with both inevitability and nobility. Time and again women splay themselves. Women share their painful stories. The world remains largely indifferent.

A year ago, when the allegations against Harvey Weinstein were first published, I wrote about what I hoped men might do in that moment of reckoning: "Men can start putting in some of the work women have long done in offering testimony. They can come forward and say 'me too' while sharing how they have hurt women in ways great and small." I was being naïve, I suppose. Or I was placing too much faith in decency. But I never imagined that instead of self-reflection, men would reflect on how they had been harmed by their own bad behavior.

I said that I watch a lot of *Law & Order: Special Victims Unit*, but for the past year, current events have offered a far more sinister version of the show, without the attractive cast or the satisfying payoff of occasional justice. Every day there is some new revelation about some man who has done some terrible thing. In this #MeToo era, women have repeatedly demonstrated the ways in which they have suffered at the hands of men. We have done so knowing we will be disbelieved, discredited and degraded. We have watched history repeat itself, time and again.

In 1991, Anita Hill testified in front of the Senate Judiciary Committee about the sexual harassment she said she experienced at the hands of

Clarence Thomas. She took a polygraph test that indicated she was telling the truth. She was disbelieved, discredited and degraded. Mr. Thomas was appointed to the Supreme Court and continues to preside.

In 2018, here we are again. Another woman, Christine Blasey Ford, testified in front of a panel of mostly men about the sexual assault she says she endured at the hands of the Supreme Court nominee Brett Kavanaugh. She too has taken a polygraph test supporting her version of events. She is speaking her truth in front of the nation. Her entire life has exploded because she had the courage to come forward out of a sense of patriotic duty, the greater good. And still there are people who doubt her. Who do not find her credible. And if they do find her credible, they don't think what she endured merits Judge Kavanaugh's losing this career opportunity.

Judge Kavanaugh did not need to write down his woes in an essay. He was able to share them in front of an international audience, in real time. When he spoke on his own behalf, he was all rage and righteousness, ego and entitlement. He cried. He glared. It was a grand performance, more implausibly dramatic than any episode of *Law & Order.* Judge Kavanaugh interrupted nearly every Democratic senator who questioned him. A year after the allegations against Harvey Weinstein were first reported, a federal judge behaved as a self-indulgent brat, unwavering in his conviction that he deserves to be on the Supreme Court.

In his statements to the committee, Judge Kavanaugh said that the allegations against him had ruined his life even though he may well be confirmed to a lifetime appointment on the Supreme Court. Mr. Hockenberry and Mr. Ghomeshi also lament how their lives have been ruined. The bar for a man's ruin is, apparently, quite low. May we all be so lucky as to have our lives so ruined.

History is once more repeating itself and will continue to do so until we, as a culture, begin not only to believe women but also to value women enough to consider harming them unacceptable, unthinkable.

Originally published in the *New York Times*, October 5, 2018

Dave Chappelle's Brittle Ego

———

We generally have the same debates about comedy over and over. Let's address those upfront: Art should be made without restriction. Free speech reigns supreme. Sometimes good art should make us uncomfortable, and sometimes bad people can make good art. Comedians, in particular, are going to punch up and down and side-to-side.

Also true: Comedy is not above criticism, even if the most famous, wildly wealthy comedians will keep insulting those who question them. It's just laughs, right? Lighten up. All criticism is forestalled with this setup, in which when you object to anything a comedian says, you're the problem. You're the one who's narrow-minded or "brittle" or humorless.

"Shut up," Dave Chappelle recalls telling a woman who had the gall to challenge his comedy, using a sexist slur and laughing at how witty he is, as if he's the first man to ever deliver such an original, funny line. "Before I kill you and put you in the trunk. Ain't nobody around here." The audience cheers, before Mr. Chappelle explains that he didn't in fact threaten the woman: "I felt that way, but that's not what I said. I was more clever than that."

Mr. Chappelle spends much of *The Closer*, his latest comedy special for Netflix, cleverly deflecting criticism. The set is a 72-minute display of the comedian's own brittleness. The self-proclaimed "GOAT" (greatest of all time) of stand-up delivers five or six lucid moments of brilliance, surrounded by a joyless tirade of incoherent and seething rage, misogyny, homophobia and transphobia.

If there is brilliance in *The Closer*, it's that Mr. Chappelle makes obvious but elegant rhetorical moves that frame any objections to his work as unreasonable. He's just being "brutally honest." He's just saying the quiet part out loud. He's just stating "facts." He's just making us think. But when an entire comedy set is designed as a series of strategic moves to say whatever you want and insulate yourself from valid criticism, I'm not sure you're really making comedy.

Throughout the special, Mr. Chappelle is singularly fixated on the L.G.B.T.Q. community, as he has been in recent years. He reaches for every low-hanging piece of fruit and munches on it gratuitously. Many of Mr. Chappelle's rants are extraordinarily dated, the kind of comedy you might expect from a conservative boomer, agog at the idea of homosexuality. At times, his voice lowers to a hoarse whisper, preparing us for a grand stroke of wisdom—but it never comes. Every once in a while, he remarks that, oh, boy, he's in trouble now, like a mischievous little boy who just can't help himself.

Somewhere, buried in the nonsense, is an interesting and accurate observation about the white gay community conveniently being able to claim whiteness at will. There's a compelling observation about the relatively significant progress the L.G.B.T.Q. community has made, while progress toward racial equity has been much slower. But in these formulations, there are no gay Black people. Mr. Chappelle pits people from different marginalized groups against one another, callously suggesting that trans people are performing the gender equivalent of blackface.

In the next breath, Mr. Chappelle says something about how a Black gay person would never exhibit the behaviors to which he objects, an assertion many would dispute. The poet Saeed Jones, for example, wrote in *GQ* that watching *The Closer* felt like a betrayal: "I felt like I'd just been stabbed by someone I once admired and now he was demanding that I stop bleeding."

Later in the show, Mr. Chappelle offers rambling thoughts on feminism using a Webster's Dictionary definition, further exemplifying how limited his reading is. He makes a tired, tired joke about how he thought "feminist" meant "frumpy dyke"—and hey, I get it. If I were on his radar, he would consider me a frumpy dyke, or worse. (Some may consider that estimation accurate. Fortunately my wife doesn't.) Then in another of those rare moments of lucidity, Mr. Chappelle talks about mainstream feminism's historical racism. Just when you're thinking he is going to right the ship, he starts ranting incoherently about #MeToo. I couldn't tell you what his point was there.

This is a faded simulacrum of the once-great comedian, who now uses his significant platform to air grievances against the great many people he holds in contempt, while deftly avoiding any accountability. If we don't like his routine, the message is, we are the problem, not him.

This toxic performance crescendos when Mr. Chappelle shares a heartbreaking story about his trans friend Daphne Dorman, a comedian, who died by suicide—suggesting that if she was fine with his comedy, how dare anyone else have a problem? The story is bittersweet and sometimes funny, and then it is tragic, and the worst part is that Mr. Chappelle is clearly so very pleased with himself when he gets to the punchline. He thinks he has won an argument when really, he is exploiting the death of a friend. For comedy. Of course, we don't know Ms. Dorman at all; pushing back against this portrayal twists us in an impossible bind. Once more, Mr. Chappelle forestalls any resistance.

One of the strangest but most telling moments in *The Closer* is when Mr. Chappelle defends DaBaby, a rapper in the news for making pretty egregious homophobic remarks, and his fellow comedian Kevin Hart, who once lost an Oscars hosting gig for . . . making homophobic remarks. Both men faced professional consequences for their missteps, but neither was canceled: Mr. Hart remains one of the highest-paid comedians in the world. DaBaby has more than 43 million monthly listeners on Spotify.

At the end of his special, Mr. Chappelle admonishes the L.G.B.T.Q. community one last time, imploring us to leave his "people" alone. If it wasn't clear from his words, the snapshots of him with his famous pals in the closing credits of *The Closer* make it abundantly clear that Dave Chappelle's people aren't men or women or Black people. His people are wealthy celebrities, and he resents even the possibility of them facing consequences for their actions.

Originally published in the *New York Times*, October 13, 2021

Jada Pinkett Smith Shouldn't Have to Take a Joke. Neither Should You.

———

This is not a defense of Will Smith, who does not need me to defend him.

Instead, this is a defense of thin skin. It is a defense of boundaries and being human and enforcing one's limits. It is a repudiation of the incessant valorizing of taking a joke, having a sense of humor. It is a rejection of the expectation that we laugh off everything people want to say and do to us.

I think a lot about how we are constantly asked to make our skin ever thicker. Toughen yourself, we're told, whoever we are, whatever we've been through or are going through. Stop being so brittle and sensitive. Lighten up.

I'm not talking about constructive criticism or accountability but, rather, the intense scrutiny and unnecessary commentary people have to deal with when they challenge others' expectations one way or another.

Who is served by all this thick skin? Those who want to behave with impunity. If the targets of derision only had thicker skin, their aggressors could say or do as they please. If we all had the thickest of skins, no one would have to take responsibility for cruelties, big or small. It's an alluring idea to some, I suppose.

Thick skin comes up often in the context of comedy. Done well, comedy can offer witty, biting observations about human frailties. It can force us to look in the mirror and get honest with ourselves, to laugh and move forward. Done less well, it leaves its targets feeling raw, exposed and wounded—not mortally, but wounded.

It should go without saying that comedians are free to say what they please. Long live creative license and free speech. But it should be obvious that the targets of jokes and insults have every right to react and respond. There is a strange idea that there is nobility in tolerating or, better yet, enjoying humor that attacks who you are, what you do or how you look—that with free speech comes the obligation to turn the other cheek, rise above, laugh it all off. We often see this when comedians want to joke about race, sexual assault, gender violence or other issues that people experiencing them don't find terribly funny. If you can't laugh along, you are humorless. You're thin-skinned. You're a problem.

I've stopped aspiring to be thicker-skinned, and I no longer expect or admire it in others. Because sometimes, people can't take a joke. In some situations, yes, we're humorless. If our skin gets too thick, we won't feel anything at all, which is the most unreasonable of expectations. And we won't know we've been wronged or wounded until it's too late.

During the 2022 Oscars telecast, the comedian Chris Rock made a joke about Jada Pinkett Smith's closely shorn hair. "Jada, I love you," he said. "*G.I. Jane 2*, can't wait to see it." The audience, including Ms. Pinkett Smith's husband, Will Smith, laughed, but she rolled her eyes, and her face fell. Her thick skin cracked.

You probably know what happened moments later: Mr. Smith walked onto the Oscar stage, slapped Mr. Rock, returned to his seat and shouted that Mr. Rock should keep her name out of his mouth, including an obscenity for good measure. The laughs became titters, became stunned silence. It wasn't clear if this was a bit or real life, and then all was crystal clear: What we were experiencing was someone not taking the joke. We were seeing skin that had thinned to nothing.

Ms. Pinkett Smith has alopecia, a condition resulting in hair loss that disproportionately affects Black women. It was in poor taste for Mr. Rock to poke fun at her hair. He has reportedly said he did not know about her alopecia, but he probably at least knew that the joke would sting, since he produced the documentary *Good Hair*, about Black women and their often fraught relationships with their hair.

Ms. Pinkett Smith has spoken openly about her struggles with hair loss—which is difficult for anyone but especially hard in the sexist and image-conscious world of American celebrity, where women, especially, endure an endless litany of comments about their appearance, their sartorial choices, their relationships and anything else people can find to pick apart. Famous women such as Whitney Houston, Britney Spears,

Amanda Bynes, Janet Jackson, Monica Lewinsky and Meghan Markle have been pushed to the edge by such scrutiny and the unreasonable expectation that they thicken their skin to derision, disrespect, insults and jokes. Even if later, long after these public shamings, their treatment is re-examined and condemned, the measly acts of public contrition are too little, too late. The damage is done.

Violence is always wrong and solves very little. Mr. Smith could have made so many better choices that did not involve putting his hands on another person in front of the entire world. The Academy of Motion Picture Arts and Sciences opened an inquiry into the incident Monday afternoon, and Mr. Smith apologized to Mr. Rock and the world on Monday evening via Instagram.

Still, Mr. Smith most likely saw his wife's pain, and it's possible he was himself experiencing a moment of fragility, of thin skin. In his memoir, *Will*, the actor writes about the guilt he felt because, as a child, he could not protect his mother from his father's abuse. Mr. Rock's gibe was not in any way the same thing as domestic violence, but I can see how Mr. Smith might not have been able to take that joke, at his wife's expense, given the layers of context and public and private histories leading into that evening.

I am trying to hold space for all of those layers—Ms. Pinkett Smith's exhaustion with being a target of humor, Mr. Smith's series of bad decisions and Mr. Rock's trying to maintain his composure in the immediate aftermath of being a target of violence. Unfortunately, the incident has become something of a Rorschach test onto which people project their backgrounds, opinions and affinities. And what gets lost in the discourse is that, however disappointing the incident was, it was also a rare moment when a Black woman was publicly defended.

We also witnessed an example, last week, of a woman forced to wear incredibly thick skin as she was left largely undefended. During Judge Ketanji Brown Jackson's confirmation hearings for the Supreme Court, that distinguished jurist endured all manner of insult, racism and misogyny from Republican senators asking ludicrous questions that were really opportunities for grandstanding. Judge Jackson was applauded in many circles for her calm and composure.

For many Black women, it was a painful spectacle because we know what it is like to experience that kind of scrutiny, interrogation and disrespect in personal and professional settings. We know what it's like to withstand scrutiny without intervention. We understood that the only way forward for Judge Jackson was to remain composed, stoic, impervious. We also noted that other than Senator Cory Booker, Democrats failed to protect their president's nominee. The Senate Judiciary Committee apparently valued decorum over Judge Jackson's dignity.

Thick skin was also on display at the 2022 Critics Choice Awards, when the director Jane Campion made the bizarre claim that the tennis stars Venus and Serena Williams "do not play against the guys, like I have to." Whatever led to that strange, unnecessary and incorrect claim (Ms. Campion clearly had not planned her remarks, and she was caught up in the adrenaline of the moment), it forced the sisters to be thick-skinned, to take the joke made at their expense. As cameras panned over to them, the Williams sisters smiled quizzically and maintained their composure. In the aftermath—Ms. Campion apologized the next day—they were gracious beyond measure. Their thick skin held up, as it has in the face of myriad unspeakable insults and as it will many times to come. It shouldn't be this way.

Yes, these are all public figures. An imperviousness to criticism and ridicule is a necessity for celebrities or anyone in the public eye. But no matter how thick your skin is or with how much wealth, fame and power you are cosseted, being the butt of a joke isn't fun. Sometimes, it is intolerable. When you are constantly a target—of jokes, insults, incivility and worse—as most Black women are, the skin we've spent a lifetime thickening can come apart. We're only human, and so, too, are the people who love us.

Originally published in the *New York Times*, March 29, 2022

MINDING OTHER FOLKS' BUSINESS

Madonna's Spring Awakening

——

Madonna has no patience for bad wine. I learned this while sitting in a well-appointed living room at her New York City home, with Nina Simone playing softly in the background. I must tell you, Madonna's house smells amazing—something delicious, maybe roasted chicken, was cooking in a kitchen elsewhere in the manse, and there was a gentle fragrance in the air, jasmine, perhaps. While I waited for Madonna, her day-to-day manager, her publicist, and I chatted while reclining on gorgeous cream-colored furniture set upon the largest rug I'd ever seen, on top of immaculate black wood floors. On the wall behind me was a black-and-white photograph of a woman perched on the edge of a mussed bed, scantily clad, sucking on a gun, it's Helmut Newton's *Girl with Gun* photograph. Of course.

Madonna was late, but that didn't matter because she is Madonna. What is time, really? She was all apologies when she arrived, and we quickly got down to business. She was in the process of planning a fundraiser at Art Basel in Miami Beach, and like any perfectionist she wanted to taste the wines that could be served. She knelt on the floor as she considered various reds and whites and a rosé—or "summer water," as she called it. "Roxane," Madonna said. "You don't have to wear that dress tonight." That's when I exhaled. This was familiar territory. My name is part of a well-known song or two. I smiled and said, "No, I do not." At one point she asked me for my opinion on a particularly troublesome wine, handed me her glass, and swore she didn't have anything contagious. I believed her and took a sip. To be fair, the wine was terrible—it tasted like vinegar—and the year on the bottle said 2016, so it wasn't really wine yet. It was the suggestion of wine.

Madonna is very good at multitasking. While she was considering the wines, she held forth with me, and before long she was done with the bad wine. "Take the mediocre out of here," she tells Dustin, the strapping young man who served all the wine and apologized for its mediocrity even though that mediocrity was not his fault. "I'll go broke before I drink bad wine," she declared, and I was entirely in agreement. I wanted nothing more than for Madonna to offer her opinions on wine for the rest of the evening. Dustin promptly brought us the good wine, served in a crystal decanter. I drank it, and it was, indeed, good.

In the days leading up to our conversation, I kept wondering what I could possibly ask Madonna that she hadn't already been asked. She has been a figure in popular culture for more than 30 years. There was plenty I was curious about. I mean, I grew up on her music. As a good Catholic girl, I was obsessed with "Like a Prayer" and how she blended transubstantiation and eroticism. I listened to *The Immaculate Collection* nonstop. I coveted her book *Sex*, which came out just as I turned 18. I've been intrigued by her personal life. I've admired her stamina and artistic evolution. But I didn't want to ask silly questions. I didn't want to pry even though my job was, of course, to pry.

Over the course of an hour, we talked about a great many things, but we started with her upcoming movie project, *Loved*, an adaptation of Andrew Sean Greer's novel *The Impossible Lives of Greta Wells*. On her coffee table, there were binders filled with research for the project—potential settings, costumes, and so on. Madonna is thorough. In fact, she co-wrote the screenplay and will be directing the film. The novel follows the title character as she moves through time and negotiates three different lives she could have lived. The story also focuses on Greta's relationship with her gay twin brother, Felix, in those different lives. "It touches on a lot of really important topics I've always been invested in or championed—fighting for women's rights, gay rights, civil rights, always fighting for the underdog," Madonna says. "I've always felt oppressed. I know a lot of people would go, 'Oh, that's ridiculous for you to say that. You're a successful white, wealthy pop star,' but I've had the shit kicked out of me for my entire career, and a large part of that is because I'm female and also because I refuse to live a conventional life. I've created a very unconventional family. I have lovers who are three decades younger than me. This makes people very uncomfortable. I feel like everything I do makes people feel really uncomfortable. Why does this book appeal to me? Why did I want to adapt it into a screenplay? Because it touches me on so many levels and it deals with so many important topics. Right now, more than ever, it's an extremely timely story to tell."

ROXANE GAY: As an artist, whether it's in film or music or writing, do you think your work is political?

MADONNA: Completely.

RG: How so?

M: Because I'm political. I believe in freedom of expression, I don't believe in censorship. I believe in equal rights for all people. And I believe women should own their sexuality and sexual expression. I don't believe there's a certain age where you can't say and feel and be who you want to be. All you have to do is look at my career—from my *Sex* book to the songs I've written, kissing a black saint in my "Like a Prayer" video, the themes I explored on my *Erotica* album. As I get older and I get better at writing and expressing myself, then you get into my *American Life* era, and I start talking about politics and government and how fucked our country's politics are, and the illusion of fame and Hollywood and the beautiful people.

RG: It's been almost two weeks since the election. How did you feel in the wake of Donald Trump being elected president of the United States? Were you surprised?

M: On election night I was sitting at a table with my agent, who is also one of my very best friends, and we were truly praying. We were praying. She was on her computer. She's friends with someone who was working on Hillary [Clinton]'s campaign and was getting blow-by-blow reports, and at one point she was like, "It's not looking good." It was just like watching a horror show. And then she was reading from the Quran, and I was reading from the Zohar. We were doing everything: lighting candles, meditating, praying, offering our lives to God forever, if only. I went to sleep, and since that night, I wake up every morning and it's like when you break up with somebody who has really broken your heart. You wake up and for a second you're just you, and then you go, "Oh, the person I love more than anything has just broken my heart, and I'm devastated and I'm broken and I have nothing. I'm lost." That's how I feel every morning. I wake up and I go, "Wait a second. Donald Trump is the president. It's not a bad dream. It really happened." It's like being dumped by a lover and also being stuck in a nightmare.

RG: What do we do now?

M: I feel like I'm already doing it to a certain degree anyway and have been doing it. But I have to get way more vocal and become a little bit less mysterious. What I find really astonishing is how quiet everybody is in my industry. I mean, nobody in the entertainment business except for maybe a handful of people ever speak out about what's going on. Nobody takes a political stance or expresses an opinion.

RG: Why do you think that is?

M: They want to maintain a neutral position so they can maintain their popularity. I mean, if you have an opinion and people disagree with you, you might not get a job. You might be blacklisted. You might have fewer followers on Instagram. There are any number of things that would be detrimental to your career. Everyone's really afraid. Because it doesn't affect their daily life yet, no one's doing anything about it.

RG: How do you stay motivated after accomplishing so much?

M: Art keeps me alive. I've obviously been devastated or heartbroken all my life, since my mother's death. I've had so many challenges throughout my career, however successful people perceive me to be. The only way I've been able to survive the betrayal of lovers, family members, and society is to be able to create as an artist.

RG: What beyond art gives you that kind of drive to keep doing what you do?

M: Wanting to inspire people. Wanting to touch people's hearts to get them to look at life in a different way. To be a part of evolution, because, for me, it's either you're part of creation or you're part of destruction. It's inexplicable; it's like breathing, and I can't imagine not doing it. That is one of the arguments I would get into with my ex-husband, who used to say to me, "But why do you have to do this again? Why do you have to make another record? Why do you have to go on tour? Why do you have to make a movie?" And I'm like, "Why do I have to explain myself?" I feel like that's a very sexist thing to say.

RG: Yes. Because nobody asks men that.

M: Does somebody ask Steven Spielberg why he's still making movies? Hasn't he had enough success? Hasn't he made enough money? Hasn't he made a name for himself? Did somebody go to Pablo Picasso and say, "Okay, you're 80 years old. Haven't you painted enough paintings?" No. I'm so tired of that question. I just don't understand it. I'll stop doing everything that I do when I don't want to do it anymore. I'll stop when I run out of ideas. I'll stop when you fucking kill me. How about that?

RG: Do you still feel the same rush when you accomplish some new milestone? Or does it become commonplace?

M: No. When I made *secretprojectrevolution* [the 2013 short film that Madonna directed with the photographer Steven Klein, which dealt with the subject of artistic freedom], that was really exciting because it was a very political statement. And whenever I do my live shows, I feel artistically inspired and excited because I get to do and say a lot of things that I can't if I just make a record. A lot of times it's the only way people are going to hear my music because you don't get to have your music played on Top 40 if you're above the age of 35. It's always exciting for me to perform. I'm liking the idea more and more of just standing up with a microphone and talking. I like talking; I like playing with the audience. That's what I've started to do with *Tears of a Clown* [Madonna's most recent stage show, which combines music and storytelling]. I'm obsessed with clowns and what they represent and the idea that clowns are supposed to make you laugh, but inevitably they're hiding something. That's how I look at my life. I keep telling Amy Schumer and Dave Chappelle and Chris Rock that I'm going to do stand-up and they'd better watch out. I'm coming. I'm coming right behind them.

RG: What are you reading right now?

M: I'm reading several books. I cheat on my books a lot, which is not a good thing because it's good to stick with one book and get to the end of it, but I'm a book philanderer. I'm reading *The Dovekeepers*, by Alice Hoffman, and before that I was reading *All the Light We Cannot See*, by Anthony Doerr. I was also reading Isak Dinesen's *Out of Africa*, even though it's not a new book.

RG: My editor at *Harper's Bazaar* told me that you read an excerpt from *The Beautiful and Damned* for a video that you did for the magazine. I was curious as to why you chose that book.

M: I worship F. Scott Fitzgerald and I love his writing, and I felt like what we were shooting, that somehow there was some kind of connection to his stories and the decadence of that time, but also to the lack of expression. Or the inability of women to express themselves really. They were beautiful and damned.

RG: I have one last question: What do you like most about the art that you make?

M: I think it depends on what I'm making. I like pushing the envelope. But I don't like to do it just for the sake of doing it. I don't like to be provocative for the sake of being provocative. I like to be provocative. I like to make people think. I like to touch people's hearts. And if I can do all three of those things in one fell swoop, then I feel like I've really accomplished something.

Originally published in *Harper's Bazaar*, January 10, 2017

Charlie, Come In

———

In person, Charlie Hunnam is brutally handsome and pensive—a chiseled face and piercing blue eyes. He wears a dark blue cable knit sweater over a white T-shirt and jeans and it feels like he chose this outfit earnestly. We meet at Greenblatt's Deli in West Hollywood, and sit across from each other in the upstairs dining area. At a table just behind us, two men are talking, one so loudly it's clear he wants everyone within earshot to know he is a man with grand ambitions. He knows people in the business and because we're in Hollywood I can only assume that "the business" to which he refers is show business.

Hunnam, on the other hand, does nothing to draw attention. As a reasonably successful actor and incredibly handsome man, he doesn't need more notice than he already gets. He carries himself with the confidence of someone who knows just how attractive and charming he is. Throughout our conversation, he is so suave and engaged that I decide he's either being genuine or he's an even better actor than I already thought him to be. The accent doesn't hurt, either.

Certainly, we cover the expected subjects—the last book he really enjoyed (*The Sisters Brothers* by Patrick deWitt), what he's been cooking (shakshuka, which we decide is the new frittata), and the film he's been intrigued with lately (*Moonlight*, because it showed real restraint and respect for the audience). I learn he practices jujitsu and watches MMA fighting and really is tired of answering questions about why he backed out of the *Fifty Shades of Grey* franchise. (Fortunately, I Googled it prior to our conversation.)

In FX's *Sons of Anarchy*, which ran from 2008 to 2014, Hunnam played Jax Teller. As the brash leader of a motorcycle gang with something of a heart of gold, Teller tried to understand his father's legacy while raising a family, loving a woman not entirely thrilled with his gang activities, and dealing with a mother who was a force of nature. There was a lot on Teller's shoulders, and Hunnam carried that burden well. He also looked incredible in a distressed leather jacket, white T-shirt, and jeans. Even three years later, the role still affects him. "[After the show ended] it was a painful process of what felt like real mourning, of grieving to extricate him from my life," he says. "I became very conscious of what a giant impact it had on me playing that guy—being with him for so long inside of me."

Now that the role he's best known for is behind him, Hunnam is thinking carefully about the career he wants to build for himself. He wants to, in his words, "change people's perception of what I'm capable of." This moment of insight intrigues me so I ask Hunnam how he thinks he's perceived. He is quiet as he considers how to respond. Like I said—Hunnam is very pensive. He doesn't speak out of turn. He says, "I try not to think about that too much because I'm just trying to shape my own perception of myself and feel confident in my own identity. But people recognize I have some real ability and have demonstrated that. There will probably be some people that relegate me to still being sort of a pretty boy."

And there it is. It's refreshing to be able to talk openly about his obvious physical beauty. "You're seen as an attractive man, a sex symbol. Does that ever frustrate you or is it just collateral damage?" I ask. Hunnam responds with a great deal of self-awareness. "It's both collateral damage and a huge opportunity. I mean, it's a visual medium and it makes it a lot easier to get roles if you're a little easier on the eyes. But the reality is you get on set and every scene is a challenge to make work."

Hunnam is certainly finding scenes to make work with the roles he is choosing these days. In May's *King Arthur*, Charlie Hunnam takes on Guy Ritchie's interpretation of Arthurian legend. Hunnam stands out as a different kind of Arthur from the one we've come to expect. His Arthur is arrogant and reluctant, orphaned, hardened by a life on the streets and being raised by women in a brothel. It was this new take on Arthur that intrigued Hunnam, playing a "rough and ready street kid who had this call, this duty, this destiny presented to him who was not interested at all in pursuing it." More than that, though, Hunnam wanted to work with Guy Ritchie with whom he had, "a veritable love fest," when they first met. When I remarked that their first meeting sounded so romantic, Hunnam drily replies, "I know, right? It was love at first sight."

Hunnam also stars in this month's *The Lost City of Z*, based on a true story of British explorer Percival Fawcett, who, in the early 1900s was willing to sacrifice nearly everything, including his family, while searching for a fabled city in the Amazon. On the surface, it might be difficult to find the connective tissue between Hunnam's roles but in several, there are nuanced, fraught, and powerful relationships between fathers and sons. Hunnam, who cites his connection with his own father as extremely important to him, says he gravitates to such roles because, "the human condition through the prism of the male journey is something I'm interested in, which is very much I think connected, for most men, with their relationship with their father." I want to push further, ask about Hunnam's relationship with his father but as he sits, shoulders squared, he does not give the impression that he wants to open up too much.

He is, however, willing to open up about how he loves his work. "Life makes the most sense to me when I'm acting," he says. "Being engaged in the process of telling a story from beginning to end completely, totally nourishes me." Hunnam can get so absorbed in the process it's often difficult to come back to his real life. "It's brutal. Re-integration is a motherfucker. I keep thinking it'll get easier, but it doesn't. It's really hard for my girlfriend . . . there's all this expectation and longing and hope for what that reunion's gonna be. For me it's always a process of trying desperately to get back to center so I can be that person for her."

That reintegration is, in part, a challenge because Hunnam loves to immerse himself in his roles. "One of the great things about the film business is you do get to go and live a million different lives and experience different cultures and different ways of life," he says, though makes it clear he didn't get so immersed, while preparing for *Sons of Anarchy*, that he became a criminal. "No?" I ask. We laugh and finally, he admits, "Well, occasionally," revealing, once again, his dry wit that always appears if you just wait for it.

When, just before Christmas of last year, he wrapped his next film *Papillon* (a remake of the 1973 prison escape drama with Hunnam in the Steve McQueen role), Hunnam's girlfriend gave him an ultimatum—do whatever you need to do, but don't come home until you're ready to see me. Hunnam took a trip back to England first to decompress before returning home to LA to his girlfriend, which gave him time to reflect on "how fragile our connection is to anything." Our conversation is peppered with these heady asides and he admits, "I struggled through my childhood as a bit of a weird existential kid just [he laughs here] growing up into a weird existential adult. I was constantly preoccupied with trying to understand what it all meant . . ."

It was in books and, ultimately, acting that Hunnam found at least some solace. "Working in film felt like a valid and exciting use of time and a way to spend it in a way that might reduce a little bit of that existential crisis, you know? And I still feel that way. It's not by any means that I think it's important and writ large in a global sense, but it's very, very important to me."

Originally published in *InStyle* magazine, April 2017

Nicki Minaj, Always in Control

The day I wait in the hotel lobby of the Ritz-Carlton in Battery Park City to meet Nicki Minaj is the start of New York Fashion Week. I am early, and I watch as stylists push an overfull rack of designer clothes out of the elevator. I later learn they are from Alexander Wang, and are dressing Minaj for the designer's show.

In the hall entrance of her suite, there is another rack bulging with outfits. Deeper into the suite, a lean and lanky hairdresser is combing a very long platinum-blond wig. He is wearing a fascinating outfit that includes black leather pants, a description that is doing those pants a great disservice because they are fabulous. He brushes the wig so carefully, so lovingly, that for a moment, I want to be that wig. A few feet away from his gentle ministrations, a makeup artist is organizing makeup and various brushes and other tools of the trade. Everyone speaks in hushed murmurs.

When Minaj enters, from an adjacent chamber, she is a petite wonder, wearing a fluffy white bathrobe, her face naked. After we greet each other with a light handshake, she asks if I mind if she gets her eyes lined. She isn't really asking, nor do I object. She sits in the makeup chair, and the artist begins applying Minaj's trademark black eyeliner with its exaggerated cat's eye flair.

I am stunned by the number of people Minaj has at her service. I also meet her day-to-day manager and personal assistant—who are two different people—and her stylist. In the hall just outside the suite wait a tailor and a couple of other people eager for Minaj's time. She is the center of gravity for a great many professionals, and she wears that responsibility well.

When her eyes are done, Minaj sits on the adjacent couch, arranging her robe to her liking. There is regality in how she sits. That she is wearing a bathrobe is utterly inconsequential. A queen is a queen regardless. A stylist begins presenting her with options for the two events she will attend later that evening—a dinner party and a book launch. She is shown a clingy, see-through dress with a long train, a gorgeously patterned black-and-white leather Balmain gown and a couple of other options. I marvel at the sublime luxury of basically having a human closet.

Finally, Minaj turns to me, offering her full attention, and says, "You want us to start?" as if, this whole time, we've been waiting on me. I want to applaud with appreciation. Yasssss, queen, as they say.

Throughout her career, Minaj has demonstrated a discipline and intelligence that is rare among other pop stars of her generation. She has what she describes to me as "the X-factor, which is just the thing you can't put into words." Onika Tanya Maraj was born in Saint James, Trinidad and Tobago, in 1982, and immigrated to Queens, New York, with her family at the age of 5. She began her music career singing with various rappers and working odd jobs. When she waitressed, she wrote lyrics constantly on the notepad she used to take orders. There is genuine pleasure in her voice as she reminisces about this. "I would take people's order and then a rap might come to me just by what they're wearing or what they said or did, and I would go in the kitchen and write it down, put it in the back of my little thing or my apron, and by the time I was done I would have all of these sheets of paper thrown around everywhere with raps."

Since then, her career has been a checklist of milestones. In 2009, she was the first woman artist signed to Young Money, the label founded by Lil Wayne. Three mixtapes and three studio albums—*Pink Friday* in 2010, *Pink Friday: Roman Reloaded* in 2012 and *The Pink Print* in 2014—followed, and in March 2017, Minaj surpassed Aretha Franklin for the most appearances (76) by a woman on the Billboard Hot 100, a record Franklin had held for almost 40 years. She is the rare hip-hop artist who has successfully and sustainably crossed over into pop music. Minaj, M.I.A. and Madonna performed their single, "Give Me All Your Luvin," at the 2012 Super Bowl. Days later she performed solo at the Grammy

Awards. Her dance song "Starships" went platinum six times over. She even collaborated with Ariana Grande on 2016's song "Side to Side," and while the pairing was unexpected given Grande's previously wholesome image, the song went triple platinum. Minaj does not temper her swagger or sexuality. Sometimes, when I am daydreaming, I marvel at the phrases "dick bicycle" and "If you wanna ménage I got a tricycle" from "Side to Side," which are so damn clever and funny and vulgar but also accurate as hell for a song Grande once described as being "about riding leading to soreness."

Minaj's music is characterized by urgent lyrics, spitting in a range of voices and accents. Her rhymes range from bold and aggressive, to coquettish, to wanton and sultry, with a soupçon of women's empowerment. The pace of her rapping is often breathless but her diction is impeccable. There is wit and sly humor in her work. Take the 2014 single "Only" where Minaj raps, "My man full, he just ate, I don't duck nobody but tape / Yeah, that was a setup for a punch line on duct tape." She quite simply broadened the definition of hip-hop, making it more joyful, energetic and robust.

Nicki Minaj is also coming down with a cold. Yes, I know what I did there, but it also happens to be true. When we meet, she has just missed a rehearsal for an upcoming performance at Philipp Plein's runway show because of the encroaching sickness, and is medicating herself with Theraflu, NyQuil and rest. Having to fly to New York did not help. Minaj was in Miami (where she now spends most of her time) working on her fourth studio album, the title of which is, for now, a well-kept secret but is "super, super iconic."

That studio time begot the beginnings of her cold—the air-conditioning always blasting, shutting off, blasting again—a vicious cycle of climate control. Minaj ended up spending two nights in the studio because it was one of those sessions where she was able to "write and record and listen back and have excitement in all three of those stages."

It took a long time to get to that place, Minaj tells me, and now, "sonically, I know what the album's about to sound like. I know what this album is gonna mean to my fans. This album is everything in my life coming full circle and me being truly, genuinely happy. It feels almost like a celebration. The last album, *The Pink Print*, was almost like my diary, closing the chapter on certain things and not knowing if I was happy or sad about beginning new chapters. I was really writing about feeling unsure. Now, I can tell you guys what happened for the last two years of my life. I know who I am. I am getting Nicki Minaj figured out with this album and I'm loving her."

Minaj's public image and personas are carefully curated. The tabloids have assiduously tracked her professional and personal lives and I restrain myself from asking about her ex Safaree Samuels, who appears on *Love & Hip Hop*, a reality television series about the music industry, and if she would ever give Drake a shot. (I restrain myself greatly.) I don't know that anyone but her inner circle knows who Nicki Minaj really is.

This elusiveness is compounded by her fascinating catalog of performative alter egos, including Harajuku Barbie (a fashionista obsessed with pink and Minaj's longest-running persona), Nicki Teresa (known as "The Healer") and the sexually explicit Nicki Lewinsky—there is even a male persona, Roman Zolanski, a slightly exaggerated version of Minaj herself. She has a vocal range that can go from a high-pitched twittering to a growl in a few bars. In both music and regular conversation, she enjoys playing with accents, offering up valley girl–speak or island patois. During our time together, she switched to a British accent a couple of times and then effortlessly returned to her normal voice, a slightly affectless cadence that recalls her Queens upbringing. In public, she often wears dramatic makeup, dramatic outfits and a rainbow of dramatic wigs, which is to say she performs both on- and offstage. There is no point during our conversation where Minaj demonstrates anything but absolute self-awareness. She pauses briefly before she answers my questions, as if calculating every possible outcome to everything she says. By the end of the interview, I am impressed by her fierce intelligence.

But she's at her most animated and unguarded when she's talking about music, and she thinks about music in deep and complex ways. She has strong opinions on what's necessary to make a great rapper: "Do you sound intelligent? Does your flow switch up? Are you in command of the beat? I listen for things like that." Jay-Z, Lil Wayne, Foxy Brown—"Those are the three I keep in my head when I'm writing because they've influenced me so much," she says. "I feel like I'm a part of all of them."

I'm curious about whom Minaj thinks she's influenced herself. She tells me that around two years ago, Kanye West said to her, "'Every girl I hear rap, I can hear Nicki in her rap.' I didn't ask him who, but that was such a great compliment. Because sometimes you think you're the only one that can hear those types of things."

It feels like Minaj is on the verge of another big moment in her career, and she knows it. "This is definitely the most inspired and free and excited I've been since I started releasing albums through a label," she says. She is also deeply reflective about her evolution as an artist. I ask if the transition from making mixtapes to studio albums compromises the joy of creation and she answers, "Yeah, because . . . artists do it to themselves. I'm not going to blame a label. You just overthink. When you're doing your own little thing, you feel like, I can be myself, I can be crazy. When you start working with a record company, you start thinking you need a bigger sound. I wanted to get back to the place where I wasn't second-guessing things so much. Sometimes simple is O.K."

I ask her what it has taken to get to this place of newfound confidence and trusting her instincts. "I believe in my gift wholeheartedly," she says. But this self-assurance was not easy to come by. "Sometimes I wake up and say, 'I don't know if I can do this anymore,' you know? I've had those times. I've had those years where I'm just like, 'Am I good enough?'" But she believes in her "ability to withstand what would break the normal girl," she says.

At this point in her career, Minaj is able to reconcile, somewhat, her struggles. "I kind of love that I've had to go through so many hurdles to get where I am because I feel like I deserve it." She is frank about what she has been up against. "I had so much going against me in the beginning: being black, being a woman, being a female rapper. No matter how many times I get on a track with everyone's favorite M.C. and hold my own, the culture never seems to want to give me my props as an M.C., as a lyricist, as a writer. I got to prove myself a hundred times, whereas the guys that came in around the same time as I did, they were given the titles so much quicker without anybody second-guessing."

I am struck by these words because I've heard similar sentiments from other successful women in male-dominated industries—this sense that their endurance and perseverance contribute to their greatness. But, above all, Minaj has persevered because she is always in control of her craft. Neither her work nor her success are accidental. When we finish talking and I make my exit, there are more people in the hallway, waiting for their time with her. She remains in command of the beat.

Originally published in the *New York Times*, October 16, 2017

Melina Matsoukas's Fearless Vision

How does a contemporary filmmaker make entertaining black art that also responds to the world we live in? I am preoccupied with this question as I sit down with director Melina Matsoukas. Just before our conversation, I'd watched an early screening of her first feature film. I was transfixed. As the final credits rolled, I sobbed—I was utterly wrecked. *Queen & Slim*, a romantic thriller starring Jodie Turner-Smith and Daniel Kaluuya in the title roles, is by far the blackest movie I've ever seen. As engrossing as it is political, the movie is an unequivocal rejoinder to the world we live in, where police brutality is a pervasive and omnipresent reality, and where a great many people still need to be reminded that black lives matter.

I am meeting Matsoukas in a conference room at The Wing in West Hollywood. For some reason, the overhead lights aren't working. A candle flickers on the table as sunlight streams through a glass wall separating us from the rest of the space. Under different circumstances, the setting might seem romantic. Matsoukas, 38, is composed and confident. The longer we talk, the more ebullient she becomes and the more she warms to discussing her artistic ambitions.

"I would like to make history. I want to be an auteur," she says, laughing, but entirely serious. "And I want to make opportunities for other filmmakers and other people of color to create art and really give them a platform to speak. If I can do that, that's my greatest satisfaction."

Although she came to prominence directing music videos, Matsoukas sees her work in all genres of film as her greatest weapon, the one with which she can join the fight and try to change the world. "I try to walk the line between making a statement and trying to create change by creating a dialogue and having people think about what they're seeing," she says.

"The goal is always change and entertainment. If I can do both at the same time, that's my best victory.

"It's always first in the material," she adds. "I try to tell a great story that's beautiful and entertaining. Showing the struggle but also the beauty. You can be political by showing black people on-screen, because we don't get to see ourselves that much. Just by being, we are."

Matsoukas thinks carefully about how to balance artistic and political ambitions, and she comes by those instincts by way of her parents, who were both "very politically active in the '70s, very leftist," she says. "We were brought up to say something and to be part of the struggle."

Born in the Bronx in 1981 to a father who was a carpenter and a mother who was a professor of education, Matsoukas was introduced to photography by her dad. In high school, she began taking classes and would travel across the city and to the Jersey shore, shooting whatever caught her eye, honing her sense of composition, "trying to make beautiful imagery." In college at NYU, she majored in math, but "then I took Calculus II, and I decided I hated math," she says, soon transitioning from photography to film because she felt it was "elevating that as a language."

Her first film, she says, was "a really bad film" about how women are viewed in New York's Meatpacking District. "It made me fall in love with the medium," she says of the experience. "And I burned the film." No copies of that first work exist, but she began to create other films, continued taking classes and developed both her taste and her aesthetic. Sixteen years ago, she came to Los Angeles to pursue graduate studies at her mother's urging because, she told her, as a black woman she couldn't afford to not have a graduate degree (she earned hers from the American Film Institute in 2005).

Matsoukas's first professional music video after finishing grad school—2006's "Dem Girls" by Red Handed, featuring Scooby and Paul Wall—is raw but compelling. The camera draws the eye exactly where the director wants it to go. Over the next decade, she established herself as a master of the form, a prolific director with talent and imagination as ferocious as her ambition, and worked with some of the biggest musical artists in the world, including Jennifer Lopez, Ludacris, Alicia Keys, Lady Gaga, Katy Perry, Solange, Rihanna and her best-known collaborator, Beyoncé.

Like Matsoukas, I was part of the MTV generation, still a child when the network began airing music videos in the early '80s. At first, the world didn't quite know what to make of the form. Were videos a marketing tool? A creative endeavor? Some hybrid of the two? Before long, the answers to those questions did not seem to matter. Music videos made artists more accessible to their fans. They brought dimensionality to music and became not only their own genre but a showcase for directors to express their craft in short form.

Matsoukas's video work reflects all the trappings of hip-hop videos—beautiful women scantily clad, their skin dewy and clear, flashy cars, gold chains, masculine swagger and braggadocio—but amid these trappings Matsoukas always articulates her aesthetic: brightly saturated color, vivid imagery, the artist at the center of the frame always establishing a video's center of gravity. Black people and black communities are shot with profound respect. Her directorial style is confident. She is unafraid of revealing her influences. She tends toward the referential.

For a video like "Sensual Seduction," by Snoop Dogg, she uses visual wit and a throwback aesthetic. Rihanna's "Rude Boy" references dance-hall culture, the art of Warhol and Basquiat and more. In Beyoncé's "Pretty Hurts," Matsoukas crafts a powerful statement on the price women pay when trying to conform to rigid standards of beauty. She can be just as visionary interpreting the ethos of a brand in her commercial work. In "Change Lanes," for Lexus, her camerawork is frenetic, the imagery stark yet vivid. Her "Equality" video for Nike, starring some of the brand's biggest stars—LeBron James, Serena Williams, Megan Rapinoe—is more a short film than a commercial, shot mostly in Cleveland with black-and-white, unadorned imagery and sweeping tracking shots.

The narrative sophistication of her work expanded exponentially over the years, eventually landing her work as a TV director, including for several episodes of HBO's *Insecure* and two episodes of Netflix's *Master of None*. But it was 2016's "Formation," part of Beyoncé's groundbreaking visual album *Lemonade* and the culmination of years of innovative music videos, that propelled her into a new creative echelon and opened up more lucrative opportunities.

In conceptualizing "Formation," Matsoukas drew, as she does in all her work, from a broad and eclectic range of source material—everything from Toni Morrison to the film *Daughters of the Dust*. The resulting video transcends the genre: a soulful and artistic meditation on the triumphs and tragedies of blackness, set to a killer beat. "Formation" was shot over four days and, after winning a Grand Prix for Excellence in Music Video at the 2016 Cannes Lions Awards, became a resounding declaration: Matsoukas was ready to make the challenging and often fraught transition from short to long form.

Matsoukas first came to *Queen & Slim* through actor-writer-director-producer Lena Waithe, who co-wrote the critically acclaimed "Thanksgiving" episode Matsoukas directed for *Master of None*. Waithe said she had a project for her, and though Matsoukas doesn't like to make professional decisions based on personal relationships, she read the screenplay and knew she had found the right feature film to direct.

"I was looking for something that spoke to me," she says. "I was looking for something I felt was political in a way that had something to say, that was strong and unique and powerful."

Queen & Slim, which comes out November 27, is an astonishing debut, every frame resonating with Matsoukas's distinct point of view. The screenplay, written by Waithe, is intricately drawn and lyrical. Reviewers will be tempted to compare *Queen & Slim* to *Bonnie and Clyde*, but the similarities between the two are skin deep. Queen and Slim go on the run to save themselves from becoming statistics, not because of any inherent penchant for criminality. The artistry of the movie and the harrowing political reality it dramatizes resist facile comparisons. It stands unto itself.

A page in Claudia Rankine's *Citizen*, her incisive book of cultural criticism published in 2014, offers a remembrance of black people who have been murdered, most of them by police. In Memory of Jordan Russell Davis, Rankine writes. In Memory of Eric Garner. In Memory of John Crawford. In Memory of Michael Brown. In Memory of Laquan McDonald. In Memory of Akai Gurley. With each new printing, more names are added to the page, a haunting and ever-growing memorial. It is within this context that *Queen & Slim* opens. A young black couple meet at a diner for a first date. Afterward, they are driving home, sharing that awkward energy of a relationship that will never be, when they are pulled over by a white police officer. Things escalate in ways that will be all too familiar to a black audience. From there, the tension continues to build and build inexorably. I spent the rest of the movie holding my breath, hoping that somehow a new narrative for blackness could be written.

The film reflects the diversity of black America, from Slim's devout and tightknit Cleveland family to Queen's veteran uncle in New Orleans. Matsoukas lights black people in the glory of their black skin. One of the most refreshing aspects of the film is that white people are held to the margins. They have few speaking roles. The movie makes clear that this story is not about them.

Despite the inherent tensions of Queen and Slim fighting for their lives, the film is also a love story. The farther south they go, the more Queen and Slim warm to each other. "I wanted to have two dark-skinned people love each other and see the beauty in that," Matsoukas says. "I wanted young girls to see themselves in Queen and know she was stunning."

Verisimilitude was important to Matsoukas because, as she notes, "I like authentic portrayals of life and finding the beauty in that." To find as much beauty as she could, Matsoukas shot the entire movie on location; no sets were built. The South, from the humid languor of New Orleans to a back-road juke joint to the balmy ease of Florida, is as much a character in the film as any of the leading roles.

"I wanted the narrative to go from feeling very cool to warming up as their relationship warms up, visually paralleling what they're going through," she says. "And I always loved the idea that it's kind of the reverse slave-escape narrative. They're going south instead of north." Setting was not the only consideration. She shot the driving scenes in real cars so the actors could "feel the road to inform their performances."

The movie's visual language is also carefully orchestrated. In one scene, as Queen and Slim drive along a rural highway, the camera focuses on a crucifix hanging from the rearview mirror. This is juxtaposed with crosses of telephone poles along the roadside. It is a profoundly layered image. In the essay "Time and Distance Overcome," Eula Biss writes that telephone poles "became convenient as gallows, because they were tall and straight, with a crossbar, and because they stood in public spaces. And it was only coincidence that the telephone pole so closely resembled a crucifix." A couple is on the run from police, searching for faith in something, anything, flanked by quotidian markers of time and space once used across the South to terrorize black people into submission.

When she's scouting locations or developing the visual language for a project, Matsoukas always assembles collections of imagery. She loves having creative options to shape her work. And for *Queen & Slim*, she was inspired by a wide range—the funerals of Nipsey Hussle, Biggie Smalls and Fela Kuti, street art, the film *Belly*, the architecture of New Orleans, bounce music, the *Love Jones* soundtrack and Brother Vellies shoes.

Matsoukas also pays close attention to the spaces she inhabits. She remembered a location she found two years earlier, while scouting for a Nike commercial in the historically black Cleveland neighborhood of St. Clair–Superior. "There was this street we didn't shoot on," she says, "but I always wanted to go back. While we were scouting, maybe six cars had been pulled over by cops in a half hour. One of the cars that's pulled over when we were scouting, maybe two blocks from where we actually shot, was a white Accord. My production designer shot it, and we were like, 'That's Slim's car. That's it right there.'"

All of these details add up in a way that helps her convey the film's visual ethos. "You can read that in the emotion of an actor or a piece of clothing or the paint on the wall or the scratch on the floor," she says. "All of those things are telling you a story that you're not always aware of but are important to the narrative."

On set, Matsoukas is very communicative, even when she shouldn't be, a habit she developed while directing music videos where, because no sound was recorded, she was able to talk an artist through a performance. On a film or television set, "I can't speak," she says, "although I do, and my editor's always taking my voice out. I'm a New Yorker."

Daniel Kaluuya, in referencing Matsoukas's skill as a director, singles out "a lovely touch she added" to one of the film's early scenes: Slim pauses to say a prayer before he and Queen start to eat, a gesture that conveys so much about his character with so little. "She exists in the real world," Kaluuya says. "She's done all the hours and all the work a director of her ability would have done, but she still lives in the real world." It was her growth during filming that impressed Kaluuya most. "When you watch *Queen & Slim*, you're like, 'Who the hell is this?'" he says. "Why hadn't a person like this been allowed to create these images?"

Jodie Turner-Smith, Kaluuya's co-star, was initially drawn to the project because "the writing was so rich and incredibly powerful and beautiful. I loved what the story was about, who Queen was. It's a celebration of black beauty and black culture and black love," she says. Turner-Smith trusted Matsoukas because she has "a very specific vision. She's very particular about her ideas and where she's coming from, and she really brings you into her process and shows you visually and aesthetically where she is coming from. Then she lets you infuse your own interpretation."

Matsoukas herself is well aware of the value she brings to her work. "I'm not asking anymore. Now I get to demand what I know I'm worth," she says. "I feel like our culture has taken from us so much; it's our biggest commodity, and we're not paid for that. So now I'm like, 'OK, I know what I'm worth and I know what my stories are worth, and if we can't do it amongst ourselves, you're going to have to pay.'"

Like many ambitious people, Matsoukas is always moving the goal post. And she is hard on herself. "I'm not the easiest person to work with, because I have a very specific vision and that doesn't always translate with everyone." She admits to being something of a control freak because, she says, "I like consistency. Every detail is thought out. Nothing is by accident. And I want to make sure that translates on-screen or wherever you're seeing it. If I put in the work, I expect it to end up in the final product." She's aware of the limitations of this approach and that she can be a perfectionist—to a fault, she says. When *Queen & Slim* went into post-production, the editing room became "the room of what could have been, what should have been."

An accomplished career comes at a price. For Matsoukas, the art of filmmaking—managing the cast and crew and production challenges and contending with the gravity of the subject matter—is all-consuming. While on location in Cleveland, the crew shot scenes during a polar vortex and subzero temperatures. Matsoukas has to move to wherever she is working for months at a time, which can be hard on personal relationships. She hopes to head off to Jamaica soon, for research and pre-production as she develops Marlon James's *A Brief History of Seven Killings* into a Netflix series, and then to Nigeria for a film about Fela Kuti, also in development. When she returns to Los Angeles, the transitions can be rocky, which was especially the case after shooting *Queen & Slim.*

"I remember coming back and I was like, 'I feel like I just did a bid.' It took me two, three weeks to feel like a real person again. It was hard. Every day was a struggle," she says. She is circumspect about her private life because, she says, "My ambition is not for me to be seen. It's that my work speaks to people and creates a dialogue and brings about change."

Even so, toward the end of our conversation, she opens up about her desire to start a family, another project in development. She's clear about one thing, though. "I will not ever be married. I know what love is, and I have that," she says of her relationship with someone she refers to throughout our conversation only as "my man."

When we discuss the directors she admires most, Matsoukas shares her love for Hype Williams and his stylized aesthetic, and Spike Lee, especially the movie *Do the Right Thing* and how it had a "strong political, racial backdrop" while speaking to contemporary issues. She extols the virtues of Mira Nair's work and how it "gives you this window into a culture." She talks about Barry Jenkins and Pedro Almodóvar and Julie Dash.

Then she says she loves Wes Anderson. I am surprised and can't hide it. I admit to having a chip on my shoulder because white directors are able to make movies that are so specific while directors of color are expected to make art that is universal.

"I'd like to see a woman have that very specific point of view," I say.

Without missing a beat, Matsoukas says, "That might be me."

Originally published in the *Wall Street Journal*, October 30, 2019

Janelle Monáe's Afrofuture

Two days before the 2019 Grammys, much to the chagrin of her team, Janelle Monáe went skydiving. Her album *Dirty Computer* was nominated for Album of the Year, she was scheduled to perform, and still she and some adventurous friends drove two hours outside Los Angeles on a clear and sunny afternoon. They watched a training video about the inherent risks of throwing yourself from a plane with only a parachute to bring you safely back to earth. As Monáe waited at 14,000 feet, preparing to dive into the great wide blue below her, she was ready. If she died, she thought, at least she would die doing what she wanted. She stared down and marveled at how small the world seemed—tiny houses, tiny cars, tiny people—and in that moment, she felt fearless.

There was something cathartic about that jump, the exhilaration of flying through the air and the simple satisfaction of realizing she had the courage to make that leap. It was the beginning of what would become a year of introspection and evolution for Monáe. "I wanted to skydive into different parts of my life," she said when we met for dinner in L.A. We were ensconced in a booth in a darkened corner of a private club in West Hollywood where celebrities and other assorted fancy people have to put stickers over their camera lenses before they gather to eat and drink and see and be seen. It's a silly gesture, because what can be applied can just as easily be unpeeled, but, like airport security, I suppose, it allows members to feel like their privacy is safe.

Monáe was dressed sharply in a matching three-piece suit—black-and-gray pinstripes, a cream-colored silk shirt with wide cuffs, a wide-brimmed black hat, two different earrings, and high-heeled cream booties. Her hair was long, wrapped in a thick braid cascading down her back. As we walked to our table, in a city where a great many people are powerful and gorgeous, so much so that they become unremarkable, she turned heads. She is known for always sporting a different look—a red tuxedo, a thickly brocaded black-and-white dress with a wide skirt, braided buns on each side of her head, a pompadour, her hair slicked close to her scalp. She has absolutely flawless skin, and I often want to ask her about her skin-care regimen, but I never do because I only use water and shower soap and Jergens lotion. There's no use pretending I would ever expend the energy to do anything more rigorous than that.

We began our conversation talking about the stories Monáe wants to tell—stories that are bold, honest, ones that can shape the culture and have a specific point of view. In many ways, at least to me, Monáe was describing her own body of work. She is ever evolving, experimenting with her aesthetic and her sound, refusing to limit herself professionally or personally. She is daringly herself in an industry that often demands conformity and punishes originality. She actually looks like she is having fun. And still there is an interesting tension in her work: She creates music that allows people to feel seen while maintaining firm boundaries around how much of her truest self we will ever really see.

Janelle Monáe Robinson was born on December 1, 1985, in Kansas City, Kansas, where she nurtured a desire to perform, as did her large, matriarchal family. She participated in talent shows and high-school musicals to hone the ambition that, she says, was in her DNA. Monáe's mom and grandmother instilled a strong work ethic in her, perhaps too strong. When she looked back at her 2019 calendar, she realized she had gone from project to project to project and was emotionally spent. She began to recount everything she did last year; even as a workaholic myself, I found it exhausting. After the Grammys, she performed at Coachella, then she filmed *Antebellum* and then another movie, then she was in preproduction for a television show, and somewhere in there she went on tour, and then the show was in actual production.

New artists are often forced to say yes until they have the power to say no, to compromise their integrity until they have the power not to. Monáe, however, is different. "At the beginning of my career, I always said no," she said. "'Nope, nope, nope.' That was my secret weapon. Once I started to eliminate the things that didn't feel in line with where I was trying to go, and that could potentially pigeonhole me from having that freedom as an artist, it was very helpful." That selective approach to curating her early career led to the bounty Monáe is currently experiencing. She so distinctly defined who she was that the industry took notice and, in its way, bent to her creative will.

As she began to assert herself, Monáe was drawn to the idea of the android—someone who is part human, part robot—in order, she now reflected, to protect herself. The android persona gave her a mask beneath which she could hide, something more perfect to which she could aspire. With her debut, a concept album titled *Metropolis: Suite 1 (The Chase)*, she took on the persona of an android, Cindi Mayweather, and would continue to play with that persona and a musical blend of neo-soul and synthesized beats with a hard-rock edge for two more albums, *The Arch-Android* and *The Electric Lady*.

She had long been interested in science fiction and Afrofuturism, which, for Monáe, represents "the full spectrum of our blackness; where we come from, our present, and our future." She takes an expansive, imaginative view of this spectrum. When I asked her what an Afrofuture looks like, Monáe said, "Right now, it's Lil Uzi Vert being happy with orange locs, Erykah Badu doulaing, Octavia Butler's voice, Stacey Abrams being president and punching Trump out the Oval seat, black people getting passports and hanging out in Africa, black queer lovers holding hands while the pastor smiles, George Clinton's sunglasses in 1974, Prince's eyeliner in *Under the Cherry Moon*, black bodies walking away alive after a police stop, Tierra Whack and Ari Lennox joking on Twitter, black kings in nail polish, Lupita's performance in *Us*. It looks like an orgasm and the big bang happening while skydiving as Grace Jones smiles."

This eclectic vision echoes across all of Monáe's music. "Dirty Computer was really a reflection of where I was at that time. I was discovering more and more about my sexuality. I was walking into being more sex positive, also understanding different ways to love and to be loved," she said. The album was accompanied by a 46-minute "emotion picture," in which Monáe plays Jane 57821 in a society where people who don't conform are "dirty computers" and must have their memories erased to clean them into submission.

It is a vision of a dystopian society, responding to our current dystopian moment. Monáe was motivated by the fear she felt after the 2016 presidential election, fear for her safety as a black woman in a world where white supremacists were newly emboldened, fear for the political trajectory of the country. That anxiety fueled the music. She decided to make the album unapologetically black and radical. "It started with who don't I mind pissing off," Monáe said. "I don't mind pissing off conservatives. I don't mind pissing off white men. I don't give a fuck. This is about celebrating. I wanted to celebrate queer black people living outside of what it meant to be American."

Monáe has always been brash and relentless and political in her work and in how she moves through the world. In 2015, she released the song "Hell You Talmbout," on the scourge of police brutality. The lyrics demand that we say the names of black men and women who have been murdered by police. While introducing Kesha's performance at the 2018 Grammys, she said, "We say time's up for pay inequality, time's up for discrimination, time's up for harassment of any kind, and time's up for the abuse of power." Recently, she tweeted #IAmNonBinary, and, as you might expect, people wondered what she meant. When I asked, she said, "I tweeted the #IAmNonbinary hashtag in support of Nonbinary Day and to bring more awareness to the community. I retweeted the Steven Universe meme 'Are you a boy or a girl? I'm an experience' because it resonated with me, especially as someone who has pushed boundaries of gender since the beginning of my career. I feel my feminine energy, my masculine energy, and energy I can't even explain."

Over the course of our conversation, I realized Monáe is one of those artists who have an interesting response to every question. She is deliberate in what she says, purposefully provocative in ways that serve to reinforce her carefully crafted public image. She is well read and voraciously curious. There is a private person behind that image, but it's difficult to truly know who that person is, who and what she loves, what brings her true joy, what she most yearns for. This is not to say we didn't have an intimate conversation, because I think we did, but it was an intimate conversation within very specific boundaries. I very much wanted to ask her about her pansexuality and some of the famous women she has been associated with, so I asked Monáe if she was in a relationship. She smiled demurely and said, "I don't talk about the folks I'm dating," and we left it at that.

She likened the public interest in her personal life to fanfiction; people take what they think they know of her and create stories that are nothing more than figments of the public imagination. And I suppose she's right. That is what we do with celebrities. We finish the incomplete stories about their lives that they offer us in ways that fulfill our own needs and wants. Monáe wasn't closed off, though. She was merely circumspect in entirely reasonable ways. Among other things, she shared that motherhood is one of the dives into the unknown for which she is ready. Like many people, she is trying to find the right time professionally to take a step back to have a child. She wants to make sure she is healthy enough as she recovers from mercury poisoning, which she got after becoming a pescatarian. "I started feeling my mortality," she said.

Though she has been spending more time in Los Angeles, Monáe is based in Atlanta, where she collaborates with the Wondaland Arts Society, an arts collective determined to spread its reach to every aspect of the entertainment industry. Wondaland is, in Monáe's words, a "school for mutants and droids" and comprises an intimate group of young, black creatives who want to "piss off the Old Guard of gatekeepers who don't understand the value of black-renaissance artists." Monáe is a radical voice looking for other radical voices, and she has built a career on that kind of forward thinking. These days, she is trending toward being as accomplished an actor as she is a musician.

Monáe made her film debut with supporting roles in two movies—the Oscar-winning *Moonlight* and *Hidden Figures*. In April 2020, she will star in *Antebellum*, a "mind-bending social thriller" from the producers of *Get Out* and *Us*. She plays Veronica, a writer with a strong sense of social justice. Details on the film are intentionally vague, but Veronica finds herself in a horrifying reality (the trailer suggests she's trapped in an alternate reality where she is enslaved) and must solve the mystery of how she got there before it's too late. It is reminiscent of Octavia Butler's work, shaping a black future that is inextricable from our past.

Veronica was Monáe's most difficult role yet, with a rigorous filming schedule and the pressure of leading a major motion picture for the first time. These pressures were magnified by the way she works as an actor—the role tends to follow her home during filming. "I want that spirit to always stay on-camera so I don't break. I don't talk on the phone a lot . . . I don't want that to take me out of my space." Monáe allows her characters to subsume her. And that approach certainly takes its toll when she is choosing to "dig in and stay there" in a role that deals with trauma. Despite the rigors of her craft, acting is still therapeutic. "I use my pain," she said. "I use it."

The club emptied out as the evening waned, and Monáe suggested that we repair to Wondaland West, the Hollywood Hills home she rents when she is in town. As we were leaving, a seemingly drunk man with strategic scruff and a deliberately casual manner waylaid her. He introduced himself and told Monáe he wanted to talk to her as if he had something of the utmost importance to say. He did not. I stepped aside to give them privacy but did not put too much distance between us because he was clearly hitting on her and she gave no impression that she was at all interested. A few minutes later, as we walked to the curb to wait for our cars, she thanked me for not leaving her alone. Sometimes celebrities really are just like us, tolerating the attention of obnoxious men with terrible beards.

Wondaland West is one of those homes with a pristine and spectacular view of L.A. Inside the house, there was a large orange trunk I recognized immediately as Beyoncé's new Adidas x Ivy Park collection, which would drop a few days later. Janelle Monáe has got it like that, I thought to myself as I stared at the trunk and its contents covetously. I was, I felt, as close to Beyoncé as I had ever been or would ever be. It was a holy moment.

Several members of the Wondaland team gathered to greet me in a flurry of names and kind faces, and I was immediately struck by the genuine camaraderie and affection the group shared. Earlier in the evening, Monáe had said the Wondaland team is a family, but that's something lots of people say, so I didn't know it was true until I saw them together. They bantered, talked trash, and opined on any number of things, including the 2020 Oscar nominees, the joys of Peloton, and something about "daily rankings."

On a nearby kitchen counter, a fragrant dish was cooking in a Crock-Pot. There was an open Popeyes box. A man sat on the couch with his feet on a pedal exerciser, and another man was slowly cycling to nowhere on a Peloton bike. Four of us immediately sat down to play *Rummikub*. I am extremely competitive, so once I refamiliarized myself with the game's rules, I was determined to dominate. Monáe is competitive too, as was everyone else. It didn't occur to me until much later that perhaps I should not have been playing to win. The game proceeded apace. I concentrated, studying the game board and my tiles with an undue amount of intensity. My goal, mostly, was to not embarrass myself. Imagine my surprise when I won the first game. I felt stupidly flush with victory.

We immediately began shuffling tiles for a second game. Monáe remarked that the game helps her relax and focus. Sometimes, when she is creatively blocked, a good game of *Rummikub* will help her reach a much-needed breakthrough. The second game was more competitive. I ran the permutations of possible moves over and over in my head as I waited for my turn. I knew what I needed to do to win again. And just as I was ready to lay down my final tile, Monáe, who had been deliberating for quite some time, found her final move, laid down her tile, and won the game. "At least this game was closer," I quipped, and everyone began to laugh.

It was interesting, though, to see how determined Monáe was to win, that her ambition extended even to board games. Earlier in the evening, I had asked her if she could ever achieve enough, and she admitted, "I feel like there's never going to be enough." Even early in her career, she hustled, cleaning houses, working in Office Depot, starting to form her tribe, some of whom were in that house playing *Rummikub* with us. She used the money from her day jobs for studio time. She was pressing her own CDs and selling them out of her car trunk. All the while, she was thinking about the kind of artist she wanted to become. She was thinking about what she was and was not willing to compromise. She was willing to sacrifice becoming a household name to create honest work. She was not going to sacrifice her freedom for fame, and as I looked around that table, it was clear she was surrounded by people who would hold her to that. I asked Monáe what she likes most about her work. "I like how my work reveals itself over time," she said. "It's like a letter you wrote yourself ten years ago, but when you open it in the future, things start to make sense."

After the second game, it was well after midnight, time for me to go home. We assembled around the Beyoncé box, admiring the array of Ivy Park merchandise. Monáe donned a maroon parachute cape, went outside, and began running around the pool deck, the cape billowing behind her, a bright smile stretched across her face. For a moment, as she began to catch the wind in her cape, it looked like she might soar off that deck, still fearless.

Originally published in *New York* magazine/*The Cut*, February 3, 2020

Sarah Paulson Has No Fear

I hate asking celebrities about their personal lives, but I love celebrity gossip. I will happily read Bossip or Lainey Gossip or *People*, and idly speculate about celebrities and their romantic entanglements, real estate transactions, mistakes, or triumphs. And yet I don't want to be the person who extracts this information. I don't want to get my hands dirty. It makes me uncomfortable to pry, intrude, encroach. But still I am nosy. It's a real predicament.

Sarah Paulson is first and foremost an actor—and a formidable one at that. Over the course of her career, she has perfected the steely glare, the tight smile, the precisely arched eyebrow. Paulson has certainly found her lane, but when she has stretched her craft, she has done so with aplomb. In *Ocean's 8*, for example, Paulson uses her dry humor to great effect as Tammy, a wife and mother who also happens to be a fence. Or in her new Netflix series, *Ratched*, as the iconic asylum nurse Mildred Ratched from Ken Kesey's novel *One Flew Over the Cuckoo's Nest* and Milos Forman's 1975 film version, a notoriously cruel character who Paulson somehow makes human. It is because of her humor, intelligence, and creative versatility that Paulson's fans are legion, and I count myself among them. Though she may not identify as such, Paulson is also a celesbian, a self-explanatory Internet portmanteau of affection. She is in a relationship with Holland Taylor, another great actor and celesbian. I love saying the word "celesbian"—it rolls right off the tongue—and I love any and all gossip about celesbians because they are so few and far between. No one should ever be defined by their romantic life, but as a queer woman it is surprisingly wonderful to see relationships that reflect my own.

As I prepared for our interview, my wife gently insisted that I ask

Paulson how she feels about being a celesbian. I said I would try, cringing inside, but then it wasn't a problem because Paulson was forthcoming about their relationship from the outset. She and Taylor have been together for almost six years. They both own homes in Los Angeles. They go back and forth between each other's places every few days. Taylor calls everyone a "lovely girl" or "darling," and is more inclined to respond to internet trolls. They deal with the same issues any couple does trying to live a shared life. Our conversation was peppered with anecdotes about their relationship. I was delighted, I tell you. DELIGHTED.

Paulson expressed the ambivalence that I suspect a lot of celebrities harbor about being private people in a public world. "To feel that I belong to anyone other than a person I would like to belong to, like Holland or my dog or my best friend or my sister . . . A bunch of strangers claiming me as their own feels a little confusing," she told me. "Since I'm not an expert at figuring out how to move around it, I end up giving more than I want to sometimes."

Paulson and Taylor's relationship is often the source of speculation because of their age difference—Taylor is 77, and Paulson is 45. Or people speculate because they are both famous or because they are two women open about their relationship and that is still something of a novelty no matter how far we think we have come. I asked Paulson why people are so preoccupied with the age gap. An unwillingness to confront mortality seems to be part of it, she concluded, but it also reflects "our own ageist thinking and the idea that to be old is to cease to have any desire." In general, Paulson said, the attention she and Taylor receive is positive, but when it isn't she does not take to it kindly. "Anybody says anything about any person I love in a way that is disrespectful or cruel and I want to cut a bitch."

When she said those words, I absolutely believed she is capable of cutting a bitch, and I had only one ambition throughout our conversation—to not be a bitch who gets cut. We spoke for a couple of hours in August, the way nearly everything is done these days, at a distance, via Zoom. Paulson was in her L.A. home in what appeared to be her office. She sat with her legs pulled under her, in a flowy white dress, her shoulder-length hair wet and slicked back, her face unadorned by makeup. It is beside the point, but she is arrestingly beautiful—wide eyes, sharp cheekbones, and an even sharper wit. Behind her, black-and-white photos, and an Emmy statue, the golden arms reaching toward the sky—a subtle, elegant flex. Paulson won the award in 2016, for her portrayal of embattled prosecutor Marcia Clark in *The People v. O. J. Simpson*. She had been nominated four times previously, primarily for her work in Ryan Murphy's anthology program *American Horror Story* but also for her role as former Republican operative (and current MSNBC host) Nicolle Wallace in the 2012 HBO movie *Game Change*.

More recently, Paulson appeared with Bette Midler, Issa Rae, Dan Levy, and Kaitlyn Dever in HBO's *Coastal Elites*, a film comprising five vignettes that was shot in our new abnormal. Paulson plays a YouTube meditation guru grappling with Covid-19, the political climate, and her family, who ascribe to rather different politics. Paulson shot her scenes in her guesthouse, working with the director, Jay Roach, via laptop. The writer was in New York. The film crew was on her deck. It wasn't her favorite way of working. "I'm not interested in acting with me. I like to look at another pair of eyes, not my own." Paulson also leads the upcoming Hulu horror film *Run*, about the mother of a wheelchair-bound teen, played by Kiera Allen, who begins to realize that something is amiss in her life. As always, Paulson brings technical precision to the role, chilling as a woman determined to keep her daughter at any cost.

But Paulson's most interesting role to date may well be *Ratched*. Her name was the first on the call sheet, and she serves as an executive producer on the series, which premiered on Netflix in September. (They are already developing a second season.) An origin story set in the 1940s, *Ratched* is visually sumptuous—the costumes and scenery, both natural and otherwise, are impeccable. The story is quietly terrifying, but also full of unexpected empathy. We see, over the span of eight episodes, what transforms Mildred Ratched into the cold, immovable woman we'd later encounter, and the character evolves in surprising ways. She does things that seem inexplicable, until they don't. She demonstrates tenderness in harsh circumstances. "We were going for something, and I'm proud of it," Paulson said. "It's an exploration, and it has something to say, and it looks beautiful. It's dangerous. It's scary. It's sexy." Paulson was also a force on *Ratched* behind the scenes, an active participant in all the hiring decisions, with equity in the project. "I realized that not only could she be the lead actress, but I wanted her to produce with me," Murphy said. "It was this great evolution of our partnership."

And Paulson took that partnership seriously, even breaking a long-standing pledge not to watch her own performances. "I feel a real sense of accomplishment with it," she said. "I still to this day have not watched *People v. O. J.* Not seen it. That was the beginning of my commitment to not watching myself. But because I'm executive-producing *Ratched* and because it was my first time doing something like this, I watched every frame of it, dailies every single day. And it was a very confronting experience. Dealing with one's face is really something. It's really something to just be confronted with your mug."

At this point I am supposed to say that amid all this acclaim Sarah Paulson is having a moment, but Paulson has been working steadily for more than two decades. She is an avowed perfectionist and control freak. She is ambitious, but mostly about growing as an actor and being able to more easily sit in her work. She is, in her own words, exacting and self-critical, and yearns to get beyond the constant self-assessment. "That kind of freedom," she said, "it's happened to me so few times. When it has happened it's like a drug."

Looking at the map of her life, Paulson traces the origin of her perfectionism to her upbringing. "I was left alone a lot as a child," she recalled. She was born in Tampa, Florida, but after her parents split up when she was five, she moved to New York with her mom, who worked as a waitress at Sardi's while pursuing a career as a writer. As a kid, Paulson often bargained with herself, thinking that achieving perfection in everything she did would manifest the things she wanted most. "There was a wish fulfillment, magical thinking, 'If I could be X, I could have Y,'" Paulson said. "The idea that the world worked in this very cut-and-dried way seemed like a way for me to manage my fear. Perfectionism is often a real consequence of being terrified."

After working as a Broadway understudy, Paulson landed her first professional on-screen role as Maggie Conner, a teenager suspected of killing her mother, in the fifth season of the original *Law & Order*. The year was 1994. She had recently done a Horton Foote play with the Signature Theatre Company and hadn't put much effort into applying to college, maybe because she wanted to get into the work of acting immediately, but maybe because she was afraid of the unknown and of straying too far from home. That's how she found herself engaging in what has become a rite of passage for New York actors. "I didn't know you could turn your head on camera. I moved like I had a neck brace on the whole time," Paulson said. By the time she returned to the *Law & Order* universe in 2010, this time on the *Special Victims Unit* franchise, she had learned to move her head, and much more. In "Shadow," she plays Anne Gillette, an heiress suspected of murdering her parents. She takes a wonderfully sociopathic turn as Gillette—demure and elegant and assured and oblivious in the way of the wealthy and entitled. In the ensuing years, Paulson continued to grace screen and stage, but the kinds of opportunities she's now enjoying eluded her. There is a very narrow and rigid career trajectory for most women who act. They are the ingenue, and then they aren't. They are the sex object or the love interest, and then they age into onscreen motherhood, and then they age into dotage, and then they are 40 and their career ends. There are exceptions, but those are exceedingly rare. "I was very aware that the window was closing," Paulson said. "I wasn't sure I was going to be able to squeeze my body through it. But I kept trying."

The tide began to turn, Paulson said, with the trifecta of *Game Change*, *12 Years a Slave*, and *American Horror Story*. For *12 Years a Slave*, directed by Steve McQueen, she made an audition tape that McQueen's daughter actually watched. She told her father that Paulson was the scariest person she'd ever seen, so he should probably cast her. And with that endorsement, McQueen did. As Mistress Epps, Paulson is chilling, embodying the ways in which white women were complicit in slavery, especially in the subjugation of enslaved Black women. As she prepared for the part, McQueen told Paulson, "If you judge her, this will not work. You cannot do it." Paulson's performance is magnetic and appalling, compelling and repulsive. You want to look away from the brutality of the performance, but you can't. You shouldn't.

Paulson welcomes the darkness of such roles. "It's where the good stuff is," she said. "I'm much more interested in where there isn't nobility. Human beings so often are motivated by the ugliest part of themselves . . . the stuff we don't want to admit to ourselves about what we're hungry for."

"What's interesting about Sarah," McQueen said, "is that there's a fear, but that fear is overridden by her power. She gets better and better each take. When she's really comfortable, it becomes extraordinary and different and unexpected."

Paulson's costar Lupita Nyong'o won an Oscar for Best Supporting Actress for her work in *12 Years a Slave*, which was her first movie. "I was terribly nervous and shy on set, though I think I hid it well," Nyong'o said. "In walked Sarah, with a big, generous smile and warm spirit. I recall her coaxing me out of my shell by asking thoughtful questions and sharing freely of herself." Nyong'o and Paulson developed a tight bond off set. "I feel so blessed that she continues to be just a phone call away," Nyong'o said.

Ryan Murphy first worked with Paulson on *Nip/Tuck* in 2004. He later tried to work with her again on *Glee*, but she wasn't available. Their creative stars finally aligned in 2011 with *American Horror Story*, and Paulson has become something of a muse for Murphy. I tend to disdain the notion of men and their muses. It seems like quite a lot of unpaid emotional labor for women. But in this instance, the relationship has been mutually beneficial and enriching. "She knows every light, every camera angle," Murphy said. "She's a savant about memorization. She knows everybody's part. She makes other actors sit up straighter and bring their A game."

The premise of *American Horror Story* changes each season, which allows for a creatively dynamic environment for the cast. "The biggest gift I've ever been given in my working life has been what my being on *American Horror Story* has made permissible with my relationship with an audience," said Paulson. "They don't expect any particular thing with me. That's afforded me a tremendous amount of freedom."

Paulson's frequent scene partner on *American Horror Story* has been Jessica Lange, whom she'd worked with onstage, in a 2005 production of *The Glass Menagerie*. Lange appreciates the energy Paulson brings to a performance. "She comes to it with a full range of emotions," said Lange. "There's nothing artificial. There's no grandstanding. It's always coming from a place of great honesty and emotion."

Though much of her career has been spent in supporting roles, Paulson has a way of creating a center of gravity in each character. "Sarah is a ferocious actor," Murphy said. "She attacks. She doesn't sit back."

"When I started out I was playing a lot of supporting parts, and I didn't know if this was just going to be the story for me," Paulson said. "I used to think of it like a building. You need a buttress."

I asked Paulson if she ever thinks, "Fuck it, I'm going to chew the shit out of this scene." She laughed. "Can you imagine? That would be such a great way to be. Why not? Nobody wants to celebrate themselves enough. You can say as many shitty, self-deprecating things about yourself and no one would say anything other than, 'Oh, how charming.'" Indeed, Paulson is right. For women in particular, the vigorous performance of low self-esteem is de rigueur. Like many creative people, Paulson seems to balance self-effacement with the confidence of someone who is a master of her craft and is finally being recognized as such. McQueen is effusive on this point. "There are actors, and then there are artists," he said. "She's an artist."

If there is something more to want from her work, Sarah Paulson is going to find it. "It's the one place I don't feel frightened in terms of my ability to go somewhere unpleasant," she said. "I am unafraid to be ugly. I feel a certain sense of pride about being able to do that and without all the things that happen in every other aspect of my life when that comes up. But in this one area, I can actually say I feel capable of being fearless."

Originally published in *Harper's Bazaar*, September 22, 2020

The Talented Tessa Thompson

I'm not speaking to Tessa Thompson in person, and that's honestly kind of a relief. It's just before Thanksgiving, and Thompson is at home in Los Angeles, beautiful as ever, sitting in a chair with a knee pulled to her chest. We're talking over Zoom and having a great conversation, but, given that this is how interviews take place these days, there's no opportunity to witness a quirky encounter with a fan or to remark on her wardrobe or to see what and how she eats. Without superficial distractions, we're able to get real and go deep.

During the initial moments of our conversation, Thompson remarks, "'How are you?' feels like a cruel question these days," and indeed, she's right. It's late November, and while we're past the 2020 presidential election, political uncertainty lingers. We are experiencing yet another surge in coronavirus cases, and the holiday season isn't shaping up to be nearly as festive as it should be. "It feels like things have been turned inside out this year," Thompson says. The world as it really is, she explains, "has been exposed in all its glory and gore, and maybe there is hope in that, in the sense that some of us are more awake than we have been." The question becomes what we do, now that we're more awake.

Thompson is aware that she's expected to do something. After all, she is, at 37, one of the most visible performers of her generation. She is a star of action franchises like *Men in Black* and of Marvel movies; she has charmed audiences in independent films like *Sorry to Bother You* and *Little Woods*; she has appeared in TV series like *Westworld* and *Dear White People*; she records her own music; there's a Twitter account dedicated to posting pictures of her with goats (more on that later). She's got what you'd call a platform.

Thompson readily acknowledges the things that people expect of her. "We're living inside this time where there's an expectation, if you have some measure of a platform, to use it," she says. "I'm not sure it's that useful all of the time. If I have a microphone, maybe the most useful way is just to pass it on to someone that knows more than I do." As she negotiates that balance of knowing when to speak and when to listen, one thing Thompson is definitely doing is putting her whole heart into work.

In her latest film, *Sylvie's Love*—streaming now on Amazon—Thompson, who is both star and executive producer, demonstrates that. Deftly directed by Eugene Ashe, Thompson plays Sylvie, an ambitious young Black woman of privilege living in Harlem in the 1950s. She is watching television in her father's record shop when she meets Robert (played by the handsome, finely chiseled Nnamdi Asomugha), a talented jazz saxophonist. Though Sylvie has a fiancé, she and Robert fall in love, but their relationship abruptly ends when Robert has an opportunity to advance his career in Paris. Instead of telling Robert how she feels and why he should stay, Sylvie stays silent, sacrificing herself for his benefit. Years later she is a budding television producer, with a husband called Lacy (Alano Miller) and a young daughter. She is trying to balance her nascent career and her family, and struggling to "have it all," at a time when such a notion was rarely available to women. In one of the film's more powerful moments, Sylvie tells Lacy, "I can't be the woman of your dreams while also trying to be the woman of mine." It's the kind of love story Thompson never thought she would be able to make. "We haven't necessarily gotten to see ourselves as the romantic leads, and when we have, particularly in period pieces, there's less focus on the interpersonal, like how hard it is to be two humans trying to love each other," she says. "There's a lot of emphasis on historical context, which is, obviously, wildly important. I was conflicted as to whether it would work, whether you could tell a story like that." Ultimately, *Sylvie's Love* allowed Thompson to stretch her creative legs and to "do something that feels glamorous and sprawling, like the love stories you see in Hollywood iconography."

Thompson was born in Los Angeles and grew up there and in Brooklyn. She began acting in high school and went on to Santa Monica College, where she majored in cultural anthropology. She's well versed in any number of topics, and no matter where our conversation wanders, she speaks effortlessly but deliberately, clearly someone practiced in saying only what she means.

As an actress Thompson started out on stage, appearing in productions of *The Tempest* and *Romeo and Juliet* before landing her first TV role in an episode of *Cold Case* as Billie Ducette, a lesbian in the Prohibition era. In 2010 Tyler Perry was helming a film adaptation of *For Colored Girls . . .* , and Thompson auditioned for a role after another actress dropped out; she got the job, and a new phase of her career began.

In her roles since then, Thompson has attempted to balance being the woman of an audience's dreams with living a life of her own. But as her star rises, she is increasingly the woman of a great many people's dreams. She has an ardent and diverse fan base. She once mentioned in an interview that she likes goats, and since then fans have showered the internet with pictures of her next to pictures of the barnyard animals; there's a Twitter account called, as you might expect (or not), @TessaAsGoats.

No corner of Thompson's fandom is more passionate than her queer following. Though she doesn't explicitly identify as bisexual, in a 2018 interview she said she was "attracted to men and also to women." For a community that rarely gets the representation it deserves, that was all it took. Few actors publicly express same-sex desire, so Thompson was quickly elevated to icon status. It means a lot to see an openly queer actor portraying a superhero, slaying her way through imaginary worlds.

Thompson's devoted following is made up of movie fans and the fashion set alike. In 2018 she starred in Rodarte's look book and attended the Met Gala wearing Thom Browne. The following year she was back at the gala in a Chanel dress, carrying a leather whip. Playwright Jeremy O. Harris recalls, "Her bondage look for the Met Gala was both playful and transgressive . . . She looked beautiful, but she didn't look soft, which is often dangerous for a woman."

This year Thompson brings something new to the screen in *Sylvie's Love*. Her portrayal of Sylvie is as determined as any of her other performances, but she brings a tenderness to the part. There is genuine yearning woven through every move she makes. The movie is lush and beautifully shot against the backdrop of Harlem, and Thompson's subtle performance soars.

Eugene Ashe chose Thompson for the role because he "was really looking for someone who could pull off an Audrey Hepburn–esque ethereal quality," he says. "Tessa is generally supertough . . . Not that she doesn't have agency in this film, she does, but it's an arc where she gains agency over the movie. In some of her other roles, she comes as a fully formed badass. Here she grows into one."

When Thompson and Ashe first met to discuss *Sylvie's Love*, they agreed about the type of movie they wanted to make. A half-hour meeting, he tells me, turned into a two-hour lunch. They both wanted to make a love story centering Black people that was not consumed by race. And given the political climate, that is certainly . . . a choice. The movie is set before the signing of the Civil Rights Act of 1964, at the height of the movement; it seems impossible to elide race from the narrative. And at the same time, *Sylvie's Love* offers audiences what so many have been craving: a story in which Black people can just be their fullest selves, for better and worse. We do indeed know what racism was like back then, and if we can expand our imaginations to believe that Thompson is a brash and bold Asgardian named Valkyrie who rides a winged horse, or the smoothly confident Agent M in *Men in Black: International*, we can probably expand our imaginations to appreciate a midcentury love story between two Black people who keep trying to find their way to each other.

In the two *Creed* films Thompson played Bianca, a young woman dealing with progressive hearing loss who falls in love with Apollo Creed's son Adonis. Her co-star Michael B. Jordan is effusive in his praise of Thompson. "She's extremely talented, and a lot of the dynamics we had working together came from her asking the right questions and caring about the right things," he says. "She always brought so much to the table and made us think outside the box. She challenged stereotypes, and she always made sure we were being true."

Challenging norms is an integral part of Thompson's ethic. A lot of people in Hollywood say they are going to change the industry, but Thompson is one of the few people who seems as if she actually will—as though she already is changing how business is done. Even early in her career she tried, in ways both great and small, to assert her autonomy in situations where she could not necessarily expect to have any. During auditions, when she was instructed to sit in a chair, she would deliberately move that chair, because she wanted to "remind myself and the room that

I was going to take over the space." Controlling that space, she says, "was definitely out of my comfort zone," but there can be pleasure in the discomfort. "I think that's why I like what I do. I've always felt a little afraid of what happens when we get too comfortable, that we're not growing. Maybe I'm a masochist or maybe I'm a sucker for the discomfort of the first squeak."

And Thompson is well aware that sometimes, for other people to be able to change, they need to see that change is possible. She observes that "there's invariably people in the room that have been silenced. I remember a distinct moment on set. A squeak just came out of me, I didn't even mean for it to, and then I could see the secret little smile on some of the women around the room, and you realize that there's a choir of wheels waiting to squeak together. It emboldens folks, and you realize you have support and you're not squeaking just on your own behalf. You're squeaking for everybody."

The Covid-19 pandemic has, at least for now, radically changed the entertainment industry. As acting work slowed down, Thompson used the opportunity to throw her energy into developing projects for other actors, and she is thinking about how those projects are executed. As work slowly resumes on film sets, a lot more care is being taken to promote distancing and hygiene. And, Thompson hopes, maybe that care will extend to the interpersonal dynamics and power structures. "Because we're having to think about what safety looks like on set and having to be thoughtful," she says, "I'm interested if that reverberates. I hope so, because there's something audiences can sense inside of the DNA of the thing they're watching that is actually powerful and useful."

As she looks ahead and takes on more producing projects under her own banner—including a development deal at HBO and HBO Max for her Viva Maude productions that will see her producing adaptations of the novels *Who Fears Death* and *The Secret Lives of Church Ladies*—Thompson is thinking about new ways of doing business in Hollywood, and she's thinking about ownership. "That's my favorite thing to think about, particularly in building this company," she says. "Thinking around the voices I invite into it, how I allow them to retain as much ownership over their work and their ideas as possible." She hopes for film sets to become more collaborative, for them to become places where every voice can and should be heard. That may sound idealistic, but it's worth considering why the idea of treating people who work hard equitably is considered an ideal. "I'm really interested in trying to create a utopia," she says. "It's imperative, because I'm curious about being able to give opportunity to folks that people might say are less experienced. A lot of people are batting a lot higher than their average because they just, frankly, haven't been given the opportunity."

Her upcoming projects include *Passing*, an adaptation of Nella Larsen's Harlem Renaissance novel directed by Rebecca Hall and set to premiere at the Sundance Film Festival; *Thor: Love and Thunder*, due in 2022, and a third installment in the *Creed* series. A biopic of jewel thief Doris Payne (who is said to have used *Town & Country* for information about some of her greatest heists) is in development. It's a collection of interesting, carefully chosen parts, which speaks to the care Thompson takes with her work and underscores just how exciting it will be to watch her continued ascent.

"In the beginning Tessa didn't care to get too into the business side of things—having her own production company or getting more behind the camera," Jordan recalls. "But now I've seen her grow into that and realize her power. She doesn't need to limit herself by staying in front of the camera. The world needs to see her from all sides."

Originally published in *Town & Country*, January 15, 2021

Where Jordan Casteel
Sees Herself Going

———

In the fall, Jordan Casteel was finishing the paintings for her solo show *There Is a Season*, a series of portraits, still lifes, and landscapes at the Massimo De Carlo gallery in London. Casteel, who lives in New York, is one of the most vibrant and exciting artists working today, known for her bold use of color, her arresting portraiture, and her massive canvases that demand space. In the U.S., her career had been on a steep upward climb: Her shows were selling out almost immediately, and museums and collectors were clamoring for her work. *There Is a Season* would be her first solo show abroad.

A few weeks before her flight to London, Casteel received a call from an unknown number. "I didn't understand what was happening," she says. "They were saying my name. And then the woman says, 'Someone important from Chicago wants to speak to you.' And I was like, *Who's in Chicago?* I got a cousin there, but he ain't that important." The call, it turned out, was from the MacArthur Foundation: Casteel had won one of its coveted "genius" grants. It's the kind of thing most creative people don't even dare dream of receiving, let alone at the age of 32. "I shat myself, basically. I felt like a balloon floating in the sky, like I was being lost to the world," she says. She'd already been struggling with the visibility of her career, feeling oversaturated with attention and the existential questions that such attention brings: "I'm young and that scared me. If you reach a pinnacle, if you reach the top of the mountain, then what? The only place is down."

Upon arriving in London, Casteel headed to her show along with her husband, the photographer David Schulze, and her father. She wasn't sure what to expect. It was a foreign art landscape, populated by curators and institutions and collectors she didn't recognize. And as a Black woman in the U.S. who paints Black people in the U.S., she was not sure how British audiences would engage with the work. When they walked into the gallery, they were confronted with the familiar sight of her paintings, which offer glimpses of everyday life and the people who inhabit New York. A young man on a subway bench, napping, a hard hat on the seat next to him. A handsome bearded man sitting on a fence before a snowy urban backdrop. An image of a windowsill, against which is propped a framed family photo and a copy of the Black newspaper *New York Amsterdam News* with Obama as president-elect on the cover. The room, however, was empty.

That night, Casteel lay in bed a bit panicked. "That was weird," she said to Schulze. She was used to her show openings in New York, which felt like celebrations, gatherings attended by her supporters and everybody she'd ever painted. But when she woke up the next morning, she thought, *Fuck yeah. I'm glad there's a space for me to still feel this.* "Because I shouldn't feel like I conquered it all, not at 32," she says. "This trip showed me how naïve I am. I haven't conquered anything at all."

"Was that a useful feeling?" I ask.

"Yes," she says. "Profoundly."

Casteel's studio is located on a quiet street of warehouses in the Bronx. When I visit her on a Tuesday in December, the room is light and airy and filled with blank canvases, stretched and primed and waiting. She is dressed comfortably in a pastel sweatshirt and joggers, her hair cropped short in a pixie cut. Near one wall is a rolling whiteboard holding two calendars full of obligations and deadlines.

Casteel is not new to this. Throughout her childhood in Denver, she was a maker, drawn to arts and crafts and creative expression, and she was always looking for a space of her own where she could make things, away from the youthful intrusions of her brothers. She grew up in a family of distinguished civil-rights activists: Her grandfather Whitney Moore Young Jr., served as the executive director of the National Urban League for nearly a decade. Her mother is Lauren Young Casteel, an activist and the president and CEO of the Women's Foundation of Colorado, the first Black woman to assume that role. Casteel attended a small women's

liberal-arts college in Decatur, Georgia, where she majored in anthropology and sociology. During a semester abroad in Italy, she began to study
art more formally. Upon graduation, she Googled "best M.F.A. program"
and showed up to Yale with three paintbrushes and no idea how to prop-
erly stretch a canvas.

After Yale, Casteel moved to Harlem. There, she began roaming
the neighborhood, camera in hand, seeking out people to sit for her
portraits—a family running a restaurant, street vendors, a woman working at a nail salon. She would photograph each person in their natural
space, taking as many as a hundred frames, which she'd then interpret
in oil on canvases that sometimes stretched from floor to ceiling. From
the beginning, Casteel sought to form relationships with her sitters that
lasted years beyond their fleeting interactions on the street. She'd ask to
stay in touch, inviting them to shows and even traveling with them to see
their portrait when it was on view. Occasionally, a sitter would decline. "I
remember there was this young man, Stanley, I photographed in front of a
barbershop. He was like, 'I'll do this, but you don't need to stay in touch.
It's fine.' And I said, 'Okay, bet,'" Casteel recalls. "I made that painting,
and he's sitting in the shadow. I painted him black and white because I
felt like he created this boundary line that only let me get so far."

That respect permeates all her figurative paintings. In 2014, for her
first solo exhibition, *Visible Man*, Casteel painted portraits of Black men
in the nude in their homes. Each image is hyperrealistic, the background
rendered with the same care and attention to detail as the foreground.
In *Elijah*, a man sits on his bed, and at the periphery of the image, we
see a desk holding a glass of water and a prayer candle. In another painting from the same period, *Devan*, a man sits sideways on a green chair,
his skin interpreted in shades of brown, purple, dark red. Behind him, a
baseball cap is flung onto a radiator; at his feet are a pair of shoes and a
stuffed animal.

Embedded in each portrait is a deep understanding of people and
the spaces they inhabit. "There is inherent to Jordan's work a profound
idea of community," says Thelma Golden, the director of the Studio
Museum, who became familiar with the artist's work when she was an
M.F.A. student. "It's evident not only in how she depicts her subjects
but the way in which she exists in community with her subjects." After

Visible Man, Casteel continued to make figurative paintings but also turned her eye to still lifes and landscapes, which shared the same visual voice—the sumptuous canvases textured with layers of paint; the earnest, unself-conscious brushstrokes. In her 2017 painting *Memorial*, a discarded funeral wreath hovers above an overflowing trash can at a Harlem intersection, strangely poignant in its stillness. In 2019, she began a series of subway paintings, unexpected images of people sharing public spaces—three pairs of legs dangling from a subway bench, the reflection of a rider in the window.

Casteel pushed herself to become intimately involved in the business side of being an artist, even before anybody knew who she was. "I remember feeling like I had to insert myself into the system and figure out how it works because they're not necessarily going to welcome me," she says. She took copious notes throughout her interactions with curators and institutions, and she created a detailed log of information about every collector ever mentioned to her and why they were interested in her work. "I want to know what the gallery's thinking: Why are you placing the work with such and such? Why are you choosing them over this person you told me about last week? You said they were important last week; why aren't they important this week?" she says. "I don't want things to happen that I don't understand."

This inclination became higher stakes as her name soared to prominence in the U.S. Starting in 2018, Casteel began showing her work at prestigious institutions across the country, from the Cantor Center for Visual Arts at Stanford University to the Museum of Contemporary Art in Los Angeles to the Denver Art Museum. Then, at the start of 2020, she staged a major solo show at the New Museum, where she exhibited nearly 40 paintings spanning her career. The month the show opened, her 2013 painting *Mom* sold at auction for a record $666,734. Last year, her painting *Medinilla, Wanda, and Annelise*—a portrait of an undergraduate art student she taught at Rutgers University–Newark sitting with her mother and sister—entered the Metropolitan Museum of Art's permanent collection.

Her explosion collided with a strange moment in the American art world. As the industry grappled with the same inequities that plague almost every aspect of our lives, there grew a rather frenzied interest in African American figuration, with works by Black artists fetching unprecedented prices and shows quickly selling out. Some of this acquisition may appear mindless, with collectors not seeming to care much about the artist or their practice, because any Black artist will do. In part because she produces only a handful of paintings a year, Casteel tries to be deliberate about where she places her work, looking for collectors interested in developing a relationship with her, not "just purchasing because they heard that it's hot or because they have a collection of African American artists and they want to add to it," she says. Her primary goal is for the work to be seen, rather than hidden away in a storage facility or sold for a large return on the secondary market.

Still, she acknowledges, there is a price to scaling so quickly, and a price to participating so fully in the business of making it happen. "I've inserted myself so much that when I'm making paintings, my relationship to the painting has changed," she says. "And there are times—it's most of the time these days—there's a sense of loss in my relationship to this object." It's a peculiar tax to pay, particularly because this was always her dream. And it's a lonely problem, too, often impossible to express to those close to her. Frequently, her parents call and ask, "'Are you having fun, baby? Are you enjoying it?' And I'll say, 'I'm just thinking about a deadline, and I have a ton to do, and I'm only getting this much of the painting done, and I haven't slept, and blah, blah, blah,'" Casteel says. "They'll ask, 'But are you feeling grounded?' And I don't always think that answer is 'yes.'"

These days, Casteel is splitting her time between an apartment in Harlem she shares with Schulze and a home upstate, a small farmhouse that sits on three acres of land. She is building a new studio and tending to a verdant garden. She is channeling her love of making into gardening and baking, activities in which her hands are active but the stakes don't feel so high. She is investing in herself.

Her primary ambition today is to reset other people's and maybe her own expectations about how much work she can produce and why. Toward the center of her studio is a worktable with a note that lists five questions she must answer when considering professional opportunities, the most important of which is, "Will I enjoy it?" If she cannot answer "yes" to three of those five questions, she declines. She is making the time to nurture her personal relationships: "For the past few years, I've been the friend you call and say, 'Oh, I'm surprised you picked up.' I don't want to hear that. I don't want to feel that." What she's looking for now is longevity: "a career that can sustain itself so that I don't have to necessarily break my back forever. At what point can I rest? What does that look like? Is there such a thing as rest as things grow?"

She is also beginning to think about her next show, scheduled for September at New York's Casey Kaplan Gallery. "I was squiggling some notes this morning," she tells me. She needs to consider which subjects she'd like to paint. But she's also asking, "How many paintings are we talking? What's actually realistic? What does it mean to look at my calendar for 2022 and put in vacations to look forward to?" For the first time in her career, Casteel believes her pace of work is something she can maintain.

Last year, Casteel was in the thick of finishing *There Is a Season*, contending with the pressure of deadlines and feeling miserable. Schulze said to her, "You need to paint something you're enjoying in life right now." At the time, that enjoyable thing was her garden. But she fought against the idea: She wasn't sure how a painting of her garden would fit into the show she was making, or how it'd fit into the expectations that others had for her as an artist. Finally, on a canvas she had originally planned as a subway painting, Casteel painted *Nasturtium*, a vivid explosion of purple and green with splashes of red and orange. The painting, she says, "evoked a certain freedom that I didn't want to lose in the way that I tell stories." It ended up serving as the headliner of the show. She was so pleased with the result that she chose to keep the painting, wanting to hold on to it a bit longer.

Originally published in *The Cut*, February 16, 2022

This Is Pamela, Finally

——

While watching *Pamela: A Love Story*, the new Netflix documentary about Pamela Anderson's life, I was struck by interview clips at the height of the model turned actress's career. The mostly male interlocutors were bizarrely obsessed with her appearance (her breasts), and they leered and ogled and asked vapid, degrading questions that Anderson largely tolerated with an almost preternatural patience and humor. She knew her lane and was willing to stay in it. In several interviews, she reaches a point where she is clearly done with the condescension and lets them know she is more than fodder for male fantasy. Sadly, these valiant stands were mostly ignored. How could the interviewers recognize her humanity while so fixated on her buxom assets?

After a sex tape, compiled from stolen home videos made by Anderson and her then-husband Tommy Lee, was released without the couple's consent, the interviews became even more ridiculous. And it was clear everyone thought it was fair and reasonable to treat Anderson like a hypersexual punch line. She had posed in *Playboy*, after all. She dared to have sex with her husband and document it. She dared to exist. She was a public figure with a publicly coveted figure, and that superseded her right to privacy or respect. Even a judge said so when Anderson and Lee tried to adjudicate the matter of the sex tape.

For Gen-Xers like me, Anderson was either the *Playboy* centerfold or the *Baywatch* babe or the celebrity with the sex tape. That's a narrow way of thinking of someone, but popular culture has a tendency to distill its most prominent figures down to the shallowest, most consumable versions of themselves. Decades in retrospect, many people are realizing just how terribly Anderson has been treated juxtaposed with the extent of her cultural impact. They are searching for that redemptive arc or trying, in some way, to right a wrong.

Anderson rose to fame in the late 1980s and 1990s, posing for *Playboy* and appearing on the cover a record 14 times over nearly 30 years. As an actress, she was Lisa the *"Tool Time* girl" on two seasons of *Home Improvement*. She starred in *Baywatch*, a show about attractive Los Angeles lifeguards and their misadventures. The series did everything it could to exploit her good looks, and given the show's premise, she spent most of her time scantily clad, running along the beach, practically bouncing with each step, or emerging from the water as if nary a drop had touched her. She appeared in a few movies, but acting was not her forte. That did not matter. She had charm and charisma and, of course, her looks. That was more than enough. For a time, she was one of the most famous and recognizable women in the world.

In *Pamela: A Love Story*, we follow Anderson as she narrates her life from her childhood to the present day. She now lives in Ladysmith, British Columbia, where she was born and raised. We meet her sons, Brandon and Dylan. We watch as she stands in the kitchen with her mother, talking. We see her rehearsing for and performing in the Broadway musical *Chicago*. The present-day narrative is interspersed with clips from her life and career. She has hundreds of videotapes in her personal archive documenting nearly everything, which the director draws from liberally. And then, of course, there are the media clips of mostly men making absolute fools of themselves in her presence. It would be funny if it weren't so embarrassing and repulsive.

While Anderson has enjoyed a bounty of privilege, it has come at a very high price. She has sacrificed her privacy and had to endure a bewildering amount of bad behavior. At one point in the documentary, she discusses her finances, and we learn she has made no money from the sex tape. She earns little money from *Baywatch* despite her singular role in making that series hugely popular. In 1996, it was the most widely seen show in the world with more than 1.1 billion people tuning in each week. It is inexplicable that she has little to show for that. Bad management, exploitation, naïveté—an all too familiar story. Anderson doesn't seem particularly angry about any of this, but in media appearances, her son Brandon is more than willing to carry that torch on her behalf.

Alongside the documentary, Anderson has released a new memoir, *Love, Pamela*. From the outset, she makes it clear she wrote the book herself despite the protestations (underestimations, likely) of others. She tells her story, in her own words, with a blend of not-very-good-but-refreshingly-earnest poetry and capable, equally earnest prose. The memoir offers what seems like a rather gilded set of memories, even though many of the experiences Anderson details are traumatic or troubling. She has clearly known more than her fair share of suffering—childhood poverty, domestic violence, multiple incidents of sexual violence, abusive boyfriends, lousy husbands, the injustice of the court of public opinion. And still she shares these disturbing stories with an almost Zen attitude, as if she has made peace with it all. Anderson makes her life read like a fairy tale—the dark, gritty kind in which still, at the center of it all, there is a princess searching.

As with many celebrity projects, there are intriguing revelations. If your interest is prurient, you won't be disappointed, but, again, you will only learn so much. While a significant amount of the narrative is given over to her childhood, she rushes through most of her romantic relationships and their dissolutions. After Tommy Lee, the love of her life, there are all kinds of lovers and husbands and ambiguous assignations including Kid Rock, Rick Salomon, Jon Peters, David Charvet, Scott Baio, Dean Cain, even Julian Assange. She talks about Hugh Hefner as if he is something of a deity, and that is fitting, I suppose, given the role he played in her stardom. She writes about selling her Malibu mansion (for $11.8 million) and how that has set her up for the rest of her life. She talks about her activism, mostly centered on animals, and all things considered, she seems content, at peace, living on her farm with her parents and her dogs.

And yet, in 2022, Hulu released *Pam & Tommy*, a miniseries fictionalizing Anderson and Lee's relationship, the theft of the sex tape, and the aftermath. Once again, a version of Anderson's story was told without her input or consent. Once again, she did not benefit financially from the exploitation of her story. We are open to cultural redemption until we aren't, I suppose.

Meanwhile, Anderson's memoir and the documentary are complementary, curated artifacts of a life lived. For nearly 30 years, Anderson has seen alternate versions of her reality distorted by the media—a Playmate multiverse, if you will. In the acknowledgments of *Love, Pamela*, Anderson says, "It is a celebration, a scrapbook of imperfect people living imperfect lives and finding the joy in that." The phrasing is an apt encapsulation of both the book and the documentary. In both projects, Anderson is telling her own story in her own words in her own way. That is to say we see and learn only what she wants us to see and learn. That circumspection is not unique to Anderson; any time someone shares pieces of themselves with the public, they are curating how they present themselves. That Anderson curates her life so carefully across these two projects is incredibly fitting, a small justice.

Originally published in *The Cut*, February 3, 2023

[SOLICITED ADVICE]

Yes, Your Job Is Important.
But It's Not All Important.

———

Though I receive a lot of questions as your work friend, there are a few common themes. Mostly, people want something different, something more. They want more satisfaction or more money or more respect. They want to feel as if they're making a difference. They want to feel valued or seen or heard. They want the man in the next cubicle to chew less loudly so they are afforded more peace. They want to have access to drinking water outside of the bathroom. They are employed at a family business and are ambitious but there's no room for advancement for nonfamily members. They work at a very small company without a formal H.R. department so there is no recourse for the many work issues that arise. They want to have more time for themselves and interests beyond how they spend their professional lives. They want and want and want and worry that they will never receive the satisfaction they seek.

Mostly, people are worried. They have families and mortgages or rent and student loans and car loans and all the other financial obligations that consume our lives. They are in their 60s and don't know how to navigate the contemporary job market, or they are in their 20s and worry they will never be taken seriously. They are two years away from vested retirement and can't afford to make a career change. They are just out of college without a strong résumé and can't afford to be selective. They've been working for 30 years but never had the chance to save for retirement. They have a disability but don't want to disclose that to their employer for fear of reprisal. They want to bring attention to a terrible wrong but are their family's breadwinner.

Mostly, people are trying to figure out how to navigate ever-evolving workplace norms. As the ongoing pandemic waxes and wanes, they want to work from home forever, or they miss the din of the office and happy hours with their best work friends, or they want flexibility to enjoy both working from home and spending time in the office. They want to unionize for better working conditions, and they want parental leave, and they want to know they won't be fired for simply being who they are. They want to stop living paycheck to paycheck but are making minimum wage and can't see a way past that.

We all have different circumstances, but most of us contend with the same stark reality—we don't have as much control over our professional lives as we want and need and deserve. A lot of the time, we are stuck. We might be able to leave a terrible job or a terrible boss, but rarely is there a guarantee that the new job or new boss will be an improvement. This is not to say that work and misery are synonymous. The luckiest among us love our jobs and feel valued and respected and well-compensated. That should be the rule but in many cases, alas, it is the exception.

A new year holds opportunity, a fresh start, a time to change. But most of us are returning to the same old jobs where we will deal with the same old frustrations. I love giving advice but the real challenge in being your work friend is that few people are in positions to realistically make the changes that would improve their professional lives. There's too much at stake.

Yes, you should quit your job. Yes, you should call out the overbearing colleague who steals your ideas and talks over everyone. Yes, you should go back to graduate school. Yes, you should make a drastic career change and pursue your passion. Of course you should make the risky, terrifying choices with absolutely no guarantee of success. But what we should do and what we can do are two different things.

And still. It is a new year. However challenging change in our professional lives might feel, we are not just cogs in the machine, trapped in unfortunate circumstances. In these early days of 2023, I've been thinking a lot about how who I am and what I do for a living are two very different things. I'm a writer and professor and editor. I love my work, but it is still work. I am, admittedly, a workaholic. Like many people, I am overextended and overcommitted. I work far more than I should, even though my time is finite and apparently, I do need sleep. I am ambitious, yes, but ambition alone is not responsible for the intensity of my professional life.

The older I get, the more I question why. At the end of my life, will I want to be remembered for who I was or what I did for a living?

I am far from alone. In the United States, we have an obsession with work as a virtue—the harder we work, the closer we are to God. It's a toxic cultural myth that contributes to the bizarre valorization of people sacrificing almost everything at the altar of an extractive economy. It's why an entire discourse rose around labeling people who are simply doing the jobs they were hired for, nothing more and nothing less, as "quiet quitting."

The expectation that we should go above and beyond for employers who feel no reciprocal responsibility is a grand, incredibly destructive lie. We may not have a lot of professional flexibility, but we do not need to believe anything that is so fundamentally detrimental to well-being.

The pandemic has given us the opportunity to rethink almost everything from where we live to how we work. Employees in all kinds of industries are organizing themselves into labor unions to advocate for equitable working conditions. People are taking the big risks and leaving terrible jobs, and employers are having to rise to the occasion to recruit and retain talented people.

These glimmers of progress are incredibly encouraging. As we think about this new year and what we want our professional lives to look like, we should all take some time to reflect on who we are and what gives us meaning beyond what we do. We should think about how to nurture who we are beyond what we do. The greatest shame would be to reach the end of our lives and have the epitaph read, "They worked really hard."

Originally published in the *New York Times*, Work Friend, January 8, 2023

Ask Roxane: Is It Too Late to Follow My Dreams?

—

I love advice columns, always have. Growing up, I read "Dear Abby" and "Ask Ann Landers." I enjoyed the voyeurism—glimpses into the lives and troubles of others—and I appreciated the steady, practical advice as if truly, for any problem, there was a solution. Giving advice is nearly as satisfying: the simple pleasure of offering counsel and hoping that you are helping in some small way.

Not long ago, I put out a call for questions and heard from a range of people. (If you have something you want to ask, send an email to askroxane @nytimes.com.) As we look to the new year, and all the hope that brings, I answer two letters—edited slightly, below—from writers of a certain age wanting to know if they still have a chance to make their dreams come true.

Dear Roxane,

I'm a writer who just turned 65. I've written two as yet unpublished books. Numerous excerpts have been published. I'm working on another book despite feelings of failure and despair. Am I too old to have a career in writing? Does age play a part in artistic success?

Signed,
Just Turned 65

Dear Roxane,

I'm a 47-year-old writer who lives in North Carolina. I have three children, a partner and a full-time job.

My job recently reclassified me (demoted me), and I've taken it as a sign to get out of my profession and get my writing life started.

I'm just getting my feet wet. I've written some essays and some blog pieces, but I haven't been paid for them. I want that to change. I know I have a lot to say, but will anyone want to pay me to say it if I'm closer to 50 than I am to 35?

Signed,
Closer to 50

Dear Just Turned 65 and Closer to 50,

Throughout my 20s and most of my 30s, I was convinced I was never going to make it as a writer. My writing was constantly rejected, and I took the rejection personally, as one does. I'm stubborn, so I kept writing and reading and writing some more. It was the earlier days of the internet, before the rise of social media but after the dawn of blogs. I was fortunate in that I was aware of the writing community I wanted to be a part of, but I wasn't inundated by the details of anyone else's writing life and successes. If I wanted those details, I had to seek them out, which, of course, I did, and covetously.

I was incandescent with envy—so many breathless stories about people my age and often younger who were discovered by a hotshot agent, who sold a book for six or seven figures, who created a popular blog and parlayed that success into a full-time writing career.

The writing world was passing me by. I was never going to be noticed. I was going to spend my life working mediocre jobs, writing in obscurity, and before long it was going to be too late. I was going to turn 30 and then 35 and after that, I couldn't even speculate because I was either going to have a best-selling book by the age of 35 or my dream would be not merely deferred but dead, dead, dead.

Even as I met with less rejection, I found reasons to worry about getting my shot. It took a long time to sell my first novel, *An Untamed State*, nearly two years, two agents, two revisions, countless rejections.

I kept whittling down my dream from literary fame to modest riches to just getting a book deal to, finally, simply writing a good book. And still my dream did not come true. I had done my best, and my best was not good enough. I nearly gave up, but I had someone in my corner who told me to get ahold of myself, to have faith, to keep writing and hustling because I was going to get my chance. She was right. She is always right. Now as she waits for her shot, I get to tell her to keep writing and hustling and having faith until she gets her chance. And she will.

When I sold that first novel, I had to reshape my understanding of artistic success. I signed a contract for an advance of $12,500. In a strange confluence, around the same time I also sold an essay collection, *Bad Feminist*, to a different publisher, for an advance of $15,000. I was 38 and living in rural Illinois, teaching full-time. Instead of glory, I got a chance. The rest was out of my control.

It is easy to fall prey to the idea that writing success is intrinsically bound to youth. Publishing loves a literary ingénue, as if no one over the age of 40 or 50 or 60 has anything worthwhile to say. Such is not the case. The older I get, the more I have to say and the better I am able to express myself. There is no age limit to finding artistic success. Sometimes it happens at 22 and sometimes it happens at 72 and sometimes it doesn't happen at all. No, you are not too old to have a writing career, no matter your age. Yes, it is perfectly reasonable to feel defeated when you've worked so hard at writing and have yet to make your mark so long as you don't stay defeated. No, you are not promised artistic success simply because you want it.

What I wish I could have told myself when I was hopeless about my writing prospects is that I should have defined artistic success in ways that weren't shaped by forces beyond my control. Sometimes, success is getting a handful of words you don't totally hate on the page. Sometimes success is working a full-time job to support your family and raising your kids and finding a way, over several years, to write and finish a novel. Sometimes it's selling a book to a small press for 25 copies of your book and a vague promise of royalties you may never see. And sometimes, if you are very lucky, artistic success is marked by the glittery things so many of us yearn for—the big money deals, the critical accolades, the multicity book tours, the movie options.

The older we get, the more culturally invisible we become, as writers, as people. But you have your words. Writing and publishing are two very different things. Other writers are not your measure. Try not to worry about what other people your age or younger have already accomplished because it will only make you sick with envy or grief. The only thing you can control is how you write and how hard you work. The literary flavor of the week did not get your book deal. All the other writers in the world are not having more fun than you, no matter what it might seem like on social media, where everyone is showing you only what they want you to see.

Write as well as you can, with as much heart as you can, whenever you can. Make sure there are people in your life who will have faith in your promise when you can't. Get your writing in the world, ideally for the money you deserve because writing is work that deserves compensation. But do not worry about being closer to 50 or 65 or 83. Artistic success, in all its forms, is not merely the purview of the young. You are not a late bloomer. You are already blooming.

Originally published in the *New York Times*, December 30, 2017

Ask Roxane: I'm Outraged but Failing at Activism. Why?

———

Dear Roxane,

Back in January, I emailed a group of friends asking if they planned to attend the Women's March in New York City. A progressive black woman like myself replied: "Can't make it. Completely swamped this weekend :(." My first reaction was irritation. Are we going to look back at this moment in history and say, "We could have resisted but we were really swamped that weekend with brunch plans and deadlines?"

In the months since then, I've slowly realized, with considerable shame, that I am no better. I've been harboring equal measures of apathy since November 2016. I have what seem like good excuses: having a baby, illness and death in my family, a challenging job, etc., but the truth is, these mask my underlying condition of paralysis. I have made some weak attempts to engage (joining a call, buying a book, following the play-by-play of the Alabama special election) but nothing approximating real action. I have considered that I'm coping with the allostatic load of living as a black woman during what feels like a heightened moment of racism in the country by retreating, but I think that is only partly true.

I continue to be outraged by this administration's treatment of Latinos, Native Americans, Muslims, L.G.B.T. folks, women and so many others. But I'm struggling to summon a response. Do you have words of wisdom to help me understand and perhaps overcome my feelings of apathy?

Signed,
Apathetic Idealist

Dear Apathetic Idealist,

I have no doubt that many people can relate to your letter. I can relate to it. It is difficult to balance activism and investing in the greater good with the demands of an ordinary life. It's hard to know what to pay attention to and what to respond to and how. It is hard to bear the allostatic load of living as a black woman in a country where we continually have to assert our right to personhood. It is damn hard to expand the limits of our empathy when our emotional attention is already stretched too thin in a world run through with inequity, strife and suffering.

Every day since the 2016 election there has been some terrible new story about the havoc wreaked by the current administration. It's not just overwhelming, it is exhausting.

And of course, President Trump is not the only problem, though he is, socio-politically, one of the most pressing and distressing. This week, I am thinking about 14-year-old Brennan Walker, who was shot at when he knocked on someone's door in a Detroit suburb to ask for directions on his way to school. I am thinking about two men who were led out of a Starbucks in handcuffs because they were waiting for a friend while black.

I am thinking about Saheed Vassell, mentally ill, black and killed by New York City police officers after reports he was wielding a gun; he wasn't. I am still thinking about Stephon Clark, killed by the police in his grandparents' backyard because the police thought he was holding a gun when he was holding his cellphone. I am thinking about devastating recent reporting on the role racism plays in black women's maternal health. I am thinking about the legislation the president recently signed that purports to prevent sex trafficking. It also hurts sex workers' ability to make a living and safely vet clients online, and is a thinly veiled form of censorship.

The United States just bombed Syria, and Mr. Trump, with no sense of irony or recent history, declared, "Mission accomplished." The head of the E.P.A. is spending money as if he is printing it in his basement, while pushing his agency to do the opposite of its mandate.

The fired F.B.I. director, James Comey, said in a recent interview

that Mr. Trump is "morally unfit" for the job, and Mr. Trump pre-
dictably replied by ranting about him on Twitter. Meanwhile, the
Pittsburgh police are preparing for the protests they anticipate if
Mr. Trump fires the special counsel, Robert Mueller.

My point is, there is a lot going on in the world. There is a lot
going on in my world. There is a lot going on in your world. This
is the nature of life. We try to find ways to balance taking care of
ourselves and our families, with caring about the world we live in
and the greater good. Sometimes, we will fall short in one of these
areas. Sometimes we will fall short in all of these areas. Most of the
time, we do the best we can.

I don't have an easy answer for you, but I do think many of us get
overwhelmed because we think we have to care about everything
all the time, as if that's even possible. We get mired in solipsism and
delude ourselves into believing that the proverbial struggle cannot
go on without us. This is rarely the case. The grand thing about
collective effort is that we can generally trust that someone is out in
the world, doing important social justice work when we are too tired
or burned out to join in.

Your friend didn't go to the women's march in New York this
year, but hundreds of thousands of other people did. Every day,
everywhere, people are doing the work of resisting oppression and
tyranny in ways great and small.

Lately, I've been doing two things to maintain my sanity without
checking out completely. I've stopped watching cable news because
the 24-hour news cycle has become an incoherent mess. There are
plenty of ways to stay well informed without listening to lazy pun-
ditry and an endless regurgitation of only the most salacious news.
I've also been trying to pick one issue at a time in which to invest my
social-justice-oriented energy.

If I focus on just one issue and apply genuine effort and attention
to it, I just might contribute something useful. I choose to invest
that energy in different ways, whether it's writing about a pressing
issue, amplifying the voices of others, donating money and time to
nonprofit organizations, or whatever I can think of that might be
useful. Sometimes, I have no idea how I can be useful, so I ask

people who are well positioned to point me in the right direction because I recognize that I don't have to have all the answers.

What you describe in your letter is not apathy. You aren't indifferent to the current state of the world. You are human, a woman trying to balance your own needs with doing good in the world, and right now, your own needs are winning out. Take the time you need. There is no shame in that so long as you remember to extend your empathy as far as you can when your emotional stores have replenished.

I would worry if you didn't care about the state of the world. I would worry if you didn't ask this question.

Originally published in the *New York Times*, April 20, 2018

Ask Roxane: Where the Hell
Is the Love of My Life?

——

Dear Roxane,

I am a 43-year-old, single, never-been-married, educated mother of one and would like advice on love. I'm navigating dating life and need to fully understand the difference between loving someone, being in love and having a soul mate. I love the idea of love and would very much like to spend the rest of my life with a man, but find myself having commitment issues because I am afraid of choosing wrong. I see couples that have been married 10, 15, 20 years who get divorced and seem to be completely fine with it. It's scary to me because I would like my marriage to last a lifetime. Am I overthinking this totally or being too paranoid? Or do you really never know, because only time will tell?

Sincerely,
Where the hell is the love of my life?

Dear Searching for the Love of Her Life,

We live in a culture that idealizes the idea of love, and the idea that there is one true person who will complete you, fulfill all your dreams and love you forever. We are told from an early age that our true love is out there, waiting for us and so we yearn to find them, to know what it feels like to experience true love, to know you have made the right choice. The truth about love is that it is often bewildering and unknowable. You may never know if you have made the right choice. But when love is true, you embrace all the unknowns, regardless.

I am 44, in a complicated romantic situation, never been married. I am no expert on love. I love the idea of love but I have lived and loved long enough to recognize that there is a difference between the idea of love and the reality of love.

You never really know if a marriage or relationship will last a lifetime. You can want that. You can work hard to make a relationship work and have the best of intentions and still, things might not work out but that doesn't mean you have wasted your time or failed. Many people who choose divorce are completely fine with it because they know the difference between the idea of love and the reality of love. They know there is nothing to be gained from staying in a marriage simply because the idea of love demands pretending everything is fine when such is not the case. What may seem cavalier to you is most likely a decision that has been agonized over. Few people take divorce lightly because it is a profoundly painful thing to end a commitment you nurtured and fought for and hoped would last a lifetime.

In your letter, you are very much focused on what could be rather than what is. You worry about choosing wrong but are not considering that you might choose right for a lifetime or right for a moment. When you meet someone and start dating, you have no idea where things will lead. You have hopes, yes, and dreams, but you also have to get from one day to the next, getting to know a person, deciding to deepen the relationship and, sometimes, choosing to formalize a commitment. It is so very important to know what you want from a relationship but you also have to create space for a relationship to develop without worrying about what the relationship will or won't become. You have to be in the relationship in the present, from one day to the next, and some of those days will be glorious, but some of them are going to be a complete disaster. You would like a marriage to last a lifetime, but you are, perhaps, overlooking what it takes to love someone for a lifetime. You are overlooking the small joys and sorrows and frustrations of threading all the days that make up a lifetime of loving someone.

Ask 33 people about the difference between loving someone, being in love and soul mates, and you will get 33 different answers, so I will simply tell you what these things are to me. I must also warn you, I am a passionate, foolish romantic. I believe in love and grand gestures. I am all about the chase, seduction and woo, not just during the shimmering early days of a relationship but also years in when you're thinking about the maddening ways your person behaves but still, isn't today a good day to send them some sunflowers or bring them their favorite coffee?

When you find the one you just know. But that isn't guaranteed. Some people never find the one, or there are several people for whom you have such feelings or you think you have found the one and they change or you change in ways you can no longer tolerate. Love is so damn messy. There are days when I hate love as much as I love it, when I just want to walk away, give up but still, something holds me there, to the center of my gravity.

Loving someone is recognizing the role they play or have played in your life and honoring that presence. Sometimes, love feels like an obligation but it is one you are willing to fulfill. Sometimes it takes hard work but you are willing to put in that work. Love is the constant you hold on to when you don't particularly like the one you love. Love is recognizing the ways in which, for better and worse, someone has contributed to your life.

Being in love is wild, breathtaking, infuriating. It is butterflies in your stomach when you think about your person, when you see them, when you hold them. It's the electricity when your skin meets. It's smiling at your person with wide eyes and an open heart and seeing them smile back at you in the same way. It's wanting to hold someone's hand, even when your hand is hot, a little sweaty. It's lust and the heat of wanting, wanting, wanting. It's seeing who someone truly is, the best and most terrible parts of them, and choosing not to look away from everything you see, actively embracing everything you see. It's the willingness to have difficult but honest conversations. It's compromising on the structure of your relationship. It's about patience and being flexible and getting irritated or furious with a person but still holding on. It's wanting to be the best version of yourself for your person but also for yourself, especially for yourself. It's the pride you feel in their accomplishments and being as happy for their successes as you are for your own, if not more. It's their hurts becoming your hurts. It's feeling their absence when you are apart and the rush of joy when that absence ends. It's liking someone as much as you love them, being interested in who they are, marveling at the ways they are interested in you. It's a gut instinct. You just feel it. You know it in your bones. It isn't perfect, not at all. It doesn't need to be. It is, simply, what fills you up.

As for soul mates, I did not believe such a thing existed until I did. A soul mate is someone so deeply part of you that they feel like a vital organ, living outside of your skin. They are the hottest part of the sun, your true north, your home, the one from whom you will never walk away, no matter what the material conditions of your relationship might be. Your soul mate is the one you wait for knowing no matter what happens, that they are worth the wait. Your soul mate is the person you choose because you look at them, always and think, "You . . . there you are."

But it truly doesn't matter how I or anyone else understand love. You get to decide what loving someone, being in love with someone and having a soul mate mean. You get to choose the kind of person you want to spend your life with and for how long and what that relationship looks like. You get to fight for what you want so long as the person you love is fighting alongside you.

I hope you find that person you are looking for. I hope when you meet him, you don't worry about how the relationship might end. I hope you find joy and fulfillment in the very act of loving and being loved, no matter what may come.

Originally published in the *New York Times*, October 18, 2018

Acknowledgments

———

I have been incredibly fortunate to work with astute and generous editors over the course of my career. Thank you to Jessica Grose, Megan Carpentier, Sewell Chan, Rachel Dry, Jenée Desmond Harris, Indrani Sen, and Vanessa Mobley, for the opportunity to write for you and for your work editing most of these essays and helping me grow as a writer. Your guidance has been invaluable. Thank you also to others who supported me in the early years that led to the work that made this book possible—Blake Butler, Gene Morgan, Isaac Fitzgerald, Julie Grecius, and Dave Daley. Thank you, Ashley Ford, Tracy Gonzalez, Randa Jarrar, Saeed Jones, Alexander Chee, Jami Attenberg, Matthew Salesses, Aubrey Hirsch, Matt Bell, Brian Oliu, Lidia Yuknavitch, and anyone else I'm forgetting, for being such generous friends and the best writing community I could hope to be a part of.

My agent, Maria Massie, has shepherded my career since 2013, and I am lucky to call her a friend, too. Thanks also to Kevin Mills, Trinity Ray, Sylvie Rabineau, and Lev Ginsburg, the rest of my professional team. My editor, Emily Griffin, is patient and insightful and kind and I love working with her. Thanks also to Kate D'Esmond and everyone in Harper's publicity, marketing, and academic sales departments who make sure my books find their way into the world. I work with two awesome women every day, who provide all kinds of support you may not always see but that makes my work possible—Kaitlyn Adams and Meg Pillow.

As always, thank you to *Law & Order: Special Victims Unit* but thanks also to *House Hunters* and all HGTV programming, really, for sharing the virtues of an open-concept life.

———

Last but not least, thank you to my family, who has been entertaining my opinions for nearly five decades, sometimes willingly—Michael and Nicole Gay, Joel Gay, and Michael Gay Jr. and Aide Gay, as well as my nieces and nephews who are each the cutest in their own special way. Thank you to my dog, Maximus Toretto Blueberry, who unexpectedly revealed that there is a dog person inside me. I had no idea. And thank you most of all to my wife, Deborah Millman Gay, who is just as opinionated as me, loves me as fiercely as I love her, is my first and most trusted reader, and makes every single day a joyful adventure.

About the Author

———

ROXANE GAY's writing has appeared in the *Best American Nonrequired Reading 2018*, the *Best American Mystery Stories 2014*, the *Best American Short Stories 2012*, the *Best Sex Writing 2012*, *Harper's Bazaar*, *A Public Space*, *McSweeney's*, *Tin House*, *Oxford American*, *American Short Fiction*, and the *Virginia Quarterly Review*, among many other publications. She is a contributing opinion writer for the *New York Times*, for which she also writes the "Work Friend" column. She is the author of the books *Ayiti*, *An Untamed State*, the *New York Times* bestselling *Bad Feminist*, the nationally bestselling *Difficult Women*, and the *New York Times* bestselling *Hunger: A Memoir of My Body*. She is also the author of the Eisner Award–winning *World of Wakanda* for Marvel and the editor of *Best American Short Stories 2018*. In 2018 she was awarded a Guggenheim Fellowship. She is the Gloria Steinem Endowed Chair in Media, Culture and Feminist Studies at Rutgers University's Institute for Women's Leadership.